Lecture Notes in Computer Science 791

Edited by G. Goos and J. Hartmanis

Advisory Board: W. Brauer   D. Gries   J. Stoer

Rachid Guerraoui Oscar Nierstrasz
Michel Riveill (Eds.)

Object-Based Distributed
Programming

ECOOP '93 Workshop
Kaiserslautern, Germany, July 26-27, 1993
Proceedings

Springer-Verlag
Berlin Heidelberg New York
London Paris Tokyo
Hong Kong Barcelona
Budapest

Rachid Guerraoui   Oscar Nierstrasz
Michel Riveill (Eds.)

Object-Based Distributed Programming

ECOOP '93 Workshop
Kaiserslautern, Germany, July 26-27, 1993
Proceedings

Springer-Verlag
Berlin Heidelberg New York
London Paris Tokyo
Hong Kong Barcelona
Budapest

Series Editors

Gerhard Goos
Universität Karlsruhe
Postfach 69 80
Vincenz-Priessnitz-Straße 1
D-76131 Karlsruhe, Germany

Juris Hartmanis
Cornell University
Department of Computer Science
4130 Upson Hall
Ithaca, NY 14853, USA

Volume Editors

Rachid Guerraoui
Département d'Informatique, Laboratoire de Systèmes d'Exploitation
Ecole Polytechnique Fédérale de Lausanne
CH-1015 Lausanne, Switzerland

Oscar Nierstrasz
Centre Universitaire d'Informatique, Université de Genève
24 rue Général-Dufour, CH-1211 Genève 4, Switzerland

Michel Riveill
Laboratoire de Génie Informatique de Savoie, Université de Savoie
Campus Scientifique, F-73370 Le Bourget du Lac, France
and: Bull-IMAG/Systèmes
2 rue de Vignate, F-38610 Gières, France

CR Subject Classification (1991): D.1-4

ISBN 3-540-57932-X Springer-Verlag Berlin Heidelberg New York
ISBN 0-387-57932-X Springer-Verlag New York Berlin Heidelberg

CIP data applied for

© Springer-Verlag Berlin Heidelberg 1994
Printed in Germany

Typesetting: Camera-ready by author
SPIN: 10132118   45/3140-543210 - Printed on acid-free paper

Contents

Preface

There has been a noticeable trend over the past dozen years from traditional, single-platform applications towards the development of more distributed, open applications. Such systems are open not only in terms of network topology and heterogeneous hardware and software platforms, but they are open especially in terms of flexible and evolving requirements. Open applications must be developed in a way that can meet unforeseen requirements. As a result of this trend, there has come a gradual realization that object-oriented technologies offer the best hope for meeting not only the computational requirements of open systems (i.e., in terms of providing good models for distributed computations), but they offer the most promising foundation for building open systems from systematically developed software components.

The rapidly growing interest in the application of object-oriented programming and methods to the development of open systems provided the perfect background for organizing a workshop as part of ECOOP 93 (the European Conference on Object-Oriented Programming), to assess the current state of research in this field and to facilitate interaction between groups working on very different aspects of object-oriented distributed systems. Response to the call for contributions to this workshop was overwhelming, with over fifty people submitting position papers and participating in the workshop, and almost half presenting papers.

The goal of a workshop is somewhat different from that of a conference: work in progress is emphasized over stable research results, and informal interaction is emphasized over formal presentations. Nevertheless, much of the work presented was at a very mature level, and indicated that the research community was moving in some very distinct directions. As a result of the high quality of the contributions, we felt that a "postceedings" was in order to serve as a more concrete record of the workshop. Authors who had given presentations at the workshop were invited to submit full papers, and these submissions were then subjected to a full review process. Fourteen papers were then selected for publication in this volume.

Though the papers selected cover a broad range of issues, and participants in the workshop offered very different views of what they considered to be the most important problems to be resolved, it is interesting to group these contributions into three broad categories. First, several authors focused on object models: What are the salient characteristics of objects from the point of view of building open, distributed systems? What are objects as opposed to components? What granularities of objects are important to take into account? What models of objects are suitable for distributed and concurrent computations?

Second, much of the research focused on object management issues: How to manage objects in the presence of hard and soft real-time constraints? How to support transactions in distributed environments with multiple concurrent clients? How to support object migration, replication and granularity control?

Finally, several of the participants presented concrete systems for developing distributed applications, in which object-oriented concepts and mechanisms are used to factor out useful abstractions for distributed programming. The approaches varied considerably, relying on specific languages or features, or relying more on a toolbox approach. In all cases, however, the emphasis is not on providing raw functionality for supporting distributed computation, but on how object-oriented technology provides the means for encapsulating useful, higher-level abstractions for programming distributed systems.

We would like to thank Dieter Rombach, who was responsible for coordinating the workshops at ECOOP 93 in Kaiserslautern, Walter Olthoff, the local organising chair, and the student volunteers. We would also like to thank all of the participants of the workshop for making this such a successful event, and the contributing authors for their very efficient help in the (distributed) task of putting together this volume in such a short time.

January 1994

Oscar Nierstrasz
Rachid Guerraoui
Michel Riveill

Models and Paradigms of Interaction

Peter Wegner (pw@cs.brown.edu)
Brown University, Providence, RI, 02912

Abstract:

Objects have inherently greater computation power than functions because they provide clients with continuing services over time. They determine a *marriage contract* for interactive services that cannot be expressed by a pattern of time-independent *sales contracts*. Objects express the programming-in-the-large paradigm of software engineering, while functions express the programming-in-the-small paradigm of the analysis of algorithms. Objects have a *functional semantics* specified by their interface, a *serial semantics* specified by traces of interface procedures, and a *fully abstract semantics* that specifies behavior over time for all possible interactions. They assign meaning to the time between the execution of interface procedures as well as to algorithmic effects. Church's thesis that computable functions capture the intuitive notion of effective computation for algorithms cannot be extended to objects.

Components are defined by generalizing from accidental to necessary properties of persistent interaction units. Scalability for software problems, defined as "asymptotic openness", is shown to be the analog of complexity for algorithmic problems. Paradigms of interaction are examined for functions and procedures, objects and processes, APIs and frameworks, databases, GUIs, robots, and virtual-reality systems. Early models of computing stressed computation over interaction for both theoretical reasons (greater tractability) and practical reasons (there were no software components with which to interact). However, scalable software systems, personal computers, and databases require a balance between algorithmic and interactive problem solving. Models of interaction express the behavior of actual software systems and therefore capture the intuitive notion of truly effective computation more completely than mere algorithms.

Keywords: model, interaction, object, component, interface, algorithm, problem, complexity, scalability, computability, semantics, API, framework, database, GUI, robot, virtual reality

Models and Paradigms of Interaction

1. Models of Interaction

1.1. Objects as Marriage Contracts

The observable behavior of objects cannot be expressed by computable functions because objects in software systems have a physical existence in time, called persistence, that causes them to have time-dependent physical properties. Functions capture the transformation power of objects at an instant of time but not their interaction power over a period of time. Objects determine a continuing *marriage contract* for interactive services over time that cannot be captured by a pattern of one-time *sales contracts*.

The recognition that functions are too weak to express the observable behavior of objects over time has far-reaching consequences. The gulf between algorithmic programming in the small and interactive programming in the large becomes one of expressive power rather than merely of scale. Functional and logic programming languages are seen to express the observable behavior of functions but not of objects. The Turing Test is interpreted as an attempt to express intelligence in terms of the computing power of objects rather than of computable functions. Church's Thesis that Turing machines capture the intuitive notion of effectively computable functions loses its force because functions do not model software systems.

Objects generate complex interactive behavior from simple computation rules. Objects with an interface of AND and NOT operations and no internal state have the interactive power of a Turing machine (see Figure 1), since every computable function can be generated as a sequence of AND and NOT operations. The interactive power of Turing machines can be realized from incredibly simple computational mechanisms by "temporal composition". We shall show that objects with an internal state, such as a *bank-account* object with *deposit and withdraw* operations, can express behavior that is richer than that of computable functions:

object *bank-account*
  interface
  procedure *deposit (argument: Money);*
  procedure *withdraw (argument: Money);*
  body
    includes procedure bodies and encapsulated (locally accessible) state

     Each procedure invocation is an instantaneous event in the lifetime of a bank-account object. Sequences of procedure invocations, called traces, approximate the behavior of bank account objects over time. The behavior of objects with state cannot, however, be completely described by sets of traces for two distinct reasons:

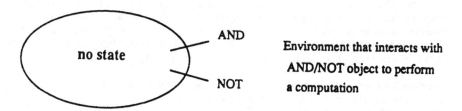

Figure 1: Agent with AND and NOT Operations and No State

different traces may have the same effect
deposit(100); withdraw(50) = deposit(50)

the same traces may have different effects
consider bank accounts with an internal interest computation
deposit(100) in 1980 is not equivalent to deposit(100) in 1990

     The time at which procedures are executed can be explicitly specified by time-stamps:

deposit(100, timestamp); withdraw(50, timestamp) -- time-stamped procedures

     Time-stamped traces can unambiguously express computation histories of objects whose executed procedures are instantaneous events in the lifetime of the object. Objects can be viewed as computable functions from initial states and time-stamped traces to outputs and final states:

  functional semantics = *F(initial state, time-stamped trace)* → *(output, final state)*

     However, this reduction of object semantics to computable functions has limitations:

executed procedures are not necessarily instantaneous, atomic, or serializable
imposing a time stamp on an operation changes (overspecifies) its semantics
the interface operations of an object may change over its lifetime

The view of procedures as instantaneous (time-stamped) events in the lifetime of an object is an inadequate abstraction objects with real-time interaction requirements. Non-serializable concurrently executed procedures cannot inherently be modeled by a trace semantics.

Time stamping is a fundamental rather than cosmetic change in the model of interaction, mapping the implicit notion of interactive time into an explicit algorithmic notion of time. Time stamping messages changes their semantics by prematurely binding their occurrence in time. The conversion of a trace into a time-stamped trace overspecifies it by forcing a temporally implicit specification of behavior to become temporally explicit.

Active objects that model cities, banks, and airline reservation systems may have both interface functions and autonomous internal activities that can cause changes of interface behavior. For example, an airline reservation system can add or delete flights, airports, and airlines that change the functionality of its interface. Such changes can be realized by second-order, procedure-creating procedures that cause new interface functionality to be created. Changes of interface functionality cannot be handled by traces or time-stamped traces.

The behavior of an object for all possible interactions is called its *fully abstract behavior*. Fully abstract behavior in algorithms corresponds to a sales contract. Fully abstract object behavior cannot in general be modeled by computable functions, though certain subclasses of objects can be modeled by traces. Of the four levels of semantics listed below, only fully abstract semantics is rich enough to capture interactive semantics for all objects.

interface behavior: response to messages (observations, events) at a given instant of time
serial behavior: the set of all sequences of events (traces)
time-stamped serial behavior: the set of all time-stamped traces
fully abstract behavior: observable behavior over time for all contexts of interaction

The inadequacy of computable functions as a basis for specifying objects mimics the inadequacy of sales contracts for specifying marriage contracts. Sales contracts are unnatural for behavior over time even when in principle possible because specifying preplanned behavior for all contingencies is combinatorially unmanageable, as in chess. They break down entirely for nonserializable concurrent interactions or when the terms of the contract can change over time.

Though the inadequacy of functional behavior is most evident in situations that involve the interaction of persistence and concurrency, the fundamental cause of the breakdown of the functional model appears to lie in the failure to model persistence. The fully abstract behavior of shared variables in sequential Von Neumann machines cannot be specified functionally since for any given functional trace of behavior over a finite period of time the behavior at the next instant of time can be chosen so the function must be changed. Milner [Mi] has discussed the inadequacy of functional models for concurrency. Our analysis suggests that the cause of this inadequacy is the inability to capture interactive real time for persistent objects, and that problems in modeling concurrency are a consequence of this fundamental inadequacy.

Rules of interaction are simpler than rules of computation because they are temporally local. They give up on temporally remote consequences of actions to provide timely and "spontaneous" local responses. Interactive time is represented by the passage of real time rather than by a simulated time parameter internal to the model of computation.

Time in models of computation means the inner time of execution of an algorithm, while time in models of interaction means external real time of the application being modeled. The notion of external time of the modeled application differs fundamentally from inner computation time for algorithms. In particular, interactive time cannot be captured by simply adding an explicit time parameter to algorithms, since this captures only temporally deterministic computations like those of physics and cannot handle nondeterministic interaction like airline reservation.

Objects are persistent entities that continue to exist between the execution of their interface procedures. They model not only the behavior of algorithms in their interface, but also the periods of time between the execution of algorithms. Whereas algorithm behavior is defined only for one input at a time, object behavior is defined for multiple interacting messages executing in sequence or concurrently. By explicitly modeling persistence and concurrent (overlapping) execution, objects can capture the behavior of real-time actions in a concurrent world.

Models of interaction generally treat algorithms as occurring instantaneously in real time. When this assumption breaks down because concurrently executing procedures of an object interfere with each other or because time critical requirements do not allow execution of an algorithm to be completed, then models of interaction become intractable. Treatment of algorithms as though they occur at an instant of time can be guaranteed by imposing requirements of atomicity on actions and of serializability on transactions.

1.2. Context-Dependent Procedures and Interpreted Actions

Real-life actions like *running* with a simple dictionary definition may have complex inner side effects when interpreted as context-dependent actions of particular individuals (running can enhance fitness or cause shortness of breath or a heart attack). The external effect of running depends in a complex way on inner athletic abilities and stamina.

Procedures of an object specify *context-dependent actions* whose effect depends on the object's state. An object's procedures may have inner side effects on the object's state and external effects determined by the state. The behavior of a *withdraw* procedure in the context of a specific bank account is richer than its effect as a disembodied action, having side-effects on the bank balance and on subsequent withdraw operations. The dependence of an object's procedures on inner context is realized by nonlocal variables that share the local state of an object:

procedure *P(visible parameters p, hidden local state variables v)*
  external interaction with environment through parameters
  internal interaction with inner state through variables

Functions specify the relation between visible input parameters and outputs on the assumption that there are no internally unpredictable actions. They specify fixed relations between inputs and outputs, and cannot handle unpredictably changing inner contexts, especially if the context can change during a given invocation of the function.

A procedure $P(p, v)$ with hidden variables v is an unknown function of its parameters p, especially if the state can be modified by other procedures during the execution of P. The interface $P(p, -)$ may be viewed as the exposed part of an iceberg as in Figure 2.

The behavior of the context-dependent procedure P1 depends on a hidden state in the submerged part of the iceberg that may be unpredictably (nondeterministically) modified by another procedure P2, thereby changing the algorithmic behavior of P1. The procedure $P1(p1, v1)$ is nondeterministic when considered as a function of its parameters $p1$ because its context dependence cannot be determined, and is enirely nonfunctional if P2 can concurrently interfere with P1.

The multiple procedures of an object provide both an opportunity for harmonious cooperation and the potential for chaotic disharmony. The worst-case scenario of nonserializable interference leads to noncomputability, while harmonious cooperation usually yields computable behavior. Physical objects subjected to conflicting stimuli, such as steel balls subject to two magnetic fields, exhibit chaotic behavior that mimics the noncomputable behavior of corresponding software objects.

Object behavior can sometimes be represented as a computable function from time-stamped traces to outputs, but are model persistent interaction and an external notion of "real" time that cannot be specified in terms of computable functions. Even when the object as a whole can be modeled as a computable function, the component context-dependent procedures of the object considered in isolation cannot be modeled as computable functions.

The object of Figure 2 can be viewed as a context-dependent form of composition of its component procedures *P1, P2*.

object-creation composition = compose(P1, P2, context(shared state))

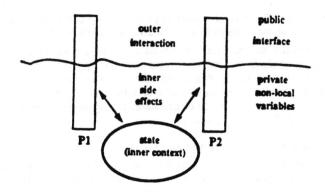

Figure 2: Iceberg Model of Context-Dependent Procedures

Object-creation composition determines a new kind of structure qualitatively different from the procedures and state that are being composed. The coordinated external interface presented by the object to its clients is more regular than the internal interfaces between procedures and their shared state. Dependence on the state that is unpredictable for isolated context-dependent procedures becomes more predictable in the context of the object as a whole, just as the effect of running becomes more predictable if we know previous performance and the state of health of the individual who is running. The effect of a withdraw operation likewise becomes predictable if we know the current balance of the associated bank-account object.

Well-designed systems should strive for tidy internal interfaces. However, goals of tidiness conflict with goals of flexibility. Procedures of an object sacrifice context-independence to permit sharing of an object's state for purposes of effective interaction. The intractability of interfaces among procedures of an object is necessary to realize sharing of the object's state. Nondeterministic noncomputable interfaces of objects are due not to bad design, but to inherent modeling requirements for interaction and persistence.

Context-dependent actions can be viewed as *interpreted actions* whose semantic effect must be expressed in terms of a context of interpretation. The notion that interpreted function symbols have greater complexity than uninterpreted ones is familiar from mathematical logic, where the uninterpreted semantics of first-order logic is simpler than the interpreted semantics. Interpreted actions have a more complex semantics than uninterpreted actions in algebra and logic, where "+(3, 4)" has the value 7 when + has its standard interpretation as an operation that transforms pairs of integers into integers, and "+(3, 4)" has the literal value "+(3, 4)" when + is the uninterpreted operation of concatenating the operator with its operands.

Context-dependent interpretation of procedures is similar to interpreted semantics of functions for first-order logic, though contexts of procedure interpretation are less mathematically tractable than function interpretations. It is not surprising that operations interpreted in the context of an object have a more complex semantics context-dependent actions. Since objects are concerned with the effect of actions over time and time has no role in context-independent action specifications, the semantics of context-dependent actions cannot be expressed in terms of context-independent semantics.

Variables are essentially objects with get and put (read and write) operations. Though get and put operations have a simple uninterpreted behavior, their interpreted behavior in the context of a specific variable cannot be modeled by functions. The set of all potential interactive behaviors of variables, like that of objects, cannot be fully captured by computable functions. Functions were simply not intended to capture the exponentially growing set of all possible interactive behaviors of a variable or an object over time. They were intended for quid-pro-quo contracts at an instant of time rather than life-cycle contracts.

The temporal behavior of physical objects can be specified algorithmically by differential equations because it is noninteractive. The temporal behavior of interactive objects like bank accounts is inherently less tractable because it depends on unpredictable (nondeterministic) interactions. The interface of interactive objects can be viewed as a select statement that listens for incoming messages and selects an action $acti$ determined by the incoming message mi.

$$select(m1|act1, m2|act2, ... , mN|actN)$$

The semantics of an interactive object can be captured by the trace of its interface operations by constraining interactions so that execution is equivalent to some sequence of noninteracting procedures (corresponding to serializable transactions). But unconstrained interaction can be fully captured only by actual computing systems. The only complete (fully abstract) model of an unconstrained interactive software system is the system itself.

1.3. Object Models in Software Design

The sales contract versus marriage contract metaphor corresponds precisely to that of programming in the small versus programming in the large:

programming in the small: functions, algorithms, sales contracts
programming in the large: software systems, objects, marriage contracts

The distinction between programming in the small and the large is not primarily one of program size, but of expressive power. Software utilities and control systems for nuclear reactors that provide services over the lifetime of the system have a qualitatively richer behavior than computable functions. Moreover, they must handle not only normal behavior but also overload and time-critical situations. Embedded software systems must serve their clients "in sickness and in health, till death do them part", like marriage contracts. These paradigmatic differences imply that the analysis of algorithms is concerned with inherently less expressive behavior than software engineering.

Object modeling techniques in software engineering provide a practical application domain for models of interaction. The object modeling technique OMT [Ru] includes *object models, dynamic models,* and *functional models* that correspond to the fully abstract, serial, and functional behavior of objects. *Object models* of OMT define the overall computation space, *dynamic models* specify traces (scenarios) for particular dynamic paths in that computation space, and *functional models* specify the functionality of events:

object model: describes the computation space of all potential interactions
 fully abstract space of all possible computations (possible worlds)
dynamic model: describes sequencing of events (procedures) for specific tasks (scenarios)
 projection onto a subspace of computations (candidate actual worlds)
functional model: describes dependencies, mappings, constraints for specific events
 projection of temporal sequences of events onto a single (instantaneous) event

Serial and interface projections of fully abstract behavior for objects correspond to dynamic and functional models of the object modeling technique OMT. The close correspondence between fully abstract, trace, and interface semantics with software engineering design models is an unexpected bonus that enhances the practical relevance of our approach and provides empirical evidence for its correctness.

Programming in the small focuses on the input-output behavior of algorithms, while programming in the large is concerned with the interactive behavior of objects and software systems over time. The difference between programming in the small and programming in the large is essentially that between sales contracts and marriage contracts or equivalently between algorithms with inner time and objects with external interactive time. It is not therefore surprising that models of interaction provide a framework for programming in the large.

The object model determines a system-wide computation space for all possible computations, the dynamic model defines a projection from the space of all possible computations onto particular dynamic computation paths (scenarios), while the functional model determines a further projection from the time line of a scenario to the behavior of instantaneous events.

Sequential computation scenarios partition global sequences of procedure calls into subsequences (traces) on individual objects. Objects in the context of sequential scenarios behave like coroutines. Dynamic models are useful in checking that that software systems are capable of certain forms of dynamic behavior. But the behavior as a whole, for all potential contexts of execution, cannot be expressed as a tractable composition of its dynamic models.

The technique of projection from fully abstract computation spaces to tractable subspaces occurs in a variety of object-based design methods. Jacobson's notion of use cases [Ja] generalizes the notion of scenarios from single execution paths to a broader set of contexts associated with a mode of use. A use case provides an imperative view of an object-based program that supports a particular class of computations. Use cases are important in validating that a system accommodates the needs of specific users. They serve as design-time test cases analogous to execution-time test cases for algorithmic debugging.

Use cases are projections of the computation space of all possible worlds onto a subspace of "similar" possible worlds, while test cases are a projection of the space of all possible computations of an algorithm onto a specific computation. Use cases project the object model onto the dynamic (procedural) model, while test cases project the functional model of a procedure onto a specific execution instance: An object-based system specification cannot be entirely specified in terms of its desired use cases, just as an algorithm cannot be proved correct by testing.

Airline reservation systems have a variety of clients and associated use cases:

passengers: smooth interaction with travel agents and airlines in making reservations
travel agents: reliable service to customers
desk employees: user-friendly access in serving travel agents, passengers, flight crews
flight crews: helpful support during the flight itself
shareholders: making sure that the system enhances profitability
system builders: access to the system for modification and during emergencies

An airline reservation system must serve the needs of these clients but has a fully abstract behavior that transcends its uses by these classes of clients, just as an object has an existence and behavior that transcends its use for any particular purpose. The airline reservation system can be viewed as a single composite object with multiple projections (views) that determine use cases.

An airline reservation system is a server object with a multifaceted that can serve many kinds of clients. Each client/server combination determines a projection of the complete semantics for a particular use case. In Figure 3, the server is shown with a jagged interface, while the clients C1, C2 determine a smooth interface with the end user. This shows that systems presenting smooth interfaces to end users may have complex and fuzzy internal interfaces among their components. Interfaces that provide services to many kinds of clients are inevitably less tidy than interfaces tailored to a specific client.

The computation space of an object-based software system can be viewed as a two-dimensional space with functionality at an instant of time along the horizontal axis and time along the vertical axis (see Figure 4). Scenarios and use cases are vertical slices of the two-dimensional space for similarly structured sets of computations. Interfaces correspond to projections onto horizontal lines that specify options at a given instance of time. Points in the computation space correspond to the execution of a specific procedure for a specific object.

Simula, the first object-oriented language, explicitly established a connection between objects and temporal modeling through the simulation of global time and through coroutines for realizing local temporal independence of objects. The connection between object persistence and real time was blurred in later languages, where objects were simply viewed as autonomous chunks of modular behavior. Since most software systems are concerned with modeling the

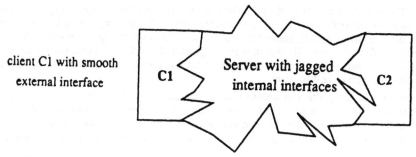

Figure 3: Smooth End-User Interfaces from Jagged Internal Interfaces

interaction of entities over time, and since fully abstract behavior requires the temporal duration of state to be considered, time should be reintroduced as an explicit primitive into object models.

1.4. Object Composition

The four forms of composition below compose two entities to create a composite entity of the same kind as its components. There is a fundamental distinction between function and procedure composition, which compose sales contracts to produce a sales contract, and class and object composition, which compose marriage contracts to produce a marriage contract:

function composition f.g: F-compose(f, g) → Function
procedure composition P;Q: P-compose(P, Q) → Procedure
class composition inherits(class, subclass): C-compose(C1, C2) → Class
parallel object composition O1|O2: O-compose(O1, O2) → Object

The composition *f.g* of two functions *f* and *g* is the function that results from applying g followed by f. The composition *P;Q* of two procedures is the procedure that results from executing P followed by *Q*. The composition *P1;P2* of two procedures, like the composition of machine language instructions, specifies a non-commutative sequence of actions. The effect of a sequence of actions *A1;A2;...;AN* depends on the order in which the actions are specified. The effect of adding a new action *A* to a program depends on where the action is inserted into the program.

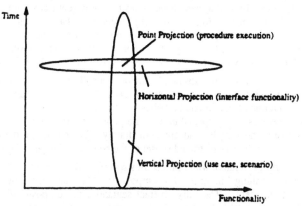

Figure 4: Computation Space for Object Behavior

The composition *O1|O2* of two objects is an unordered union, specifying the interface behavior and internal interaction of a composite entity. Object composition is commutative, since the composite interface does not depend on the order in which objects are listed. The composition *O1|O2|...|ON* of a collection of objects depends only on the listed components and not on their order. Composition specifies a set rather than a sequence, more precisely a *bag* because objects can appear more than once.

Sequential composition of actions restricts interaction by placing procedures in a unique context of execution. It is suited to the specification of non-interactive processes with a known sequential execution order. But objects require a looser composition mechanism that captures the autonomous services provided by persistent interaction units independent of their execution order.

composition of procedures: P1;P2
sequential, noncommutative: procedure P1 followed by P2
composition of objects: O1|O2
interactive, commutative: combined interface of objects O1 and O2

The looser coupling of objects compared with that of procedures makes it easier to manage incremental change. Adding an object to a collection is not affected by where it is added or on whether the component is already in the collection, while adding an action to a program is affected by where in the action sequence it is inserted.

Compositionality for functional languages means that composite expressions have a semantics definable as a simple function of their component subexpressions. Object composition cannot be expressed by function composition. The criterion of composition for objects must express the interactive interface of composite objects in terms of the interfaces of component objects by nonfunctional composition mechanisms like inheritance:

composite expression = Function(subexpression1, subexpression2)
composite object = Compose(object1, object2)
composite class = inherits(class, subclass)

The difference between procedure-oriented and object-based programs is captured by flow diagrams versus object diagrams (see Figure 5). Flow diagrams model the dynamic flow of control of a sequence of actions, while object diagrams model static relations among a collection of dynamically evolving entities. The interpretation of the nodes and edges in these two kinds of graphs is entirely different. Flow diagrams have nodes that represent transformations and edges that specify the sequencing of transformations. Object diagrams have nodes representing persistent, time-varying entities and edges representing resource dependencies, interactions, and constraints among entities. Edges of a flow diagram are one-directional control paths, while edges of an object diagram have a variety of bidirectional as well as one-directional interpretations.

Object diagrams specify the fully abstract behavior of a collection of objects in terms of the behavior of constituent objects, while flow diagrams are a special case that specifies composite functional behavior in terms of the functional behavior of constituents. The sequential composition *P1;P2* can be viewed as a very special case of the parallel composition *P1|P2* (when all the operations of P1 precede those of P2 and are immediately followed by the operations of P2). Thus flow diagrams describe a very restricted subset of the behavior of object diagrams.

Objects specify things (nouns), while procedures specify actions (events). Object composition defines a composite "thing" in terms of a composite interface and interaction (synchronization) constraints of components. The fully abstract semantics of composite objects cannot in general be defined as a computable function of components, since synchronization requires coordination between external and algorithmic time that cannot be expressed algorithmically. While composition mechanisms can in general be very complex, certain specific patterns of composition, like producer-consumer and client-server interaction, can be specified simply.

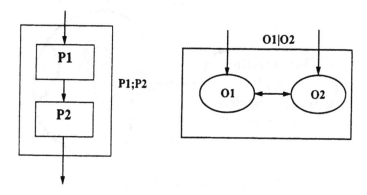

Figure 5: Flow Diagrams Versus Object Diagrams

In many contexts objects are considered to be resources that perform tasks for clients, leading to models such as linear logic that view objects as (non-reusable) resources. However, objects admit richer interpretations than their interpretation as functions in traditional logic or as reusable resources in linear logic. It is inevitable that models with the richness of interpretation of object diagrams are mathematically less tractable than narrowly interpreted flow diagrams.

1.5. Irreversible Projection

Objects describe an incredibly rich space of potential interactions whose full range of behavior is richer than that of computable functions. Clients constrain the interaction space to tractable subspaces (use cases) that provide useful services. Constraints on fully abstract object behavior that yield tractable interactions are called projections. Since fully abstract behavior cannot be recovered, projections are inherently irreversible simplifications of fully abstract behavior.

The actual path taken by an ant on a beach can usually be explained by hindsight even though its behavior for all possible beaches cannot be tractably specified. The balance of a bank account for a particular sequence of transactions can likewise be explained by hindsight, since nondeterministic choices of the computing system can be determined by examining the behavior. The explanation of actual behavior by hindsight is easier than the advance specification of all possible interactive contingencies, just as in real life:

models of computation focus on tractable projections of intractable behavior
interactive behavior tractable by hindsight may be intractable by foresight

Projections of fully abstract behavior onto particular tractable contexts can be viewed as a computational analog of Plato's parable of the cave (see Figure 6). Plato contends that humans can perceive only projections of reality onto their sense-perceptions (shadows on the walls of the cave in which they live). Noncomputability of fully abstract behavior of an object corresponds to inherent unobservability of real (Platonic) objects, while tractability of projections corresponds to observability of projections of Platonic reality onto sense perceptions.

Plato viewed his parable as a pessimistic demonstration of the futility of trying to perceive reality. His pessimism was in part responsible for the decline of empirical attempts to understand reality over the next 2000 years. Modem science reverses Plato's pessimism, showing that observability of projections of reality allows us to manipulate and control reality (though we cannot perceive God, we can describe God's shadow). The tractability of projections of software objects, like that of physical objects, is a positive result that makes the intractability of fully abstract behavior irrelevant. The ability to manipulate and control objects through their interactive projections makes it unnecessary to specify or comprehend their fully abstract behavior.

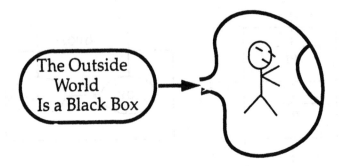

Figure 6: Projection in Plato's Cave

Real-world entities cannot be completely observed for precisely the same reason that objects cannot be mathematically modeled: their behavior in all possible contexts cannot be completely described. There is a deep correspondence between projections of real-world entities on our sense perceptions and projections of objects onto tractable subspaces. In both cases projections may be used to understand and control inherently indescribable phenomena.

Projection is closely related to abstraction, since both preserve relevant attributes of an entity or situation while ignoring others. Models of computation for algorithms are the result of a three-level projection (abstraction) process:

Platonic projection: of real-world entities onto human sense perceptions
computational approximation: of continuous physical models by discrete computational models
functional projection: of behavior over time onto behavior at instances of time

Each abstraction step loses essential information that cannot be recaptured. Platonic projection irreversibly restricts perceptions to those projected on the walls of our cave, object models irreversibly replace continuous physical perceptions by discrete approximations, and functional models irreversibly project object behavior in time onto behavior at instants of time.

1.6. Church's Thesis and the Turing Test

Church's thesis asserts that every effectively calculable function is expressible in the lambda calculus. The equivalence in expressive power of lambda expressions, Turing machines, and recursive functions provides evidence of the robustness of the class of lambda definable (Turing computable) functions. We do not directly contradict Church's thesis, but suggest that this robustly definable class of functions is too weak to capture the intuitive notion of effective computability because effective computations include computations of software systems that cannot be expressed by functions.

Church equates effective computability with functions that specify sales contracts, while computers exist in time and can effectively compute behavior over time expressible by marriage contracts. Since software systems can *effectively* compute behavior over time not expressible by computable functions, Church's thesis equating functional and effective computability is inapplicable to software systems. The argument that the Church/Turing notion of computable functions is too weak to capture the intuitive notion of computability has two steps:

1. The interactive behavior of objects and software systems cannot be completely specified by computable functions.
2. Objects and software systems determine effectively computable behavior

The first step can be established by technical arguments. The second step depends on the intuitive notion of being effectively computable. Most people would agree that automatic teller machines and airline reservation systems represent effectively computable behavior, and Church himself would probably have concurred with this view. The arguments for accepting the second step of this argument are thus quite strong, though not subject to technical proof.

The inadequacy of algorithms for modeling interaction and the inadequacy of computable functions as a model of effective computation is not merely a cute technical result. It is a technical characterization of the inadequacy of current models of computation as a basis for specifying practical software systems. The extension of the notion of effective computability from functions to persistent interactive entities is of central practical importance in describing the behavior of actual software systems.

The argument that computable functions cannot specify effective computation is also an argument against Turing's view that computable functions can model human intelligence. The interaction protocol of the Turing Test presumes a model of interaction whose computational power transcends that of computable functions. The questions posed in [Tu] are chosen to have time-independent algorithmic answers, though the suggestion that answers be delayed to model human response time borders on the non algorithmic. The test would become entirely nonalgorithmic for concurrently interactive and potentially nonserializable questions and answers from multiple questioners. Thus an argument against Turing's view is that the Turing test tests computation power stronger than that of computable functions and therefore addresses a different question from that posed by Turing.

This argument against Turing's limited characterization of intelligence shares with Penrose the view that computable functions are not rich enough to express intelligence [Pe]. However, Penrose justifies this position by strong claims about the empirical noncomputability of physical laws, while our arguments are entirely in terms of the properties of models of interaction, without any direct appeal to laws of physics. Our argument in fact implies that the laws of physics are noncomputable because they are interactive. But this strong conclusion is derived entirely from an abstract argument concerning the inability of computable functions to express interaction that has nothing to do with empirical properties of physical objects:

object behavior cannot be captured by computable functions
physical behavior can capture object behavior
therefore physical behavior cannot be captured by computable functions

The questions of whether software objects can model intelligence or physical objects, which are considered open questions for the purposes of this discussion, are distinct from whether computable functions can model intelligence or physical laws, which are answered negatively.

Software objects mimic the interactive behavior of physical objects so closely that their properties can be used to infer interactive physical laws. The behavior of physical objects cannot be expressed by computable functions because the fully abstract behavior of physical objects, like that of software objects, is not expressible as a function. Though physical behavior is computable in most everyday situations, it can give rise to noncomputable behavior like chaos or nondeterminacy when concurrent interactive conflicts cannot be resolved. For example, the chaotic motion of a steel ball in a force field determined by two magnets can be attributed to the fact that the independent effects of the two force fields on the steel ball are not serializable. This example suggests that empirically observed chaotic behavior can in at least some cases be attributed to conflicting interactive stimuli.

2. Software Components and Software Problems

2.1. Components as Persistent Interaction Units

Components generalize the notion of objects to a broader class of interaction units:

atomic interaction units: objects, processes, agents, robots
composite interaction units: application program interfaces, frameworks, databases

Our notion of components spans the above atomic and composite interaction units and captures the essence of persistent interaction over time: Components are defined by generalizing from accidental properties of objects to necessary properties of persistent interaction. Necessary properties of interaction are developed below by distinguishing between the properties of objects and procedures.

Objects have interfaces that capture interaction over time while procedures specify actions at an instant of time. Objects are noun-like entities while procedures are verb-like actions.

objects → nouns → interactions, interfaces
procedures → verbs → actions, transformations

The insight that objects behave like nouns and that interactive interfaces are the essence of being noun-like provides a good starting point for a list of necessary properties of units of interaction. Objects are nouns that interact, while procedures are verbs that compute.

Objects have the noun-like quality of being persistent, while procedures have the verb-like quality of being transient. Object and procedure specifications in libraries are comparable static constructs, while object instances and procedure invocations are comparable dynamic entities.

Objects achieve their persistence and temporal modeling power by separating existence and execution, while procedure invocations self-destruct when their execution is completed because they tie existence to execution. Separation of existence and execution allows time to be a first-class notion and introduces new kinds of (serial and fully abstract) semantics for objects that has no analog for procedures.

Autonomous existence is the basis not only for persistence but also for concurrency. Persistence implies concurrent existence of the persistent entity and its environment, while concurrent existence in turn provides a framework for concurrent execution. Object composition is based on the notion that objects being composed exist concurrently and can therefore execute concurrently. The composition of procedures aims to capture the effect of their sequential execution and is therefore noncommutative, while the composition of objects aims to capture their concurrent existence and is therefore commutative.

Procedures and objects are distinguished by the following six properties:

Properties of procedure invocations:
 procedure invocations are actions, they are like verbs, they do *something*
 they specify a one-time response to a stimulus, like a sales contract
 they tie existence to execution, terminating when an invocation is completed
 their composition is sequential and non-commutative
 their models of computation are based on functions and algorithms
 their cost is measured by execution-time resources

Properties of objects:
 objects are entities, they are like nouns, they are *something*
 they specify interactive behavior in time, like a marriage contract
 they separate existence from execution, persisting over multiple invocations
 their composition is concurrent and commutative
 their models are based on interfaces that provide persistent services to clients
 their cost is measured by life-cycle resources

The categories used to distinguish objects from procedures are the following:

Categories of comparison:
 ontology: verbs versus nouns
 interaction: sales contract versus marriage contract
 persistence: transient versus persistent

composition: sequential versus concurrent
behavior model: functions and algorithms versus interaction and interfaces
cost model: execution-time resources versus life-cycle resources

The features listed above for objects are also possessed by components of distributed networks, databases, command and control systems, airline reservation systems, robots, and virtual reality systems. By elevating this list of features to the status of required properties, components capture essential properties of persistent interaction units.

Properties of components:
ontology: components are entities, they are like nouns, they **are** *something*
interaction: they specify persistent behavior in time, like a marriage contract
persistence: they separate existence from execution, persisting over multiple invocations
composition: their composition is concurrent and commutative
behavior model: their models specify interfaces that provide persistent services to clients
cost model: their complexity is measured by life-cycle resources

The first three properties, which specify components to be interactive, persistent nouns, are clearly the core properties of persistent interaction units. The remaining properties relate to systems of components, since the impact of components on the cost and performance of complete software systems is a primary goal. Component composition, behavior models, and cost models are necessary properties in understanding the effectiveness of components as primitive building blocks in problem solving.

Object-oriented programming was for many years criticized on the grounds that "everyone is using it but no one knows what it is". Such comments, also applicable to components, are inherently unfair since significant new concepts like objects and components are *natural kinds* inherently undefinable by already existing concepts, and at best approximately definable by a number of attributes. Our approximate working definition focuses on significant software-engineering properties common to all large component-based software systems that are helpful in understanding the inherent nature of components, their mechanisms for modeling applications, and their models of computation. An approximate definition of notions like *object* and *component* by a set of necessary but not sufficient attributes is the best we can hope to achieve.

2.2. Algorithmic Problems and Complexity

Problem solving is the central goal of both algorithms and software systems. Agorithmic models of computation have a precise notion of "problem" that determines the role of behavior and complexity in the problem solving process. Component-based problem solving has many of the high-level features of algorithmic problem solving in spite of the fact that the primitive programming mechanisms may differ. We develop a notion of "software problem" by analogy with the more precise notion of "algorithmic problem" and a notion of "software scalability" that is an analog of "algorithmic complexity". An algorithmic problem is defined as follows [GJ]:

An algorithmic problem is a general question usually possessing a size parameter
Examples: sorting problem, traveling salesman problem

Algorithmic problems are expressible by algorithms implemented by procedures. The complexity of an algorithm is defined by the rate of growth of computation time and memory resources as the problem size increases. The complexity of an algorithmic problem is defined by the rate of growth of resources with problem size for the best possible algorithm:

computational complexity:
problem size n: size of data input (number of elements to be sorted)
algorithm complexity $A(n)$: growth of resources with problem size for specific algorithm
problem complexity $C(n)$: growth of resources with problem size for best possible algorithm

The behavior of an algorithm is specified by a function (every algorithm computes a function that is a subset of the computable functions). The correctness of an algorithm can be defined in terms of equivalence to a functional specification:

algorithm correctness: equivalence of functional and algorithmic specification

Behavior specifications for algorithms specify *what* is to be computed independently of *how* it is computed. "What" specifications may in general be realized by many different kinds of algorithmic "how" specifications with the same functional "what" specification. Sorting can be realized by many different kinds of algorithms, including merging, insertion sort, bubble sort, and each algorithm can in turn be realized by many different programs in many different programming languages. Much effort has been expended on the analysis of algorithms for sorting [Kn], and the space of equivalent algorithms for sorting is very large. The set of all algorithms or programs that correctly realize a function specifying a computational problem is not only infinite but not even enumerable. Additional requirements for selecting a particular program from this very large space of possible programs include execution-time efficiency and aesthetic requirements relating to program structure and documentation:

problem requirements = correctness + efficiency + aesthetics

Correctness is an absolute (binary) requirement for mathematically specified problems, while efficiency and aesthetics are a matter of degree. We are not satisfied with programs that are almost correct but are satisfied with good rather than optimal efficiency. Small increments in efficiency can be traded for other kinds of convenience, such as modularity or user-friendliness.

Correctness requirements are *hard* requirements while efficiency and aesthetics are *soft* requirements (see Figure 7). The problem of programming may be viewed as a constraint-satisfaction problem whose hard requirements determine a space of feasible solutions and whose soft requirements determine desirability criteria for selecting among feasible solutions.

Hard requirements are absolute constraints that determine a subspace of the set of programs in which the solution must lie, while soft requirements are desirable additional constraints that determine a *desirability metric* on the space of correct solutions. Some soft requirements like efficiency have a precise metric, while others like aesthetics have only subjective metrics but are nevertheless important in assigning an index of quality to a program.

Though correctness is a hard requirement in the mathematical world of algorithm analysis, it may become a soft requirement for embedded systems that must provide their results in real time. Real-time requirements arise in control applications where information needed to control an airplane in flight or a nuclear reactor must be provided with very low latency. Low latency is also required in user interface and virtual reality applications to provide users with a look and feel of continuity and realism. Real-time applications distinguish between soft and hard real-time requirements, defining requirements as *hard real-time* if timeliness replaces correctness as the hard constraint (see Figure 8). Control and virtual reality applications must provide approximate methods that trade off accuracy for speed to achieve the best possible results for dynamically determined hard real-time constraints.

Soft real-time responses may compromise correctness by computing approximate or heuristic responses when exact or complete solutions cannot be computed fast enough. Combinatorially intractable problems like the traveling salesman problem and chess are generally solved by heuristic programs that do not guarantee correctness. Correctness is compromised in logic programming by giving up logical completeness to realize heuristic flexibility. Real-time simulation of the interaction of a large set of balls or particles requires approximate computation of collisions, where the fineness of approximation may be tailored to the irregularity of particle motion.

2.3. Software Problems and Scalability

Software problems can be defined by analogy with algorithmic problems:

A software problem is a general question whose instances may be arbitrarily complex

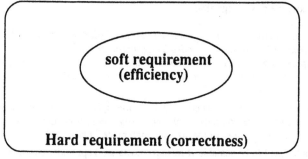

Figure 7: Hard (Absolute) and Soft (Desirable) Requirements

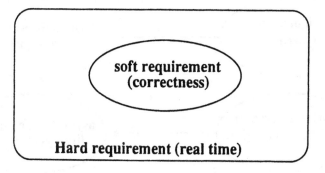

Figure 8: Hard Real-Time Constraints

Examples: airline reservation, banking, command and control

Airline reservation systems can be very simple toy systems that can be made more complex without limit by adding rules for seat cancellation, flight cancellation, airline reorganization, emergency rescheduling, and even weather prediction. Such increasing complexity has no neat size parameter or complexity metric, but the problem size can be related to the problem specification and a complexity related to the life-cycle cost in a carefully specified life-cycle model can be defined.

The growth in resource utilization as software problems become more complex is analogous to the growth in resource utilization of algorithmic problems, though the nature of the resources is very different. Resources for algorithms are space and time resources during problem execution, while resources for software problems are life-cycle costs of development and maintenance. Instances of an algorithmic problem are execution instances, while instances of a software problem are development instances.

The problem of controlling the costs of software resources for large instances of a software problem will be referred to as *scalability* to distinguish it from the problem of controlling computer resources for large instances of an algorithmic problem:

Computational complexity: growth of computer execution resources as problems grow large
Software scalability: growth of life-cycle resources as problems grow large

Scalability of a software problem can be defined in terms of a size parameter and a size-dependent scalability metric, though the size and scalability metrics are not as precisely defined as size and complexity metrics of algorithms:

software problem: a general question to be answered (application to be modeled)
size: length of a problem specification encoded by agreed-upon rules
scalability: asymptotic growth in life-cycle costs as the problem size increases for an agreed-upon paradigm of problem solving and model of life-cycle-cost estimation

Software scalability analysis is concerned with the life-cycle costs of airline reservation systems as they grow in size, just as computational complexity theory is concerned with the behavior of sorting algorithms for large values of the size parameter (see Figure 9).

Architectures are said to be scalable if resource costs are kept under control as system size grows. Scalability of hardware architectures is concerned with communication costs between

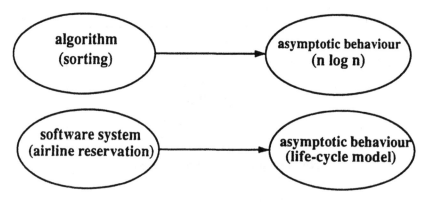

Figure 9: Algorithmic Complexity and Software Scalability

''adjacent'' processes as the number of processes becomes large. The *n-cube* is considered less scalable than the *mesh* because communication costs between adjacent processors grow as the dimensionality increases. Moreover, the mesh preserves locality of structure as the system size increases and can be scaled up incrementally without changing already existing structure.

Scalability is a central question for large software systems, just as it is for large hardware systems. As systems become large, local computational features of systems become less important and the architecture of component interconnection and interaction becomes more important. Scalability for software architectures cannot be measured by a simple metric like communication cost. Instead, it must be measured by life-cycle cost, since this is the dominating cost of software architecture. According to this measure, the data-abstraction model is the most scalable in the sense that data abstractions are autonomous components and systems of objects or distributed components can be scaled up more easily than other architectures because their components are autonomous and have few constraints in adding new components. Each of the other architectures has forms of sharing and system interconnection that violate the principle of locality of incremental modification for certain kinds of incremental modification.

Scalable software architectures should preserve locality of structure as the system size and complexity increases. Component-based systems based on data abstraction preserve locality of structure under incremental modification to a greater extent than other architectures, playing a role similar to that of the mesh in hardware architectures.

Scalability measures the asymptotic growth of software systems as they become large in much the same way that asymptotic growth of the sorting problem is measured by *nlogn*, but is less precise. Different design architectures of software systems may have different scalability properties, just as different sorting algorithms have different computational complexity. We say that one software architecture is more scalable than another if its life-cycle costs grow more slowly as the software systems grow in size.

The scalability of component-based systems is largely independent of the inner computation structure of components, depending almost entirely on their interaction mechanisms. Component-based architectures are more scalable than procedure-oriented architectures, providing a uniformly better framework for controlling the complexity of large software systems.

Thesis: Component-based architectures provide a more scalable framework for controlling the complexity of large software systems than procedure-oriented architectures.

This thesis cannot be conclusively proven because it compares inherently qualitative categories like procedure-oriented and component-based architectures. In this respect its status is similar to that of Church's thesis. However, the evidence that component-based architectures are more scalable is quite strong:

Evidence: Components capture the behavior in time of autonomous interactive entities. They allow incremental changes by adding new components and incremental changes in existing components. Component-based models are widely used in scientific models of physical, biological, economic, and social phenomena. Experience with computing systems clearly demonstrates that large systems have a component-based structure that accords with the specified necessary properties of components.

Scalability determines a hard constraint on reactive, embedded software systems that plays a similar role to that of correctness for algorithms (see Figure 10). The conjecture suggests that scalability may be replaced by component-based architecture as a hard constraint for the development of large software systems.

Conclusion: Large software systems are inevitably component-based to ensure scalability.

As systems become larger, internal small-scale properties of programs inevitably play a smaller role and the large-scale topography of program components increasingly blurs internal small-scale distinctions. Requirements of scalability are similar for large classes of systems including airline reservation systems, command and control systems, banking systems, and economic forecasting systems, resulting in robust software systems over a wide range of applica-

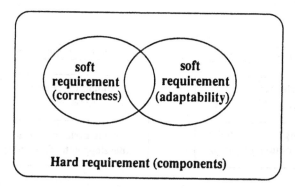

Figure 10: Component-Based Structure as a Hard Constraint

tions. However, large-scale software requirements are component-based rather than procedure-oriented and their fully abstract semantics will require temporal specifications that go beyond those of computable functions.

2.4. Requirements for Software Problems

Requirements for software problems have broader behavior and resource requirements than algorithmic problems:

requirements = behavior requirements + resource requirements
behavior requirements = functional requirements + time-varying requirements
resource requirements = computing requirements + life-cycle requirements

The behavior requirements of software problems include time-varying as well as functional requirements, while the resource requirements include life-cycle as well as computing requirements. Life-cycle costs generally dominate computing costs for large software systems and are the bottleneck in large system development. It is for this reason that scalability becomes a hard requirement, imposing a component-based architecture on software systems. Algorithm requirements are a special case of software requirements in which time-varying requirements are inapplicable and life-cycle costs are ignored (see Figure 11).

Software problems cannot generally be implemented by algorithms or specified by functions, since their time-varying behavior and life-cycle management requirements cannot be functionally specified. Their complexity cannot be specified by execution-time resource requirements because life-cycle costs generally dominate computation costs. Bottlenecks in computation speed can be eliminated by faster hardware, approximation, or heuristics, while bottlenecks in development cost have no easy resolution and are sometimes insurmountable.

Because maintenance and enhancement are dominant parts of the software life cycle, resource requirements have as much to do with the capacity of the system to change its behavior as with the delivery of a given behavior. Adaptability to change is determined by locality and depends on inner system structure as well as interface behavior. The non-algorithmic nature of system requirements is due to two independent factors:

the temporal fully abstract behavior of context-dependent procedures is non-algorithmic
the system structure requirements for adaptability and evolution are non-algorithmic

Large software systems are non-algorithmic, open, and distributed:

non-algorithmic: they model temporal evolution by systems of interacting components
open: they manage incremental change by local changes of accessible open interfaces
distributed: requirements as well as components are locally autonomous

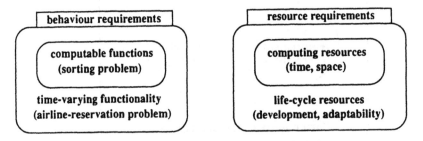

behaviour requirements

computable functions
(sorting problem)

time-varying functionality
(airline-reservation problem)

resource requirements

computing resources
(time, space)

life-cycle resources
(development, adaptability)

Figure 11: Behavior and Resource Requirements of Software Systems

Maintenance and enhancement requires easy access to the internals of a system just as maintenance requirements for an automobile require easy access to the components of a car. A system that is adaptable to change is referred to as an *open system*:

Definition: A system (or system component) is *open* if its internal structure is accessible for the purpose of changing it.

Open systems should not be confused with open standards. Open standards are publicly accessible system interfaces developed for the benefit of users rather than for system evolution. They freeze system interfaces so that users can rely on their behavior:

open standard: publicly accessible, nonmodifiable interfaces
open system: publicly accessible, incrementally modifiable interfaces

The conflict between openness for widespread use and openness for further improvement arises in many contexts. It is essentially the conflict between consumer-oriented and capital-intensive utilization of resources. Openness is a synonym for accessibility, open systems provide accessibility for incremental modification, but open standards conflict so strongly with open systems that they cause potentially open systems to become closed:

open standards → closed systems

Openness of computing systems can be captured by the notions of encapsulation and reactiveness, where encapsulation captures static notions of spatial partitioning and reactiveness captures dynamic notions of temporal evolution:

Definition: A program constituent is said to be *encapsulated* if its interactive behavior is captured by an interface that hides its implementation from clients.

Definition: A program constituent is said to be *reactive* if it is a time-varying, persistent entity whose lifetime is longer than that of the messages (atomic interactions) that it executes.

Encapsulation and reactiveness are complementary mechanisms for incremental modification. Encapsulation supports *spatial incremental change* by external agents such as programmers and software engineers, for example by adding new modules or modifying existing ones. Reactiveness supports *temporal incremental change* by internal mechanisms of change and is the natural mechanism of physical and biological change. For example, human development over a single lifetime and biological evolution are instances of reactive change.

Software engineers are particularly interested in the openness of large systems to incremental modification as they grow in size. Asymptotic openness corresponds to scalability:

Openness and Scalability: A system that remains open to unrestricted, unpredictable incremental modification as it grows in size is scalable. Scalability is an asymptotic form of openness.

Software requirements for open systems are distributed in that different clients of a system have different needs and the needs of one class of clients may conflict with those of another, as we saw above in the conflict between openness for developers and users.

Open systems require that components be autonomous rather than interdependent. The term *open system* was applied to physical, biological, and political systems long before it was used in the context of computing systems. For example, Karl Popper's *The Open Society and Its Enemies* [Po] is concerned with open political systems that provide freedom (autonomy) for their individuals (constituents), and democratic mechanisms of change. A definition of openness broad enough to encompass both political and computing systems can be phrased as follows:

Definition: Systems of interacting constituents are open if they can autonomously adapt to changing environments.

Experience with democratic and totalitarian societies suggests that short-term optimizations of totalitarianism constrain longer-term adaptation, and that a high degree of autonomy of constituents is required to sustain long-term survival. Autonomy, which is viewed as an end in itself by individuals, serves evolutionary goals as well as goals of self-gratification. Biological systems likewise require a balance between autonomy and coordination to sustain evolution, suggesting that the human urge for autonomy has evolutionary value. Computing systems, like social and biological systems, require a balance between autonomy and coordination to balance short-term functionality and long-term adaptability.

3. Paradigms of Interaction

Algorithms support a restricted paradigm of interaction, being triggered by an input in its domain and producing an output that may in turn be the input of another algorithm. Components support more flexible forms of interaction that can sometimes be specified as sequences of interactively invoked algorithms but are in general not specifiable by any simple composition rule for primitive external interactions because of unpredictable internal interactions:

algorithm: sequence of noninteractive computation steps triggered by a single interaction
atomic component: context-dependent procedures that share a persistent state
composite component: persistent interaction units with complex internal structure
stand-alone component: interacts with active or passive non-computer clients

Each of the paradigms of interaction examined below has characteristic interface protocols, composition mechanisms, and internal component structure:

algorithmic interaction units:
 autistic component: computation with no interaction
 function: input stimulus → output response, direction of computation
 predicate: stimulus → binary response, relation among arguments
 finite automaton: predefined input stream → final state or output stream
 Turing machine: input tape → output tape, computable functions
atomic components:
 object: interactive input stream → output stream + interactions
 process: nondeterministic input stream → output stream or broadcasting
composite components:
 application program interface (API): interface of tasks and services for programmers
 frameworks: virtual procedures in subclasses → application program interface
 databases, multidatabases, and information systems: information repositories
external interfaces:
 graphical user interface (GUI): interactive input stream → stream of 2D images
 robot: concurrent multiple sensors → concurrent multiple actuators
 virtual reality: multisensory stimuli → multisensory responses

Algorithms focus on inner computation for mathematically tractable, context-independent algorithms. Objects and processes have a characteristic mechanism for composing context-dependent procedures that interact through a shared state. Composite components have a persistent interactive interface and inner component composition mechanisms. We examine the properties of APIs that provide interfaces tailored to specific applications, frameworks whose inner composition mechanism is based on inheritance, and databases with a variety of internal composition mechanisms tailored to the management of large repositories of information. External interfaces include graphical user interfaces for end-user interaction, robot interfaces for intelligent interaction with passive or active environments, and virtual-reality systems that provide immersive multisensory user environments.

3.1. Algorithmic Interfaces

Algorithmic behavior is dependent only on input parameters and not on the context of execution or the time at which the algorithm is executed. The interactive behavior of algorithms is context independent.

Functions specify a direction of computation, since outputs are uniquely computed from inputs while inputs cannot be uniquely recreated from outputs. Predicates can be viewed as functions from inputs to binary outputs, or as bidirectional relations that do not distinguish between inputs and outputs.

Finite automata map a predefined read-only input stream into an output stream or onto a designated final state. Turing machines place the state-transition mechanism of finite automata in a more powerful interactive environment that allows machines to write on their tape as well as read it, thereby amplifying what can be computed. Both finite automata and Turing machines have a functional rather than interactive semantics. Finite automata and Turing machines determine functions from input to output tapes:

automaton: F(tape) → tape'

Computations of automata and Turing machines are context-independent functions that do not admit autonomous interaction. They are closed systems whose behavior is entirely determined by their tape and initial state. Their semantics does not admit a notion of interaction with autonomous clients once a computation is underway. Conversely, the semantics of objects that interact with autonomous clients while they compute cannot be described by Turing machines.

Paradigms of computation and interaction have fundamentally different notions of time. Algorithms that compute outputs from given inputs are oblivious to external notions of time. They are context independent and impervious to the slings and arrows of outrageous contexts. Context-dependent procedures are vulnerable to contextual changes of state arising in real time caused by internal object dynamics as well as to real-time interactions with other objects. Because algorithms are oblivious to real time they cannot be extended to time-dependent interactive actions without a radical change of the underlying modeling paradigm.

Unpredictable nonalgorithmic behavior in context-dependent procedures is caused by conflicts between algorithmic time and real time. Hard real-time requirements are likewise caused by incompatibility of algorithmic time and real time requirements. Interactive models view algorithms as instantaneously executed actions, and require special precautions when this assumption does not hold for actual computations.

The treatment of algorithms as instantaneous events in concurrent computations can be realized by atomicity requirements. Atomicity of primitive operations like P and V allows higher-level atomicity of actions to be defined. Serializability of transactions is a high-level atomicity requirement that allows transactions to be treated as atomic and therefore instantaneous events. Serializability, which requires concurrent computations to be equivalent to a sequential order of execution, at first appears to be a somewhat strange requirement, but becomes natural when viewed as a requirement for context-dependent actions to appear instantaneous.

Turing machines capture programming in the small at the level of algorithms but not programming in the large at the level of software systems. Since practical computation is at the level of software systems rather than algorithms, Turing computability is too weak to capture the notion of effective interactive computation. The traditional theory of computation cannot deal with questions of interaction over time that arise in "real" software systems.

Church's thesis asserts that the functions computable by Turing machines are the effectively computable functions according to an intuitive criterion of effectiveness. However, if we extend the notion of being effectively computable from functional behavior to behavior over time of persistent interaction units, computable functions no longer capture effectively computable behavior and Church's thesis is no longer applicable. Software systems of interacting components determine a larger range of computational behavior than the class of Turing-computable functions because interaction over time is effectively computable by software systems but not by Turing machines.

3.2. Objects and Processes

Objects model the behavior of periods of time between the execution of algorithms as well as the interface behavior of algorithms. Procedures embedded in an object are context-dependent algorithms whose semantics is specified in a state that may be modified as a side-effect of procedure execution and by other procedures of the object. Objects model behavior over time through the following mechanisms:

their identity persists for multiple procedure invocations
multiple procedures provide algorithmic diversity at a given instant of time
time-varying behavior and evolution in time are supported by an internal state

The effect of a procedure is specified by its effects for all possible arguments, while the effect of an object at a given point of time is defined by its interface procedures:

procedure = forall arguments. effect
object-interface = forall procedures. procedure
= forall procedures. (forall arguments. effect)

The serial behavior of objects over time is specified by sequences of procedure invocations called traces. The set of all serial behaviors is the trace of its individual procedures:

serial behavior over time = forall sequences-of-procedures. object-interface
= forall sequences. (forall procedures. (forall arguments. effect))

Traces are a powerful mathematical technique that can generate complex behavior from very simple interface operations. Objects with an interface of *and* and *not* operations and no internal state have sufficient interactive power to generate all computable functions. However, an object's interactive behavior cannot be captured by its serial behavior. Fully abstract semantics for all possible interactions is an empirical rather than mathematical property of objects, defined by analogy with operationalism in physics and behaviorism in psychology.

Composition mechanisms of object models include functional and context-dependent procedure composition as well as composition for objects and classes:

procedure composition: P1 followed by P2
context-dependent procedure composition: compose procedures with a shared state
object composition: many ways of composing objects, including parallel composition
class composition by inheritance: composition scheme for classes with subclasses

Sequential object-oriented computations partition the global time line of an object into temporally disjoint local time lines. Objects "describe" entities in terms of the *effects* of all potential observations, where effects may be both a response and an internal change of state:

effects = external-effect(response) + internal-effect(state transition)
global time line → temporally disjoint local time lines for individual objects

A sequential computation can be partitioned into temporally disjoint local computations and a sequence of send/receive interaction events that transfer control among objects. The effects of a particular sequential computation can be described by a sequence of local effects. But the set of all possible interactions of an object with other objects, or even the set of all interactions of a context-dependent procedure over time, cannot be functionally described.

Concurrent computations among processes require more complex projections of the computation space onto time lines than sequential computations. Processes must handle synchronization among competing waiting messages that may involve nondeterministic choice among alternative courses of action. Concurrent object-oriented systems generally adopt irreversible *don't-care nondeterminism* as opposed to reversible *don't know nondeterminism* of logic programming [We]. Message sending can be synchronous or asynchronous and can be point-to-point or by broadcasting.

The simplest form of process concurrency consists of internally sequential processes that accept messages sequentially. However, processes may be internally concurrent and may have interfaces that can handle multiple concurrent inputs. Internal and interface concurrency are independent (orthogonal):

neither internal nor interface concurrency: concurrent object-based languages
internal concurrency, sequential interface: user interface to complex system
internal sequentiality, concurrent interface: simple behavior in complex environment
both internal and interface concurrency: people, intelligent robots

Milner [Mi] and other researchers in the semantics of concurrency have indicated that computable functions are an inadequate model of concurrency for the following reasons:

inner breakdown: internal process concurrency causes unpredictable (nonfunctional) behavior
outer breakdown: composition of processes cannot be functionally defined

However, this inadequacy already arises for sequential objects because it is caused by the inability of functions to model unpredictable interaction over time. Procedures of sequential objects are already nonfunctional because their unpredictable (nondeterministic) interaction with an inner state and outer environment cannot be modeled functionally. A better understanding of the semantics of interaction over time can serve as a common semantic foundation for the interactive semantics of both sequential and concurrent software systems.

3.3. Application Program Interfaces and Frameworks

Application program interfaces (APIs) are interfaces to systems that encapsulate the complete functionality of an application domain. They generally require components with greater complexity and granularity than simple objects or processes. Frameworks are APIs whose inner structure is specified by a class inheritance hierarchy. They are composite components specifiable by the composition of simpler components. Moreover, framework interfaces generally contain vertical function specifications that change the balance of responsibility between developers and users of a component by requiring users to specify subclasses that implement virtual function symbols.

APIs provide a collection of services and tools for creating user application interfaces. The functionality of APIs is made available to users through a user interface with the following levels of functionality [BC]:

device drivers: for managing keyboards, mice, cursors, printers etc
resource managers: for managing windows and other background resource interfaces
interaction objects: for handling menus, scrollbars, and other widgets
dialog controller: for sequencing user interactions and system responses
application functionality: that implements the functionality of the application domain

The first four categories (devices, windows, widgets, dialogs) are concerned with interaction independently of the domain of application. Graphical user interfaces require more support mechanisms than sequential keyboard interfaces of traditional programming languages. Interaction becomes a first-class phenomenon whose smooth domain-independent realization is the analog of compiling.

APIs serve the same purpose as that served by programming languages, namely the specification of tasks by programmers for execution by computer. However, programs specify complete tasks in advance for non-interactive execution, while APIs facilitate the interactive execution of tasks. APIs permit algorithmic interaction by writing and executing complete programs but also support entirely new modes of interaction. Algorithmic interaction can be specified by traditional programming language semantics, but sequences of interactions, especially by autonomous potentially concurrent users, lie outside the realm of programming language semantics. For example, use of an airline reservation system by multiple concurrent reservation agents can be handled by an API but cannot be described by algorithmic semantics.

Interaction entities called widgets have a visual geometry that can be accessed by users to perform system actions. Widgets provided by APIs such as Motif can be classified as follows:

display widgets: buttons, fields, labels that display information
manager (container) widgets: combine widgets into composite structures (panels, menus)
dialog widgets: for creating dialogs (bulleting boards, error dialog etc)
menu widgets: for the construction of pull-down, pop-up menus
gadgets: realize efficiency by not having a separate window

Widgets are activated by mouse or keyboard actions. Actions associated with a widget are specified by *callback functions*, called when the widget is activated. Conversion from visual interaction with widgets to internal callback actions is similar to but simpler than human conversion of visual interactions into internal representations and actions of the brain.

visual interaction with widget → internal callback action

The collection of widgets of an API generally have a uniform *look and feel* that allows widgets of one API to be distinguished from another. For example, Motif widgets have a characteristic form of shading that suggests they are three-dimensional.

The collection of tools in an API is generally quite complex, and is frequently implemented by an operating system with non-component-based structure in the interests of efficiency. However, there are advantages to implementing APIs as open systems with a well-defined component-based internal structure. APIs can be implemented as collections of independent components, as class libraries with well-defined interaction protocols, or as frameworks that organize classes into inheritance hierarchies:

frameworks are inheritance hierarchies of abstract and concrete classes
virtual functions defined in subclasses allow frameworks to be systematically specialized

Frameworks are object-oriented class hierarchies that require virtual operation specifications of the framework to be defined in subclasses before objects that use the functionality of the framework can be created. They are partial specifications of the functionality of an interface that prescribe a specific form of completion by the user to specialize the framework for particular purposes.

Frameworks change the balance of interaction between the system and application developer, shifting part of the burden of defining interactive functionality onto the application programmer. This places a greater burden on the application programmer but provides considerable additional flexibility in tailoring the application environment to the needs of the user. The technique of supplying specialized functions for a generic system specification is supported in object-oriented systems but can also be used in systems that are not object-oriented to tailor the environment for specific uses.

Frameworks determine a flexible paradigm of interaction with a systematic method of building composite components as inheritance hierarchies of classes. This paradigm is useful in defining flexible APIs that allow the user to tailor widgets to particular hardware or to the look and feel of a particular style of interaction, and can be used to design and implement a variety of other complex interfaces.

3.4. Databases, Multidatabases, and Information Systems

Paradigms of interaction for databases are concerned with querying, navigation, and management of information rather than with algorithmic computation. Databases are quintessential persistent interactive components for which our semantics of persistence is especially applicable.

Interaction paradigms for databases focus on flexible retrieval and safe updating for large volumes of information that may be concurrently accessed by multiple users. Databases emphasize security, consistency, and integrity of the data as a primary requirement. They are composite components whose interfaces and internal structuring principles reflect their security and retrieval requirements. However, there is considerable debate concerning the details of interaction and internal structuring paradigms for databases:

interaction paradigm: specification, manipulation, and transaction processing language
inner structure: network, relational, or object-oriented structure

Relational databases store data as records, specify retrieval by formulae of a relational calculus, and perform computations on retrieved information by a separate programming language after the information has been retrieved. Object-oriented databases are repositories for objects with their operations rather than for records of raw data, and support computation, data types, and schema evolution more directly than relational databases.

The need to handle concurrent access by multiple users requires concurrency control and recovery mechanisms that are unnecessary for components that restrict access to one user at a time. Transactions for tasks like transferring money from one bank account to another or making an airline reservation for a sequence of flights must be performed on an all-or-nothing basis, aborting the transaction if it cannot be completed.

Multidatabases have components which are local databases coordinated by transactions executed by a global transaction manager. Transactions specify tasks which may involve the execution of operations in more than one local database, and commit only when all operations of the task have been successfully performed.

For example, a travel agent who makes airline, hotel, and car reservations for a travel itinerary can be modeled by a global transaction manager of a multidatabase. The global transaction *arrange travel itinerary* requires the execution of operations (transactions) in airline, car rental, and hotel databases. The travel agent must compete for local database resources with other travel agents and private individuals and must lock resources when exclusive access is needed. It can commit only when all stages of an itinerary have been booked.

Local databases can communicate only through the global transaction manager and not directly with each other. Local databases can be accessed by multiple global transaction managers and also by applications which can compete with global transactions for resources. For example, an airline reservation database can be accessed both by travel agents (global transaction managers) and by private individuals (applications).

The balance between coordination and autonomy is a primary concern for local databases. Local databases are autonomously created and owned and provide services whose degree of autonomy is locally determined. Some local databases may be prepared to participate in the coordination while others may not. It is useful to distinguish three kinds of autonomy associated respectively with design, execution, and communication:

design autonomy: local control of program and system changes by each component
execution autonomy: local control of execution, no unauthorized interrupts
communication autonomy: no direct access to nonlocal data (distributed components)

Multidatabases have a global interaction paradigm for interaction among databases and one or more local interaction paradigm among the components within each database. The detailed description of these interaction paradigms is beyond the scope of this paper. However, the multiplicity of interaction paradigms for information systems and the different interaction paradigms for objects, processes, APIs. frameworks, and databases, suggests that the comparative study of interaction paradigms may be worthwhile.

3.5. Graphical User Interfaces (GUIs)

GUIs provide the user with a two-dimensional graphical interface that takes advantage of parallelism in human sense perceptions but constrains users to sequential actions. The human user is permitted parallel *read actions*, but is constrained to sequential *write actions* that reflect the sequentiality of human interactions with computers (see Figure 12).

The impedance mismatch between GUIs and APIs can be bridged by a dialog manager that mediates between a *presentation component* that controls end-user interactions and *application interfaces* that control internal communication among application components (see Figure 13).

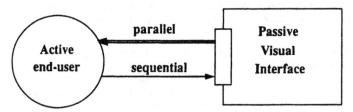

Figure 12: Graphical User Interfaces

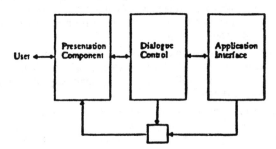

Figure 13: Conversion between GUI and API Interfaces

Mediation between user interfaces and application functionality requires both spatial matching of external with internal representations of object interfaces and temporal matching of user dialog and communication protocols with internal system communication protocols.

The relation between user and application interfaces is similar to that between high-level and machine language. The dialog manager can be viewed as a compiler/interpreter that maps between user and machine representations of interfaces in both directions. Both compilers and dialog managers must transform low-level lexical inputs (characters or mouse clicks) into semantic actions. But dialog managers must handle unpredictable interaction in time, while compilers handle predefined symbol strings. Syntactic analysis of screen interaction is generally simple since the interpretation of a mouse click is determined by its location on the screen rather than by its syntactic form. But timing and synchronization constraints with no counterpart in traditional compiling must be handled.

The GUI desktop paradigm models the human/computer interface visually as a desktop containing collections of documents. Folders containing documents are retrieved by pointing to their icons with a cursor controlled by a mouse. Desktop interfaces are called WIMP (Window, Icon, Menu, Pointer) interfaces because *windows* contain *icons*, *menus* are the primary mechanism for selecting actions, and the cursor is moved to *point* to the region of the screen on which an action is to be performed. Interaction is usually, though not necessarily, sequential.

The desktop paradigm is a document-management paradigm for documents that may contain text and pictures as well as programs. Data is stored in a network of nodes connected by links called a *hypertext*. There are some similarities between networks of nodes in a hypertext and collections of interacting objects but also some differences.

Nodes of a hypertext, like objects, exist over time and are therefore components. Links among hypertext nodes are used both for navigation and read-only browsing and for modifying the state of a node. Nodes are generally passive in the sense that they do not change unless explicitly modified. However, nodes can represent cinematic projectors, animated processes, or other temporally changing entities.

Hypertext and object networks thus have more similarities than is generally realized. Both are linked document structures that may be traversed and modified and may change autonomously over time. The fact that program components execute instruction sequences while documents generally have the purpose of displaying their contents rather than computing is for many purposes secondary.

Hypercard is a specific desktop-management system with a particular document structure, interface structure, and mode of use:

documents are stacks of cards (sequences of screen images)
card interfaces have fields for data, buttons for actions, and menus for editing
modes of use include browsing, authoring, and scripting

Each card is effectively an object with fields as its instance variables and buttons as its procedures, while menus, scrolling, and window-management tools, provide a global mechanism for object manipulation and management. Browsing and authoring provide modes of interaction that allow the creation and reading of text and picture documents without a knowledge of programming, while scripting (programming) is needed only in special circumstances for creating new forms of interface behavior.

The GUI, robot, and virtual reality paradigms can be distinguished by the degree to which the computer, its environment, or both are active agents (see Figures 12, 14, and 15):

GUI paradigm: computers are passive agents that provide services to active human agents
robot paradigm: computers (robots) are active agents that interact through sensors and actuators with passive environments
virtual reality paradigm: both computers and environments are symbiotic, active agents

GUI interfaces normally respond passively to stimuli from an active environment, though they may also operate in an *active prompting mode* requesting inputs from the user in performing an inherently interactive task. Robots are normally proactive, gathering data through self-activating users to realize a goal or perform a task. Agents with purely reactive interfaces simply respond to whatever demands the environment happens to make upon them, having no mechan-

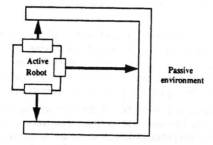

Figure 14: Robot Interaction

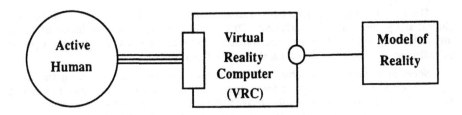

Figure 15: Virtual-Reality Interaction (single participant)

ism for independent environment exploration. Proactive agents generally need a model of the environment to guide their exploration and their interactions with the environment.

3.6. Robots and Virtual Reality

Robots have sensors for perceiving their environment, actuators for performing actions, and processing mechanisms for utilizing data gathered by sensors to influence their actions. Robot interaction is inherently concurrent, approximating the concurrent sensory interactions of humans with their environment. The complexity of robot behavior is determined in part by the complexity and adaptability of its inner computation behavior and in part by its interaction behavior.

Most everyday tasks, like traveling from home to work, involve a balance between empirical interaction with the environment and computational cleverness. Robots aim to enlarge the set of tasks computers can perform from pure problem-solving tasks to interactive tasks, and therefore require problem-solving paradigms that combine computation and interaction.

Brooks [Br] refers to complex purposive behavior generated by simple reflex actions as *intelligence without reason* and conjectures that human behavior is based more on simple interactive reflexes than on complex reasoning or computing processes. The power of mindless reflexes in generating apparently intelligent behavior was illustrated by the Eliza program, whose simple simulation of a psychiatrist by stereotypical reflex responses was remarkably realistic.

Complex behavior can be realized both algorithmically by computation or interactively by flexible interaction primitives. We distinguish between computational intelligence of computing engines and interactive intelligence of adaptive interaction mechanisms:

Computational intelligence: computation power, computable functions
Interactive intelligence: interaction power, intelligent interfaces

Intelligent problem solving should ideally combine computation and interaction power:

problem solving = computation + interaction = algorithms + interfaces
intelligence → computation power + interaction power = cleverness + responsiveness
model of problem solving → model of computation + model of interaction

Turing's notion of *Turing test intelligence* as well as the notion of intelligence tested by IQ tests is computational rather than interactive. Pure problem solving, like checking whether a large integer is prime, involves little interaction with the environment and is therefore well-approximated by Turing's notion of intelligence. However, interactive problem solving like running a business is not captured by Turing intelligence or by algorithmic behavior.

The interplay of computation and interaction in problem solving is illustrated by chess, where look-ahead is computation-intensive and position evaluation is interaction-intensive. Chess-playing programs are better than humans at look-ahead and worse at position evaluation so they emphasize computation over evaluation as compared with human chess players, but nevertheless balance computation with interaction. However, the real world is not governed by predictable rules to the same extent as chess. Robots for problem solving in the real world, as well as human problem solvers, must therefore rely to a greater extent on interaction over computation as a primary tool for realizing goals and solving problems.

Virtual reality systems aim to provide human users with the illusion of immersion in a fictitious or remote environment. The illusion is created by a variety of mutually reinforcing forms of multisensory stimulation. Some of these, like olfactory and gustatory stimulation, are not yet state of the art:

forms of sensory stimulation:
  visual sensors for visible and electromagnetic stimuli
  auditory sensors of sound waves
  olfactory sensors of chemicals in atmosphere
  gustatory sensing of chemicals by simulated tongue
  haptic sensors of touch including
    tactile sensors of temperature, texture, pressure
    kinesthetic sensors of force by muscles, joints, tendons
    spatial sensors of limb/torso positions and angles
    motion sensors of linear and angular acceleration (inner ear)

A virtual-reality computer (VRC) has two clients (users and models) with entirely different interfaces. It plays different roles in relation to its two clients, using the model as a source of information to transmit high-bandwidth information to the user:

principal roles of a VRC:
  user interface manager: transmit multisensory view of model to the user
  model manager: manage real-time model updating and environment interaction

It is convenient to distinguish two sources of temporal change in the relation between users and their virtual environment:

sources of temporal change:
  change of perspective: due to motion or attitude change of the user
  change of model: due to change of the virtual environment

The notion of models as first-class objects that can be manipulated and modified is an important research area that needs to be further explored. Models can take many different forms, ranging from explicit visual representations of airplanes or geometric objects that aim to be life-like to sets of rules of expert systems in performing medical diagnosis or welding on an automobile assembly line. Models that specify actions for all possible environment interactions can be implemented by objects.

Figure 16 illustrates two users U1, U2, associated virtual-reality computers VRC1, VRC2, and a remote environment with a telepresence computer TPC interacting through a common network. Virtual-reality computers have a virtual-reality interface to users that handles realistic multisensory immersion and a network interface that handles communication with other users. For telepresence, a telepresence computer TPC handles interaction with the remote environment. Each VRC must have real-time access to a model either locally or through the network, transmit multisensory information to its user at the rate of at least ten frames a second, and transmit user responses over the network to update the model and perform remote user actions. The model itself can either be stored at a single location or replicated at each VRC.

Virtual-reality systems may be classified along the dimensions of ontology, dynamicity, aggressiveness, and multiplicity:

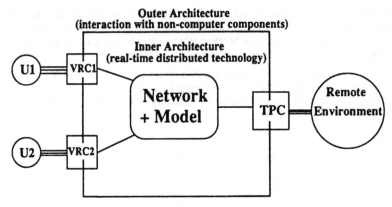

Figure 16: Virtual Reality Architecture

ontology: the degree of reality of the virtual world
 fictitious, real, augmented
dynamicity: mechanisms that determine change of the model
 static, predictably changing, unpredictably changing
aggressiveness: effect of the agent on the virtual world
 passive, active non-critical, real-time critical
multiplicity: the number of interacting agents and virtual worlds
 single agent, multiple agents sharing one world, multiple agents and worlds

Ontology and dynamicity specify properties of the model, while aggressiveness and multiplicity relate to properties of agents. The simplest case of interaction by a single passive agent with a simulated static model allows realistic interaction to be explored independently of modeling and real-time problems. The separation of user interface and model management issues provides a divide-and-conquer framework for separate exploration of user interface and model management issues.

4. Conclusion

Interactive systems are the de facto basis for application programming, embedded computing, and software engineering. They support an inherently richer class of computational behaviors than Turing-computable functions that accord a first-class status to time and persistence in computational modeling. The three parts of this paper deal respectively with models of object interaction, software system requirements for interaction and persistence, and interaction paradigms for application programming.

The computation space of models of interaction encompasses the time-dependent behavior of objects in the real world rather than merely the time-independent behavior of algorithms. The space of all possible interactions of an object is generally too rich for neat mathematical characterization. But projections of the interactive computation space such as client-server interaction or particular computation scenarios and use cases determine tractable subspaces of the space of all possible interactions. Functional behavior can be viewed as a projection onto behavior at a particular instant of time.

The fully abstract behavior of an object specifies "what" an object is as an entity and may be viewed as its declarative semantics. Projections onto specific scenarios or instantaneous actions determine imperative consequences of the fully abstract declarative semantics. Models of computation also view declarative semantics as a "what" specification that is a fully abstract behavior specification. But fully abstract functional specification have an imperative flavor even in their fully abstract form and have a how specification in terms of an algorithmic implementation. Fully abstract specifications of components have a richer what specification that gives rise to a richer class of temporal how specifications than functional specifications.

Components determine contracts between the component and its clients. Algorithms determine a relatively simple contract with a direct quid-pro-quo like a sales contract, while objects determine a much more subtle lifetime contract that is like a marriage contract. Application programming has evolved from the delivery of stand-alone algorithms specifiable by computable functions to the delivery of interactive embedded systems whose behavior over time is specified by models of interaction. We have examined both inherent differences from models of computation and theoretical tools and practical techniques for coping with models of interaction.

5. References

[BC] Len Bass and Joelle Coutaz, Developing Software for the User Interface, Addison Wesley 1991.

[Br] R. A. Brooks, Intelligence Without Reason, Proc 12th International Joint Conference on Artificial Intelligence, August 1991.

[GJ] M. Garey and D. Johnson, Computers and Intractability, Freeman 1979.

[Ja] I. Jacobson, Object-Oriented Software Engineering, Addison-Wesley/ACM-Press, 1991.

[Kn] D. E. Knuth, The Art of Computer Programming, Volume I, Addison Wesley 1969.

[Mi] Robin Milner, Elements of Interaction, *CACM*, January 1993 (1992 Turing Lecture).

[Pe] Roger Penrose, The Emperor's New Mind, Oxford 1989.

[Po] K. Popper, The Open Society and its Enemies, Princeton University Press, 1966.

[Ru] James Rumbaugh, Michael Blaha, William Premerlani, Frederick Eddy, and William Lorensen, *Object-Oriented Modeling and Design*, Prentice Hall, 1990.

[Si] H. Simon, The Sciences of the Artificial, MIT Press, Second Edition, 1982.

[Tu] A. M. Turing, Computing Machinery and Intelligence, Mind 1950

[We] P. Wegner, Tradeoffs Between Reasoning and Modeling, in Research Directions in Concurrent Object-Oriented Programming, Eds Agha, Wegner, Yonezawa, MIT Press, November 1993.

Architectural Convergence and The Granularity of Objects in Distributed Systems

Robert J. Fowler

DIKU (Department of Computer Science), University of Copenhagen,
DK-2100 Copenhagen, Denmark

Abstract. Recent dramatic speedups in processor speeds have not been matched by comparable reductions in communication latencies, either in MIMD systems designed for parallel computation or in workstation networks. A consequence is that these two classes of concurrent architectures are becoming more alike. This architectural convergence is affecting the software techniques and programming styles used: the distinctions are beginning to fade and all software systems are looking increasingly "distributed." We discuss these architectural trends from the standpoint of providing a single, uniform object-based programming abstraction that accommodates both large and small objects.

1 Where We Were

One major goal of computer systems research is to design and build systems based on powerful, general, and easy-to-program abstractions. The other major aim is to build systems with good price/performance properties. The most interesting systems research focuses on the tradeoffs that arise when these goals conflict with one another. These tradeoffs are not as simple as choosing between "truth and beauty" and "the bottom line"; since the quality of a programming model affects the cost of building and maintaining a software system, the total cost of a system can be decreased and its utility increased by making it easier to program and to use, even if this means that fewer instructions are executed each second.

Choosing an abstract model for an object-based programming environment, setting the object granularity the model will support, and creating an object-based design for an application are design activities that require evaluating the tradeoffs between the quality of the programming model and raw system performance. Usually, the latency of communication limits the frequency at which processes can interact while still providing an acceptable level of performance. Since coarse-grain concurrent programs have, by definition, the smallest number of interprocess interactions, programmers seeking the ultimate in performance will tend to adopt a coarse-grain design strategy, at least as far as that strategy is compatible with load balancing. Unfortunately, the natural granularity[1] of the problem at hand may be finer than that for which the system performs well. In

---

[1] For example, the partitioning of a problem into objects using the principles of an appropriate object-based design methodology.

this case, the programmer has the unfortunate choice between using a natural, clean design and meeting some performance requirement. To reduce the need to make such tradeoffs, systems should be designed to support the finest granularity of interaction that is compatible with good performance. Furthermore, application programmers need an understanding of the issues involved and of the limitations of the system with respect to fine-grain interactions.

1.1 The Problem

The main performance issue of "object granularity" is not the size of the programmer-defined objects. Rather, it is the cost and frequency of internode interactions within a physically distributed system. As long as the average cost of an operation in the abstract model is sufficiently small, a system can provide a single, uniform abstract object model that spans a range from very small objects, such as hardware-defined primitive data types, up to very large objects that themselves may be distributed and replicated for performance as well as for reliability. The problem with fine-grain interactions is that the most straightforward implementations map each abstract operation to one or more physical operations. Each physical operation incurs a certain fixed cost that must be amortized over the useful work performed. Whether the implementation medium is hardware or software, it is necessary to build the system (1) so that fine-grain abstract interactions are rare, (2) so that only a small fraction of the fine-grain abstract operations are implemented as physical operations or so that the abstract operations are consolidated into larger physical transactions, (3) so that the latency of each individual physical operation is reduced, or (4) so that the latencies are hidden by other concurrent activity. For example, a system might export a uniform object model while providing multiple underlying implementations for the sake of performance. Techniques such as in-line expansion of method bodies, local procedure call, object migration, remote memory access, and remote procedure call each can be used profitably in object invocation, depending on object size and the complexity of the method as well as on the respective locations of the invoker and the invokee.

A strict interpretation of "uniform object model" would imply that implementation details should be hidden from the programmer. Performance [2], however, depends upon implementation detail. If the programmer cannot choose an implementation for each object explicitly, either the system must choose automatically an implementation that works well in most cases or the programmer must understand enough about the implementation to write programs that the system can handle well. This is a common situation. For example:

- Early vectorizing FORTRAN compilers could only recognize certain idiomatic loop constructs. These idioms were publicized to ensure that programmers would use them.

---

[2] Reliability depends upon implementation detail also, but reliability issues are beyond the scope of this paper.

- The time to execute a Prolog program depends critically upon the order in which clauses are presented to the interpreter. Although one might argue that Prolog is a declarative language, a successful Prolog programmer must understand the interpretation process.
- Any computer system with a memory hierarchy is sensitive to the locality of reference exhibited by the programs it executes. To achieve good performance, a programmer must avoid algorithms and data structures with poor locality. The problem is especially important on multiprocessors [15].

In each case, designers and programmers strike a bargain in which an easy-to-program, general, and uniform set of abstractions is obtained in exchange for a loss of direct control over performance. As long as the system does reasonably well, this is a good compromise. If the system cannot make the right decisions automatically, then it is appropriate that the costs of exported abstractions and of operations on them be made as explicit as possible[26]. If costs depend upon dynamically changing properties of the system, if performance varies wildly with different input data, or if a particular program is intended to exhibit good performance on a wide range of architectures or multiple implementations of a single architecture, then the choice of implementation is out of the hands of the application programmer. Performance decisions necessarily must be made no earlier than at compilation time and are most likely to occur at load or execution time.

1.2   Tight versus Loose Coupling in MIMD Systems

One can classify MIMD (Multiple Instruction, Multiple Data) architectures into three distinct families. In a *multiprocessor*, the *hardware* architecture supports an abstraction of a shared memory in a global address space accessible from any processor in the system. The shared memory either can be in a separate module equidistant from all processors [an UMA (Uniform Memory Access cost), or "dancehall" machine] or it can be distributed so that each processor has some memory close to it [a distributed memory, NUMA (Non-Uniform Memory Access cost), or "boudoir" machine]. A *Multicomputer* is a dedicated high-performance interconnection network over which a set of processing elements (PEs), each consisting of a processor and its private memory, communicate using message-passing. *Workstation Networks* consist of standalone processing elements[3] joined by a commodity message-passing network. These architectures are often called "tightly coupled" or "loosely coupled", based on several criteria, one of which is the granularity of interaction the system can support [4].

---

[3] Exceptions include the Amoeba[27] "processor pool" and recently announced "workstation cluster" products. These consist of workstation-class single-board PEs sharing a common power supply and cabinet, but still connected using conventional LAN hardware.

[4] Other criteria include administrative autonomy, protection boundaries, and the possibility of independent failure.

The conventional wisdom classifies multiprocessors as tightly coupled because processors can coordinate with one another in the time that it takes to read and write a few shared variables. Memory access times are measured in microseconds. High-performance networks in multicomputers have latencies measured in a few tens or hundreds of microseconds. With optimized network protocols, the time required to pass a message over an Ethernet from user-mode code on one workstation to user-mode code on another is a large fraction of a millisecond [16,29]. The coupling becomes looser when the use of standard network protocols and commercial operating systems increases latencies to several milliseconds on local area networks, and to many times this on wide-area networks.

The relative costs of communication in each architecture class have determined the style of object-oriented systems that have been built upon them. For example, PRESTO [5] is a straightforward "threads" library that extends C++ for shared-memory-style parallel programming. It was written originally for a 1987-vintage Sequent multiprocessor, a machine with memories and bus that are fast relative to processor speed. Both PRESTO and the applications written for it on the Sequent freely used fine-grain sharing of data and C++ objects, respectively, among the available processors [7] with little concern for locality of reference. Nevertheless, its performance was considered to be acceptable.

Near the opposite extreme, both Eden[3] and Argus[24] were built on top of a loosely coupled network of minicomputers running Unix and using standard network protocols. In these systems, Unix processes encapsulated heavyweight objects, while different programming models based on lightweight objects and threads were used within the heavyweight objects. The very high cost of communication between Unix processes compared to that of local procedure calls led naturally to the use of two-level programming models that restrict internode communication to relatively infrequent interactions among the large objects.

Veterans of the Eden project found that the two-level programming model was unwieldy and that it forced the programmer to make early, often premature, decisions to use one sub-model or the other. This problem was one of the motivating factors in the design of Emerald.

The Emerald object model uniformly encompasses both very small and very large objects. To achieve reasonable performance, it uses a single abstraction with multiple underlying implementations. Invocations in the abstract model are implemented with mechanisms ranging from part of a VAX machine instruction to network messages. Considerable attention was paid to mobility mechanisms useful for co-locating objects[6,18] and to protocols to make invocation efficient, especially the local invocation of globally accessible objects. Decisions about object placement and, implicitly, about the granularity of interactions between processing nodes are strictly the responsibility of the programmer, so the Emerald programming language provides language constructs to guide the choice of underlying mechanism.

In summary, cost models vary dramatically among the various classes of MIMD concurrent systems, leading to a wide range of approaches in the programming environments built on top of them. The Emerald experience shows that, with careful attention to implementation, and especially by providing mechanisms that substitute local actions for remote operations, a uniform object model can achieve a reasonable level of performance on a workstation network.

In Section 2, we examine recent trends in system architecture and comment on the immediate implications for concurrent systems with uniform object models. In Section 3, we address the future of fine-grain operations in general and uniform object models in particular.

2 Where We Are

With respect to the cost of interprocessor interaction, recent trends are causing the distinctions among the three classes of concurrent MIMD systems to fade. Across the board, the latency component of cost has been increasing relative to processor power, although the absolute cost of interprocessor interaction is decreasing. In the absence of special efforts to support fine-grain interaction, we can expect the programming models used on all classes of machine to look more like those developed for distributed systems than those designed for the multiprocessors of the past.

Dramatic improvements in processor speed due to more sophisticated designs and better integrated circuit technologies require performance-conscious software designers to consider the physical distribution of the components of shared-memory multiprocessors. A bus transaction on the DEC 10000 AXP multiprocessor transfers 64 bytes and has a latency of 340 nanoseconds[10].[5] Measured by the cycle time of a dual-issue 200-MHz processor, this constitutes 68 processor clocks in which as many as 136 instructions could be issued. When viewed in these terms, the simple transfer of data in a shared variable does not seem nearly as inexpensive as it once did[6]. Systems based on very fast processors use very large secondary caches with large block sizes to reduce the number of bus operations demanded. High processor-memory bandwidth is attained by transferring a large amount of data in each operation. Write buffers allow processors to continue execution before a write operation is complete [14], thus reducing the cost of writing to memory. While these techniques are extremely successful at reducing average memory access cost in a uniprocessor, the fact remains that interprocessor communication through a shared variable still requires a relatively expensive communication operation.

---

[5] Bus transactions are pipelined. The total capacity of the bus is about 640 megabytes per second, while the bandwidth available to any one processor is about 188 megabytes per second.

[6] In terms of a hypothetical 1-MIP(peak) machine, this would be like having a 100 microsecond access time to main memory.

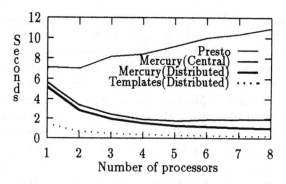

Fig. 1. Time to create and execute 100,000 tasks in PRESTO and in Mercury.

2.1 Distributed Aspects of Shared Memory Machines

Even on a "last-generation" bus-based multiprocessor like the SGI Power 4D/480[7], cache miss penalties and bus bandwidth constraints are such that indiscriminate sharing of data between threads on different processors is fatal to good performance. The smaller the objects and the less computation done on each invocation, the worse the problem becomes. While PRESTO performs well on machines like older Sequents, the comparatively poor locality is unacceptable on machines such as the SGI; it is necessary for both system and application code to be structured in response to the physical distribution of the hardware.

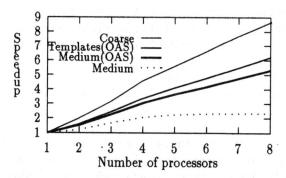

Fig. 2. A comparison of the speedups obtained for a successive over-relaxation program. A coarse-grain program is compared to fine-grain alternatives available in Mercury.

---

[7] 40-MHz R3000 processors, 80-MB/sec bus, 360-nanosecond (15 processor cycles) bus latency for a 16-byte bus transfer, 1-MB secondary caches.

For example, the Mercury runtime library [13] reimplements and extends PRESTO. The reimplementation aspect retains backward compatibility while improving locality of reference of internal mechanisms. The extensions provide a mechanism called "Object-Affinity Scheduling" (O-AS).[8] An object invocation either can be performed as a local procedure call or can be encapsulated into a lightweight task. If Mercury uses the tasking mechanism, it preferentially schedules repeated invocations of an object on a single processor, thus increasing the chance of reusing cached data. This scheduling preference is ignored only if the task is grabbed by an idle processor for load-sharing purposes. Figure 1 shows the time needed to create and execute 100,000 tasks in parallel. Each task increments a global count of the number of tasks created so far, and if more tasks still need to be created, it creates a successor task and then dies. The figure provides a direct comparison between the overhead of using the PRESTO thread mechanism with the cost of using the Mercury mechanisms. The curves labelled "Mercury" show the performance of the reimplemented thread package using centralized and decentralized task queues, respectively. The curve labelled "Templates(Distributed)" shows the additional benefit of using a continuation-passing style of invocation that schedules tasks by passing *templates*, each of which contains an activation record and explicit continuation information.

Even if a system is structured to achieve good internal locality, it may still be necessary to adopt a coarse-grain programming style to get acceptable application performance on a machine like an SGI 4D. Figure 2 illustrates the speedup of a successive over-relaxation program. The top curve is for a hand-tuned coarse-grain program, while the other curves correspond to the behavior of a fine-grain program using Mercury's invocation mechanisms. The fine-grain program creates an object for each row of a rectangular mesh and invokes each row object once per phase. The bottom curve illustrates that no useful speedup is obtained if locality is ignored in scheduling invocations. The second curve from the bottom illustrates the benefit of using O-AS when each invocation is represented as a conventional lightweight thread. The benefit of using templates is reflected in the improvement shown in the third curve from the bottom. The speedup of the fine-grain version of the program is still limited by interactions between neighboring rows of the mesh, so additional speedup could be obtained by co-locating sets of neighboring rows. Although locations can be specified explicitly, the current Mercury implementation does not make automatic co-location decisions of this kind.

Figures 3 and 4 illustrate the running times and speedups of two versions of a Gaussian elimination program. In the fine-grain version, each row of the matrix is an object and each row is invoked once for each pivot operation. In contrast to the successive over-relaxation example, the Gaussian elimination algorithm derives no advantage from co-locating neighboring rows. Thus, the fine-grain program is able to approach closely the performance of the hand-tuned program.

Fine- and coarse-grain are relative terms. The "fine-grain" programs illus-

---

[8] The COOL [9,8] programming language is based on similar, independently developed ideas.

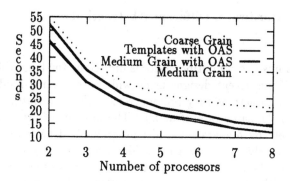

Fig. 3. Completion time for Gaussian elimination on a 640 by 640 dense matrix. A coarse-grain implementation is compared with variants of a fine-grain program.

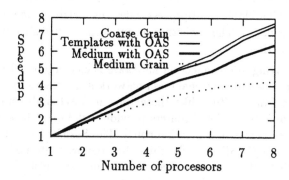

Fig. 4. Speedups for Gaussian elimination.

trated here use fairly large objects of one to four kilobytes in size and each invocation touches a large fraction of the representation. In terms of computation-to-communication ratio, each invocation executes as many as a dozen instructions for each word touched. Without Object-Affinity Scheduling, therefore, each processor would be generating a cache miss to migrate data at most every few dozen instructions. The aggregate cache miss and bus operation frequency is higher by a factor of the number of active processors. Thus, while these programs do not seem to be particularly "fine-grain" when compared with the objects typically seen in a uniprocessor C++ program, they generate enough interprocessor interaction that the physical location of data and threads is a crucial factor in obtaining good performance on recent multiprocessors.

2.2 Same Hardware, Different Abstractions

The size of a bus-based multiprocessor is limited by the bandwidth and latencies of the bus. While recent designs using wide busses, burst-mode transfers, and overlapping transactions may provide very high bandwidth, latencies are not improving at the same rate, if at all.[9] The number of processors that can be used effectively by fine-grain parallel programs will be fewer than one would expect based solely on bandwidth considerations. If multiprocessors are to scale well, they must be based on interconnection networks that scale well. Not only must bandwidth increase as nodes are added, but latencies must remain low enough to allow a sufficiently fine grain of interaction that programs can be written in a recognizably "shared-memory" style. Otherwise, one might as well just build message-passing systems.

If current trends continue, the distinction between multicomputers and scalable shared-memory multiprocessors will soon disappear. While the term "distributed memory architecture" has been synonymous in some circles with "multicomputer", all scalable multiprocessor designs distribute main memory among the processing nodes. Thus, whether or not memory is distributed will not be a relevant distinction.

The underlying interconnection hardware is converging. The MIT Alewife[2, 1] is based on a two-dimensional mesh network using Elko-series wormhole mesh routing chips from Caltech like those used in Intel multicomputers designed around the same time. These routers provide switching delays of 30 ns per hop and 60 Mbytes per second per channel[1]. The Stanford DASH[22] uses a similar network. On DASH, a cache miss that requires internode communication can be handled with a latency of about 3.2 microseconds[22], i.e., one order of magnitude larger than a miss on an SGI 4D.

Since these shared-memory systems are built upon a hardware message-passing layer, it is natural to expose this layer to the software. This strategy is part of the current Alewife design[20,21]. Detailed simulations indicate that the message mechanism will allow remote thread invocation to be done in 7.4 microseconds (time from start of call until the thread is running) as opposed to 24.4 microseconds using shared memory operations.

With both message-passing and shared memory, these systems promise the best of both worlds. Either abstraction can be used, depending on the problem at hand. The proliferation of multiple low-level mechanisms, however, has the potential to make the end programmer's life even more complex by increasing the number of available abstractions. A unified object-based programming model that automatically chooses among the underlying mechanisms is preferable.

---

[9] Compare the figures for the SGI 4D/480 and the DEC 10000 AXP presented in previous sections. The SGI Challenge series multiprocessors have similar latency figures.

2.3 Attack of the Killer Networks?

The performance gap between multicomputers and workstation networks is starting to close as well. For example, on a network of DECstations connected by a
140 Mb/s ATM network, a group at the University of Washington implemented
a network interface based on an explicitly shared memory segment model with
block reads and writes[28]. They claim an end-to-end latency of 30 microseconds to transfer a 40-byte block with a write operation[10] and 45 microseconds
to transfer the same data using a read involving a round trip on the network.
An implementation of remote procedure call (RPC) on top of this underlying
mechanism comes within a factor of 2 (93 μs vs. 57 μs) of an optimized local
RPC. The latency for small messages is less than that seen on either the CM-5
or the Intel Touchstone DELTA. In terms of sustained throughput between a
pair of nodes, this system is within a factor of two of the CM-5 and within a
factor of 3 of the DELTA[28].

2.4 What Do the Numbers Mean?

In the systems described, there is a gap of about two orders of magnitude in the
latency of minimal interprocessor interaction (including software overhead) between a bus-based shared memory system and a high-performance workstation
network. Only a few years ago, the gap was almost four orders of magnitude.
Furthermore, the gap may be as small as a factor of two for interactions such as
user-level message passing or remote procedure call. This is the good news: in response to this convergence of costs, we can expect convergences in programming
models and in system software design across the various architectural classes.

The bad news is that while communication latency has improved, processor
speed has improved at a much faster rate. A one-microsecond delay for a cache
miss on a 2-MIPS multiprocessor is the time it takes to execute two instructions.
During a 0.3-microsecond stall on a 100-MHz two-way superscalar machine, as
many as 60 instructions could have been issued. Three microseconds to handle a cache miss on a scalable multiprocessor is the time it takes to execute
six hundred instructions. In the one hundred microseconds needed for an RPC
on a workstation network, our hypothetical machine can execute nearly twenty
thousand instructions. Although the amount of data transferred may be small,
these relative latencies are like those used in a typical definition of coarse-grain
parallelism. If "fine-grain parallelism" is to be meaningful, processors must be
able to tolerate high latencies by having enough other useful work to do and an
effective mechanism for switching to it. One solution is to build processors with
fine-grain multitasking mechanisms[4,1]. Note, however, that for this strategy
to be effective, communication and computation must be concurrent. Although
software protocols for communication (e.g., programmed I/O) or for memory
management (software memory coherency, TLB and page table management)

---

[10] This write operation is not guaranteed to be reliable and can fail silently. In contrast, the failure of a read operation is easily detected because it requires round trip
communication.

can have measured latencies not much worse than hardware implementations, the potential parallelism available in the hardware implementation is lost.

3   Where We Are Going

Based strictly on measurements of communication latency, the future looks grim for all fine-grain parallel computation. As indicated in Section 1.1, however, there are several approaches that can be used to reduce the cost of fine-grain abstract operations. In an object-based system, the total cost of internode interaction is dependent upon four major factors. First, the hardware and software configuration of the underlying system architecture determines the bandwidth and latencies of interactions. The second factor is the combined ability of the compiler, the language runtime library, and the operating system to minimize the cost of each individual operation, intelligently mapping objects to nodes using static placement, static or dynamic grouping, and migration to control the total number of interactions. Third, clever mechanisms in hardware and software can tolerate interaction latencies by delaying and aggregating small operations into larger ones or by allowing other useful work to be done while one or more operations are in progress. Fourth, performance depends upon how well users choose algorithms and structure their programs to take advantage of the underlying system. Systems should be designed to make the right choices available and to make them seem natural.

Not every fine-grain interaction among objects in an abstract programming model becomes an interprocessor interaction. Compilers and run-time systems that cluster and co-locate objects have the opportunity to turn many interactions into local computations. Even though reading or writing a word in a shared memory appears to be inherently fine-grain, there are coarse-grain shared-memory programs. In such programs, spatial, temporal, and processor locality all work to control cache miss rates. If the granularity of interaction is coarse enough after the compiler and run-time libraries have done their work, good performance can be obtained from *Software Distributed Shared Memory* systems[23]. If memory need only be consistent at synchronization points, finer granularities can be handled by multi-writer protocols in hardware[17] or software[19] that can consolidate many small memory operations into a larger message. When combined with high performance (ATM) network technology, software distributed shared memory systems can perform competitively with hardware shared memory systems on medium- and coarse-grain applications[11]. Related techniques are being applied to object-based software distributed memory systems[12].

Operation latency is a problem only if that latency cannot be hidden by concurrent execution of other useful tasks. Multiprogramming to avoid the penalty of I/O latency is the oldest and most prominent example of hiding latency through concurrency. System designs that preclude effective multitasking to tolerate interprocessor communication latency should be avoided. Latency tolerance in hardware can allow very fine-grain interaction. For example, the Tera computer[4] is designed to perform an "instantaneous" context switch on ev-

ery memory operation. Less extreme designs in the hardware of Alewife [1] and
*T [25] or the software of Active Messages[30] attack both of these potential
problems by minimizing operation overhead and by facilitating concurrent activity. Future object-based systems must be designed so that applications exhibit enough concurrency at each node to hide internode latencies. The finer the
granularity of the objects, the more concurrency will be needed and the less the
system will be able to tolerate the overhead of managing it.

Prognosis

Providing a uniform object abstraction that is suitable for both large and small
objects is an important goal for designers of object-based programming systems,
whether the target architecture is sequential, "parallel", or "distributed". At-
taining this goal will become harder, however, since there is no evidence that
decreases in communication latency will be able to keep pace with increases in
processor speeds. Nonetheless, the converging performance characteristics of the
underlying systems can be used as a guide for attacking the problem. Designers
of software for parallel systems need to deal with the physical distribution of the
underlying system, and distributed system designers need to focus continually
on increasing the amount of parallelism in their designs to hide communication latencies. As the two communities converge, the solutions to their common
set of problems ultimately will be derived from techniques developed by both
communities.

References

1. A. Agarwal, J. Kubiatowicz, D. Kranz, B-H. Lim, D. Yeung, G. D'Souza, and M. Parkin. Sparcle: an evolutionary processor design for large-scale multiprocessors. *IEEE Micro*, 13(3):48–60, June 1993.

2. A. Agarwal, B.-H. Lim, D. Kranz, and J. Kubiatowicz. APRIL: a processor ar-chitecture for multiprocessing. In *Proceedings of the 17th Annual International Symposium on Computer Architecture*, pages 104–114, May 1990.

3. G.T. Almes, A.P. Black, E.D. Lazowska, and J.D. Noe. The Eden system: a techni-cal review. *IEEE Transactions on Software Engineering*, SE-11(1):43–59, January 1985.

4. R. Alverson, D. Callahan, D. Cummings, B. Koblenz, A. Porterfield, and B. Smith. The Tera computer system. In *Proceedings of the 1990 International Conference on Supercomputing*, pages 1–6, September 1990.

5. B.N. Bershad, E.D. Lazowska, and H.M. Levy. PRESTO: a system for object-oriented parallel programming. *Software: Practice and Experience*, 18(8):713–732, August 1988.

6. A. Black, N. Hutchinson, E. Jul, and H. Levy. Object structure in the Emerald system. In *Proceedings of the ACM Conference on Object-Oriented Programming Systems, Languages and Applications*, pages 78–86, October 1986. Special Issue of SIGPLAN Notices, Volume 21, Number 11, November, 1986.

7. W.J. Bolosky, M.L. Scott, R.P. Fitzgerald, R.J. Fowler, and A.L. Cox. NUMA policies and their relation to memory architecture. In *Proceedings of the 4th Symposium on Architectural Support for Programming Languages and Operating Systems*, pages 212–221, April 1991.

8. R. Chandra, A. Gupta, and J. Hennessy. Data locality and load balancing in COOL. In *Proceedings of the Fourth ACM SIGPLAN Symposium on Principles and Practice of Parallel Programming*, pages 249–259, April 1991.

9. Rohit Chandra, Anoop Gupta, and John L. Hennessy. *Integrating Concurrency and Data Abstraction in a Parallel Programming Language*. Technical Report No. CSL-TR-92-511, Computer Systems Laboratory, Stanford University, February 1992.

10. Alpha AXP architecture and sytems. *Digital Technical Journal*, 4(4), Special Issue 1992.

11. S. Dwarkadas, P. Kelleher, A.L. Cox, and W. Zwaenepoel. Evaluation of release consistent software distributed shared memory on emerging network technology. In *Proceedings of the 20th Annual International Symposium on Computer Architecture*, pages 244–255, May 1993.

12. M.J. Feeley and H.M. Levy. Distributed shared memory with versioned objects. In *OOPSLA '92 Conference Proceedings*, pages 247–262, October 1992.

13. R.J. Fowler and L.I. Kontothanassis. *Improving Processor and Cache Locality in Fine-Grain Parallel Computations using Object-Affinity Scheduling and Continuation Passing*. Technical Report TR-411, University of Rochester, Department of Computer Science, 1992.

14. John L. Hennessy and David A. Patterson. *Computer Architecture: A Quantitative Approach*. Morgan Kaufman, San Mateo, California, 1991.

15. Mark D. Hill and James R. Larus. Cache considerations for multiprocessor programmers. *Communications of the ACM*, 33(8):97–102, August 1990.

16. D.B. Johnson and W. Zwaenepoel. The Peregrine high-performance RPC system. *Software: Practice and Experience*, 23(2):201–221, February 1993.

17. Norman P. Jouppi. Cache write policies and performance. In *Proceedings of the 20th Annual International Symposium on Computer Architecture*, pages 191–201, 1993.

18. E. Jul, H. Levy, N. Hutchinson, and A. Black. Fine-grained mobility in the Emerald system. *ACM Transactions on Computer Systems*, 6(1):109–133, February 1988.

19. P. Keleher, A. Cox, and W. Zwaenepoel. Lazy release consistency for software distributed shared memory. In *Proceedings of the 19th Annual International Symposium on Computer Architecture*, pages 13–21, May 1992.

20. D. Kranz, K. Johnson, A. Agarwal, J. Kubiatowicz, and B-H. Lim. Integrating message-passing and shared-memory: early experience. In *Proceedings of the Fourth ACM SIGPLAN Symposium on Principles and Practice of Parallel Programming*, pages 54–63, San Diego, May 1993.

21. J. Kubiatowicz and A. Agarwal. Anatomy of a message in the Alewife multiprocessor. In *Proceedings of the 1993 ACM International Conference on Supercomputing*, pages 195–206, Tokyo, Japan, July 1993.

22. D. Lenoski, J. Laudon, K. Gharachorloo, A. Gupta, and J. Hennessy. The directory-based cache coherence protocol for the DASH multiprocessor. In *Proceedings of the 17th Annual International Symposium on Computer Architecture*, pages 148–159, May 1990.

23. K. Li. Ivy: a shared virtual memory system for parallel computing. *Proceedings of the 1988 International Conference on Parallel Processing*, 2:94–101, August 1988.

24. B. Liskov. Distributed programming in Argus. *Communications of the ACM*, 31(3):300–312, March 1988.

25. R. S. Nikhil, G. M. Papadopoulos, and Arvind. *T: a multithreaded massively parallel architecture. In *Proceedings of the 19th Annual International Symposium on Computer Architecture*, pages 156–167, Gold Coast, Australia, May 1992.

26. L. Snyder. Type architectures, shared memory, and the corollary of modest potential. In *Annual Review of Computer Science*, pages 298–317, Annual Reviews Inc., 1986.

27. A.S. Tanenbaum, R. van Renesse, H. van Staveren, G.J. Sharp, S.J. Mullender, J. Jansen, and G. van Rossum. Experiences with the Amoeba distributed operating system. *Communications of the ACM*, 33(12):46–63, December 1990.

28. C. Thekkath, H. Levy, and E. Lazowska. *Efficient Support for Multicomputing on ATM Networks*. Technical Report TR93-04-03, Department of Computer Science and Engineering, University of Washington, April 1993.

29. R. van Renesse, H. van Staveren, and A.S. Tanenbaum. Performance of the Amoeba distributed operating system. *Software: Practice and Experience*, 19:223–234, March 1989.

30. T. von Eicken, D.E. Culler, S.C. Goldstein, and K.E. Schauser. Active messages: a mechanism for integrated communication and computation. In *Proceedings of the 19th Annual International Symposium on Computer Architecture*, pages 256–266, May 1992.

Separation of Distribution and Objects

Eric Jul

DIKU, University of Copenhagen
Universitetsparken 1
DK-2100 Copenhagen
DENMARK
e-mail: eric@diku.dk

Abstract. Based on the experience with developing distributed applications in Emerald, this paper argues that distribution and objects are orthogonal concepts and that they thus can be developed separately: The object and process structure in many distributed application can be developed independently of distribution. We discuss this claim using the models and paradigms of the Emerald system.

1 Introduction

This paper argues that objects and distribution are orthogonal concepts in that the object and process structure of many distributed applications can be developed independently of distribution. Specifically, the process structure of an application does not have to depend on distribution. This paper describes the process and distribution models supported by the distributed, object-oriented language Emerald. One of Emerald's main features is a decoupling of processes, distribution, and objects.

2 Emerald Models

This section describes the Emerald models and paradigms of *objects*, *processes*, and *distribution*.

Before describing the Emerald object model, we argue that there should be a uniform object model.

2.1 The Problem with Hybrid Object Models

Object-oriented systems typically lie at the ends of a spectrum: object-oriented languages, such as Smalltalk [Goldberg 83] and CLU [Liskov 77], provide small, local, data objects; object-oriented operating systems, such as Hydra [Wulf 74] and Argus [Liskov 88], provide large, possibly distributed, active objects. In distributed systems, machines are physically separated by the network and programmers have to deal with two levels of operations: local, accessing shared memory, or remote, accessing data across the network. Hybrid distributed systems that support both models of computation have a separate definition mechanism for each model. For example, in the Eden system [Lazowska 81,Almes 85] a programmer can use the object model of computation in addition to the model of computation presented by Concurrent Euclid [Holt 83], which can be used within objects. Similarly, the Argus system provides so-called *guardians* for distributed computing and CLU clusters for computing locally within a guardian [Liskov 88]. The presence of two models of computation complicates programming. In Eden, the programmer could choose to use the object model almost exclusively, but in practice is prevented from doing so because Eden suffered from poor performance for objects located on the same machine. The two models differ in that one can only be used locally and is fast while the other has full generality but is much slower—usually three orders of magnitude slower. In distributed object-oriented systems, e.g., Clouds [Spafford 86] and Eden [Black 85], a *local* execution of the general object invocation mechanism takes milliseconds—even when both objects are located on the same machine. Thus a programmer can be forced to use one model of computation where another model would be more appropriate, or to accept the poor performance of the general mechanism.

2.2 The Emerald Object Model

Emerald advocates the use of a single uniform model of computation for both distributed and non-distributed programming. For many applications, distribution need not be visible. Throughout the history of computers the concept of *transparency* has been used to simplify programming (see [Parnas 75]). High-level programming languages in general make the underlying computer architecture transparent to the programmer. In Emerald, we have made the underlying distributed architecture transparent: programmers use a single object definition mechanism with a single semantic for defining all objects. This includes small, local, data-only objects and active, mobile, distributed objects.

An important advantage of this transparency is that many distributed applications can initially be programmed *without* concern for distribution; only when the program has been essentially written need the programmer pay attention to distribution: in many cases, only a few statement concerning the actual distribution of objects need be inserted. The non-transparent distribution features are described in the next section.

An Emerald object consists of:

- A unique network-wide identity.
- A representation, i.e., the data local to the object. Essentially, this consists of variables that reference other objects.
- A set of operations that can be invoked on the object.
- An optional **initially** section. When the object is created, the code in this section is executed before any invocations of the object are allowed.

Furthermore, an object has two attributes: it has a *location* and it may be *immutable*. Its location is the node where it currently resides. If it is immutable, its state is not allowed to change.

Emerald objects are passive in the sense that no process is inherently required nor specified.

2.3 The Emerald Process Model

The Emerald process model differs from many other object systems in that processes are orthogonal to objects; processes are not intimately tied to any one object. Objects are "merely" represented by some state (variables) and some operations that can be invoked. Objects are basically considered inherently "inactive": they do not contain, or need, a process.

In Emerald, the concept of a process is represented by a **process** section in an object. When the object is instantiated, a new process is created whose only use of the object is to provide the code for the process. Thus, a process originates in some object (but is not otherwise tied to this object). Emerald objects that contain a process are active; objects without a process are passive data structures. Objects with processes can invoke other objects, which in turn can invoke other objects, and so on to any depth. As a consequence, a process originating in one object may span many other objects, locally as well as remotely. Multiple processes can be active concurrently within a single object. Synchronization is provided by monitors and conditions [Hoare 74]. Other systems require a process in each object to field incoming invocations or require remote operations to pass through special *proxy* objects. The Emerald process model avoids this: a remote invocation is conceptually the same as a local and both are modelled essentially as a procedure call. When two objects are separated (by one of them being moved to another node) any local calls between them are automatically converted to remote calls by the Emerald kernel; however, conceptually, there is no change.

In terms of implementation, there is a kernel thread to implement each Emerald process. When a process makes a remote invocation, the local kernel thread is suspended and a new thread is created on the remote kernel to handle the invocation. Thus a single Emerald process may be implemented by many kernel threads residing on different nodes. The fact that the process is implemented by multiple threads is transparent to the user. The user is not involved in the implementation of distribution, e.g., as in Eden.

Some object languages have an execution model, where each object is considered to have its own internal process that repeatedly must receive incoming messages, react to them, and return a reply. Basically, this is exactly the Emerald *implementation* model. We claim that this is a low-level view of object execution and that the Emerald model of processes is high-level view more appropriate for programmers. There should only be **one** process for each concurrent activity. The fact that the high-level abstraction of a process may need to be implemented by several *kernel-level* threads residing on several different computers is an implementation detail.

An important advantage of the Emerald process model is the decoupling of processes from particular objects: there is no need to change the process structure when cooperating objects are spread across the network.

3 Handling Distribution

In the previous sections, we have argue that distribution transparency is good, because it makes programming simpler. However, there is an inherent conflict between hiding distribution and the need for some applications to control distribution. For example, it is essential for a load balancer to be able to control the location of objects and processes. In the following, we discuss our approach to distribution and describe some of the mechanism supporting the approach.

3.1 The Emerald Model of Distribution

The Emerald language was specifically designed for the support of distributed applications. A central idea is that, for most programming, distribution is transparent; it is only visible through a small set of features supporting explicit notions of distribution at the language level.

Emerald's model of the underlying hardware is that of a number of autonomous computers connected by a network. Each computer is represented by a system-defined *node*, which provides the basic operations expected of the local hardware, e.g., a *getTimeOfDay* operation. The network itself is not explicitly represented at the language level.

Our model of distribution is that the objects in the system can be freely spread out over the system and can be freely moved between nodes ([Jul 88b, Jul 88a]).

Given an object, x, the location of x (i.e., a reference to the node object where the object resides) can be obtain using the locate language construct: **locate** x. Each Emerald object resides entirely at one node at a time.[1] But it may be moved at any time by using the move statement, e.g. to move an object, x, to the location of another object, y: **move** x **to locate** y.

Each node is considered autonomous, i.e., the nodes can crash and recover independently. An important point is that *a node crash is **not** considered an error but rather a normal, expected event* in the distributed system. So-called *unavailable* handlers are used to handle such events; these concepts are elaborated upon in section 3.6.

The main idea behind our distribution model is that objects can be migrated transparently on-the-fly without being affected in any way—other than performance and fault-tolerance.

3.2 The Emerald Approach to Distribution

Our approach is that as much programming should be able to be done without concern for distribution and that the distribution dependencies be confined to a small set of features.

---

[1] To be exact, immutable objects are handled differently: they are assumed to be omnipresent.

We argue that in most cases programmers can develop their applications *without regard to distribution* and only in the latter stages of development incorporate distribution decisions (and the code to support such decisions). It is always possible to chose a suitable level of granularity for distribution because Emerald objects are fine-grained—even the smallest object can be independently moved, if desired. For example, in the design of a small electronic mail system, the designers ignored distribution during most of the design process ([Almes 84]). In the Emerald version of the system, it was only necessary to add less than *ten* keywords to the source code for the non-distributed version to obtain the distributed version ([Jul 88a]). The keywords essentially specified the co-location of objects representing mailboxes and letters, and specifying that the contents of letters should migrate along with the letters themselves.

In the following we describe some of the important distribution features that are supported by Emerald.

3.3 Migration-independent (Remote) Object Invocation

Location-independent object invocation has long been an established way of providing transparent invocation across a network ([Black 85]). In Emerald, this concept is extended to be *migration*-independent invocation. In essence, invocations work regards of the object migrations that take place before, during, or after the invocation.

This is what makes it all possible: objects will continue to work correctly regardless of migrations decided upon by distribution policies.

3.4 Mobility Primitives

As mentioned in section 3.1, Emerald has a few, simple distribution features. The **move** statement is used to move objects dynamically. Furthermore, Emerald supports the parameter passing mode *call-by-move* which can be used to provide object mobility in conjunction with remote invocations thus obtaining substantial performance improvements ([Jul 88b]).

3.5 Attachment: Getting the Best of Shallow and Deep Copy

An important issue when moving objects containing references to other objects is deciding how much to move. This issue is very similar to the question of shallow versus deep copy.

Moving an object without moving its local data structures does not make much sense because the local structures would wind up always being remotely referenced—at a potentially huge performance penalty. On the other hand, not all other referenced entities should be moved, e.g., anything local to the node, such as a node-local file system, should remain where it is. The question is, when moving an object what other objects should also be moved? In general, there does not seem to be an easy answer to this question. Our solution calls for building groups of objects that are to move together by *attaching* objects to each other.

The idea is to statically indicate (in variable declarations) which of an object's *variables* hold references to other objects that should move with it.

For example, when in the Emerald mail system ([Jul 88b]) there are *MailMsg* objects with the following variables:

> **var** *to, from*: *MailBox*
> **attached var** *text*: **String**
> **attached var** *status*: *MessageStatus*
> **attached var** *date*: *Time*

When the *MailMsg* object is moved, the objects named *at that time* by *text*, *status*, and *date* will be moved with it, while neither of the mailboxes named by *to* or *from* will be moved. If we let mailboxes store their references to their mail messages in attached variables then when a mailbox is moved, its messages and—recursively—their contents are also moved.

Attachment is transitive. Attachment is not symmetric; a mail message can be moved without its mailbox being moved (and because the *to* field is not attached). In terms of performance, the biggest win is that attachment is declarative. The attached variables are declared statically which allows the compiler to provide the attachment information to the run-time kernel without imposing *any* run-time overhead.

Attachment can be used to provide *hierarchical grouping* of objects. When a mail message moves, its attached components follow. When a mailbox moves, the underlying hierarchy of mail message objects also moves. An advantage of this approach is that it allows an object and its underlying hierarchy to be moved without breaking encapsulation.

We have found attachment easy to understand and use and believe that it is a viable method for solving the shallow vs. deep copy problem. It is also very simple to add attachment specifications to a program that has not been written with distribution in mind.

3.6   Fault-tolerance: The Unavailability Concept

In our model of computation, each node may crash (in a fail-stop manner) and may (re-)boot separately. A node is said to be *available* when it is running; otherwise, it is *unavailable*. Correspondingly, an object is regarded as being *available* when it is be located at any of the available nodes; otherwise it is *unavailable*. When invoking an unavailable object (or when a node crashes during a remote invocation) the invocation fails. In some applications, it is desirable to be able to react to such failures, e.g., a replication manager may wish to note that a replica has failed and consequently regenerate another one on another node.

Emerald provides the programmer with the possibility of handling invocations to unavailable object using so-called **unavailable** handlers. Such handlers may be defined within a scope and will field any failure resulting from invocations of unavailable objects. When a failure occurs, it is propagated back to the handler. An unavailable handler may be added to any block in Emerald. (Essentially, a block is a collection of statements surrounded by the keywords **begin** and **end** or the like.) The syntax for an unavailable handler is:

> *unavailableHandler* ::=
> > **when**[*identifier*[*":"* *aType*]] **unavailable**
> > > *declarationsAndStatements*
> > **end unavailable**

The handler specifies the action to be taken when an unavailable object is invoked. The optional identifier is assigned the unavailable object so that the handler can identify the object that caused the handler to be executed.

An unavailable handler enables a program to recover from node crashes. For example, a load balancer might protect its calls to objects on other nodes using unavailable handlers, so that the load balancer can continue execution despite other nodes crashing.

4 Summary

Based on our experience with developing applications in Emerald, this paper argues that distribution and objects are orthogonal concepts. The models and paradigms of Emerald allow programmers to develop distributed applications with little or no regard for distribution and then subsequently add in distribution policies. This works well because Emerald provides mobility-independent invocation and because Emerald processes are *not* inherently bound to any specific object nor node.

References

[Almes 84]   Guy Almes and Cara Holman. *Edmas: An Object Oriented Locally Distributed Mail System.* Technical Report 84-08-03, Department of Computer Science, University of Washington, Seattle, Washington, December 1984.

[Almes 85]   Guy T. Almes, Andrew P. Black, Edward D. Lazowska, and Jerre D. Noe. The Eden System: A Technical Review. *IEEE Transactions on Software Engineering*, SE-11(1):43–59, January 1985.

[Black 85]   Andrew P. Black. Supporting distributed applications: experience with Eden. In *Proceedings of the Tenth ACM Symposium on Operating Systems Principles*, pages 181–193, Association for Computing Machinery, December 1985.

[Goldberg 83] Adele Goldberg and David Robson. *Smalltalk-80: the language and its implementation.* Addison-Wesley Publishing Company, Reading, Massachusetts, 1983.

[Hoare 74]   C. A. R. Hoare. Monitors: an operating system structuring concept. *Communications of the ACM*, 17(10):549–557, October 1974.

[Holt 83]   Richard C. Holt. *Concurrent Euclid, The Unix System, and Tunis.* Addison-Wesley Publishing Company, Reading, Massachusetts, 1983.

[Jul 88a]   Eric Jul. *Object Mobility in a Distributed Object-Oriented System*. PhD thesis, Department of Computer Science, University of Washington, Seattle, Washington, 1988. UW Technical Report no. 88-12-6, also DIKU report 89/1.

[Jul 88b]   Eric Jul, Henry Levy, Norman Hutchinson, and Andrew Black. Fine-grained mobilty in the Emerald system. *ACM Transactions on Computer Systems*, 6(1), February 1988.

[Lazowska 81] Edward D. Lazowska, Henry M. Levy, Guy T. Almes, Michael J. Fischer, Robert J. Fowler, and Stephen C. Vestal. The architecture of the Eden system. In *Proceedings of the Eighth ACM Symposium on Operating Systems Principles*, pages 148–159, Association for Computing Machinery, December 1981.

[Liskov 77] Barbara Liskov, Alan Snyder, Russell Atkinson, and Craig Schaffert. Abstraction mechanisms in CLU. *Communications of the ACM*, 20(8):564–576, August 1977.

[Liskov 88] Barbara Liskov. Distributed programming in Argus. *Communications of the ACM*, 31(3):300–313, March 1988.

[Parnas 75] D.L. Parnas and D.P. Siewiorek. Use of the concept of transparency in the design of hierarchically structured systems. *Communications of the ACM*, 18(7):401–408, July 1975.

[Spafford 86] Eugene H. Spafford. *Kernel Structures for a Distributed Operating System*. PhD thesis, School of Information and Computer Science, Georgia Institute of Technology, May 1986. Technical Report GIT-ICS-86/16.

[Wulf 74]   W. Wulf, E. Cohen, W. Corwin, A. Jones, R. Levin, C. Pierson, and F. Pollack. Hydra: the kernel of a multiprocessor operating system. *Communications of the ACM*, 17(6):337–345, June 1974.

Integrating Structural and Operational Programming to Manage Distributed Systems

Christian Zeidler and Bernhard Fank

University of Karlsruhe, Institute of Telematics, Zirkel 2, D-76128 Karlsruhe, Fed. Rep. of Germany, zeidler@telematik.informatik.uni-karlsruhe.de

Abstract. Distributed systems have become a buzz word, well known but not well used, because of different existing paradigms for programming languages, systems, communication, cooperation, management, and because of integraton problems. From the programmer's point of view, the interesting question is how one can solve a problem specification in a distributed environment. Most of the existing distributed programming environments concentrate on two levels; First, the denotation of an operational solution in a modularized way, and second, description of an initial interconnection of these modules into a distributed application, i.e. configuration or structural programming. Both levels are kept independent as far as possible, using different notations and thus can not benefit from each other because of their separation.

This paper introduces a model which integrates structural and operational programming into a single paradigm. This paradigm is based on object-orientation and reflective programming extended by a category and annotation model realizing structural programming support.

1 Introduction

The advantages of distributed systems are well known and so it does not surprise at all that a lot of work is performed to implement distributed computing platforms [Black 87, Dasqupta 90, OMG 92, Bal 92, Borghoff 92]. Most efforts concentrate on implementing an efficient environment for interaction of distributed program parts. Few of them address problems such as application performance tuning [Haban 90], fault tolerance [Ahamad 90, Christian 91], preservation of consistency [Turek 92] and application management [Magee 90, Marzullo 91, Zeidler 92]. Even fewer consider integration of system and application tasks in one environment [Zeidler 93] or dynamic manipulation of application functionality [Foote 92, Ichisugi 92, Segal 93].

Obviously, there is still a lack of integrational work combining all these various aspects of distributed computing in a uniform manner. Most existing distributed programming environments concentrate on two levels: First, denotation of operational solution in a modularized way, and second, description of the initial interconnection of these modules into a distributed application, i.e. configuration or structural programming. Both levels are handled independently as far as possible, most of them use different notations and could not benefit from each other because of their separation.

While structural and operational programming aspects are closely related, separation of their specification and targets allows for more flexibility in combining different goals in a unified environment. Many of the aspects referred to mainly concern the structural layer of programming but these aspects also need support from the operational layer as well as from the runtime environment. Therefore, a paradigm which joins structural and operational aspects of distributed programming is indispensable for decreasing the complexity of programming distributed applications. At the same time the integration have to fulfill the need for separation of concerns, which means clear and independent description of solutions worked out.

This paper introduces a model which integrates structural and operational programming into one single paradigm, based on object-orientation and reflective programming. In section 2, we present the basic ideas. In section 3, we describe how these ideas fit together and how they have to be extended to fulfill the needs of distributed programming. The subsequent section 4 introduces the environment which serves for the validation of these concepts. Within the section 5 we present a small example, which demonstrate the advantages of our approach. We conclude this article with an outlook on future work (see section 6) and a summary (see section 7).

2 Approach

The aim of our approach is to enable a flexible and extensible framework for programming distributed applications. To achieve this goal, we need a programming paradigm which is able to satisfy the needs of distributed programming environments. One of the basic needs, identified in the early '80s, is the support of operational and structural aspects of a distributed application. While operational aspects are inherent to all programming languages, e.g. how to describe a real problem in an operational layer, up to now there are just few approaches focusing on structural aspects. The distinction between operational and structural issues is as follows:

operational issues define the functionality of an application component being offered to the distributed application user. This could be a module definition providing an interface and an implementation for procedural languages or a type definition for an object-oriented approach.

structural issues describe how the functional units, when applied or instantiated, have to be interconnected in order to realize the requested problem solution. This task is called *configuration management* within the distributed system's community. It includes the creation and deletion of application entities for the initial run as well as for the dynamic modification of an application.

Especially for large distributed applications the need for dynamic reconfiguration is obvious for the sake of reliability, long term execution, availability, and finally costs of shutting down and restarting a modified application, which has to be optimized. Unfortunately very few approaches among the research of distributed systems point out the importance of structural programming.

Progress has been achieved in the projects *Conic* [Magee 89], *Rex* [Kramer 91] and *Domino* [Moffett 92]. But from the programmer's point of view, they mainly satisfy the problem solution, without considering consistent structure of the programming models. This outlook is, however, critical to minimize the complexity of programming, instead of learning of two languages for operational and structural aspects.

Therefore, we selected the object-oriented paradigm, which is well-suited for implementing distributed environments. This paradigm includes a free-to-choose granularity of programming components (object size), a separation of specification and implementation suitable for distributed programming (encapsulation and information hiding) and an interaction pattern which is appropriate for distributed system needs (message passing).

The object-oriented paradigm lacks features considering *distribution aspects*, such as location, different kinds of method invocation, migration of active or passive objects and structural features supporting application configuration. We have, therefore, developed a concept of categories [Zeidler 90], which enables us to distinguish between objects which have relevance to the application structure and those which are used for information interchange between configuration relevant objects. Therefore we distinguish:

configured objects, which build up the application skeleton and thus have strong importance to the application and realize operational as well as structural functionality. And

generated objects, which just have an operational meaning and thus no impact on the application configuration.

This way a first step to structural distinction within application programming is made. However, with respect to the need for dynamic modification and changes to running applications, we should have a more powerful mechanism, like reflection [Caseau 88, Masuhara 92].
Here Reflection means:

- An entity's integral ability to represent, operate on, and otherwise deal with its self in the same way that it represents, operates on, and deals with its primary subject matter.
- An introspection into oneself's organization of execution and the ability to modify this organization, i.e. the possibility to modify the execution semantics by modifying the runtime environment.

Within this approach, we distinguish additionally between a structural and an operational layer of reflective programming. The structural layer addresses the creation and assembly of defined object instances to a global application, i.e. *programming in the large*, and the operational layer associates definition and modification of object denotation, i.e. *programming in the small*, which may have an impact on the structural layer. The concept presented in section 3 combines these approaches into unified and consistent programming model.

3 Concept

3.1 Separation of Concerns

It is helpful to separate denotation of targets of *existing entities* within a system [Zeidler 90]. This means clear assignment of responsibilities and good modelling. It enhances the classification ability between configured / managed objects and others. The resulting benefits are advantages with respect to stripping or adding functionality to dedicated entities etc., which may be derived from these basics.

But distinguishing between *configured* and *generated objects* is not completely satisfying. At the beginning of our work we have identified many different types of concern, we call them *categories* [Zeidler 90]. Each of these categories has been addressed to a self-contained task which was defined to be orthogonal with regard to other categories' functionality. During the DOCASE-Project[1], we found more and more that it was difficult to keep categories orthogonal and, what is more important, we became aware that we force the application designer to accept our way of thinking and actually we do not really want to.

As a consequence, a small group of categories has been identified. They are generic enough not to hinder creativity and sufficiently specific to support structural aspects of programming but they do not claim to be orthogonal. In detail, these are *configured objects*, *subsystem objects*, *logical node objects* and *generated objects*. The first three characterize a small set of types on which a configuration management may be built (see figure 1).

A configured object is a common type, realizing structural and operational functionality. A logical node object integrates a hardware independent layer onto which applications can be created uniformly despite an underlying heterogeneous distributed system. A subsystem object encapsulates some objects into one abstract set of functionality. While a generated object realizes the information flow between specific objects of a configuration.

3.2 Annotational References

There is also a need to distinguish different kinds of references. An interesting detail in our context is a classification of references. This way we gain means to express categories of referred objects, which is very useful regarding the costs of object access in a distributed environment. So we are able to distinguish between four annotations. (A) a declaration, which is a commonly used reference, (B) an aggregation, which expresses a close relation of a referred object to the reference holder, i.e. an aggregated objects always tries to incorporate the same location in case of a migration of an aggregation holder. (C) a connection, which always refers to configured objects and (D) a configuration, which always refers to configured objects which are involved in a subsystem declaration. These annotations tell us what role in the structure of an application a referred object

---

[1] DOCASE (Distribution and Objects in CASE) is a joint effort of the Institute for Telematics, the Institute of Telecooperation at the University of Karlsruhe and Digital Equipment's CEC Karlsruhe.

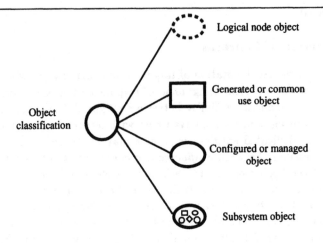

Fig. 1. Minimal subset of categories

plays. By evaluating the annotations we can compute a lot of tasks concerning configuration management avoiding many expensive distributed object accesses.

3.3 Distributed Management

According to our view of the structural features, management facilities should be attached to all *configured objects*, in the sense that each object possesses all functionality necessary for its management. Being in consensus with the object-oriented paradigm, each object must be able to manage itself. This means, a *configured object* contains all methods and data needed for its management. As already mentioned, separation of operational and structural aspects is desirable. It should also be provided within a common object-oriented model, but usually it is not. Thus, an extension of this paradigm is needed. In addition to the type hierarchy, we suggest a hierarchy of *meta types*. These meta types define, in analogy to types, structural functionality for each object instance using this definition (see figure 2).

Thus the distinction between structural and operational features depends on where (meta type or type) specific functions are inherited from. Providing this separation, structural and operational parts may be programmed independently. If this is not possible, the functions have to be adapted at the object level, i.e. conflicts are resolved within an object definition for example through redefinition, having less impact on other definitions.

3.4 What is reflection good for?

Reflection supports the dynamic manipulation of objects. The feature of computing on the self-representation is well suited for supplying a powerful configuration management. Thereby, structural aspects are satisfied by getting and

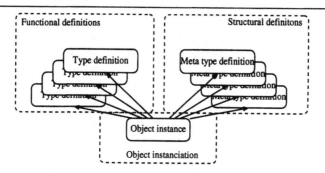

Fig. 2. Dual inheritance hierarchy

computing required facts through reflective methods. As an example, imagine a visualization of distributed applications. This task requires a selection of configured objects. Thereafter their references must be analyzed and the application's configuration must be extracted from each selected object. Whereby the annotations *connection* and *configuration* support this task. The preparation of extracted configuration data for the visualization tool finishes the process.

Using the features of reflective structural programming, configuration management is provided by realizing a subset of initial and dynamic configuration management commands. These subsets comprise basic functionality like: creation of object instances, initializing them, interconnecting them, providing name services, manipulation of their location, deleting them and replacing of object instances etc. Further, advanced functionality could be programmed using the meta level definitions, such that the configuration management is extensible in a flexible and comfortable way. Because the meta level definitions are made in the same manner as type definitions are done, the programmer just has to use his usual knowledge of operational programming in order to be able to define structural manipulations, which describe the manipulation on the object-domain made by the execution in the reflection-domain.

Operational reflection, on the other side, is responsible for the manipulation of the operational feature of an object definition, like modifying an implementation, adding or removing functionality to an object instance etc.

3.5 Integrational Solution

This section describes the interaction of the presented models, illustrated in figure 3. The object-oriented and distributed application is defined by two classes of objects. The first one – important to application configuration – is called configured objects (*configured objects, subsystems objects, logical nodes objects*) and the second one, generated objects, is important to the solution of the problem, i.e. short lifetime objects used for information exchange and transport.

Each configured object possesses a corresponding meta instance, which provides the configuration methods and includes the structural information neces-

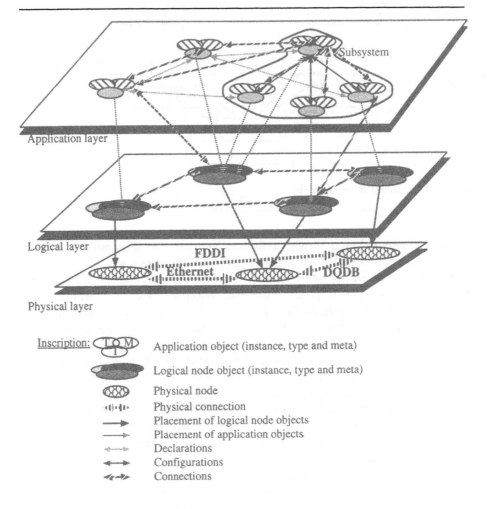

Fig. 3. A complex view on all layers of management

sary for configuration management. Thus typical configuration methods, such as creation of instances, setup of connections, replacement of objects, migration etc. are inherent to all managed objects. Meta instances are also user extensible by defining meta methods, formulated in the used object-oriented language. All meta methods profit from additional information provided by annotational references and information derived from the object type information (*runtime information*).

The application is spread over a logical system comprising a set of logical node instances. These logical nodes provide additional information, such as *name service, physical location, attributes of physical nodes* etc. which is needed by applications to fulfill the desired tasks. All interactions are "method call"-based and freely extensible according to inheritance and object-oriented programming. Further, all interaction to the physical system is managed by logical nodes, which provides the interface to the underlying system. It is worth-while to notice that this identical view is also given to the application using categories, annotations and the ability of introspection, thus advanced tools could take advantages using these integrated concepts .

To gain certain information for the configuration of a distributed application, each configured object in the application knows best the requirements need to be fulfilled by the underlying network of logical nodes. Therefore it calls methods offered by logical node instances. There, only the hardware-independent information can be found. In order to get hardware-dependent information, the logical node instance has to go a step deeper. Thus, it has to make use of a management protocol [Zeidler 93]. It interrogates the agents located on the physical nodes to contact the configured objects located in their management information bases (*MIB*). Figure 4 depicts this idea.

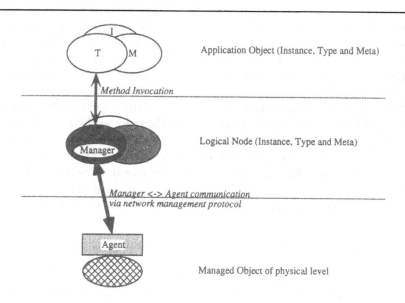

Application Object (Instance, Type and Meta)

Method Invocation

Logical Node (Instance, Type and Meta)

Manager <-> Agent communication
via network management protocol

Managed Object of physical level

Fig. 4. Integrated model of configuration management

4 Validation

The validation of the concepts presented in section 3 is done within a distributed object-oriented workspace language (**DOWL**). DOWL is derived and adapted from the object-oriented environment **Trellis** during the DOCASE-Project. Originally, Trellis was a product of Digital Equipment Corporation and has been extended to distribution mainly by Bruno Achauer [Achauer 93]. Thus, we first will describe briefly the integration of our concepts into DOWL and give further an example how this structural programming should be used.

4.1 Integration of Concepts

The integration of concepts into the runtime environment DOWL is a threefold task. First, we present the generic parts of our concepts which in general could be satisfied by almost any object-oriented language. Second, we show how we use and extend the reflective features of DOWL. This part is just for few languages generic. They must offer an adequate amount of runtime information. And in the last part we illustrate the extensions of the runtime environment needed for the concept's support.

Generic Parts The generic parts in our concept are the definitions of structural functionality, integration of categories and definition of annotational references. Their requirements postulate the necessity of defining structural types and the ability of multiple inheritance. This way, predefined types are provided which introduce the category concept. By the way, almost the whole type system of DOWL could be manipulated by the application programmer. Just device and compiler dependent parts sometimes do require support form the runtime system implementation.

The integration of annotations is made by declaration of specific component names on which the reflective configuration methods are working on. The semantics of these annotations are ensured only by using the reflective configuration language while direct manipulations of these components are still possible. For the sake of having a flexible experimental environment we rather prefer to establish a configuration management library than modifying the runtime system. Thereby the library is implemented in the reflective part of our concept.

Reflective Part The reflective part of the realization is represented by the configuration management library. This library is completely defined within the DOWL type system. It uses extensively reflective runtime informations offered by DOWL and also the developed concepts of categories and annotations. Additionally some functionality, like name service, giving the relations between names and instances, and automatic placement of objects within the distributed environment, is provided. Furthermore, the synchronization of configuration manipulation is established by allocation of manipulated objects exclusively for a dedicated activity path. Doing so, multiple different independent manipulations of configuration subsets can act in parallel. Conflicts of configuration activities are resolved by resetting the activities which were not able to allocate objects intended to be used. Therefore, the contexts of used objects are saved to be prepared for rejection of a configuration action.

The application designer is also able to define new structural methods and types. In order to keep the execution of configuration methods consistent they are marked as *meta* methods and components, like the library methods too. The extended environment of DOWL is then able to recognize the special task of attributed methods and can initiate required actions for keeping consistency, e.g. saving the context of used objects.

Environment Extension We kept the environment extensions as small as possible. At the moment we need just two extensions in order to realize reflective structural programming in DOWL. First, we had to enable the runtime system to recognize a structural expression which results in a structural action. Thus, we introduced a new attribute *meta* into the specification part of methods and components. As a consequence we had to modify the syntax checker to accept this attribute and realize the appropriate action invocation through the compiler, i.e. checking involvement in other meta activities, context preservation, reaction to exceptions, post-work etc. Secondly, we implemented reflective methods used by the DOWL code generator for meta methods. Most of them are written in the original object-oriented language and just few very specific are integrated into the runtime. So we are able to manipulate the runtime system behavior without any modifications to the runtime system, and this is what reflection intends to do.

5 Example

Having a look at a well known example we will show the described principles and ideas in this section.

The Problem Due to the lack of forks the *dining philosophers* are disturbed in having the pleasure of a tasty meal. Each philosopher tries competitively to get the two forks needed. Meanwhile s/he is considering the world and therefor using a vast amount of CPU power. The philosophers as the active objects contemplate, which means they are doing this in some time and at a location. Contemplation has the operational aspect of finding a good solution. Contemplation in some time and at a location means to find a good solution in a determined time and within a real context (neighborhood, dining–frequency, machine load). These are the structural aspects. Optimizing the number of seats on the tables and number of tables on the running systems we accelerate the access to the forks and so the pleasure of dining for each philosopher.

5.1 Modelling the Model of the Dinner

We just have to distinguish the classes "philosopher", "fork" and "table" to get all relevant objects of the application. "Philosopher" subsumes "seat" in this context. "Philosopher" and "fork" build up the application part. They are the configured objects of the application. "Table" has application relevance but also structures the distribution of the configured objects. Thus, "table" is a subtype of logical node. Furthermore we need to have a class "machine" representing the machines the processes are running on. Here we use the already implemented DOWL–type module "physical node".

Now we will have a look at the relations between the objects of the mentioned classes. The reference from a "table" to a "physical node", as well as the reference from a configured object to a "table" is called "location". "Location" is mainly a structural relation. Among the philosophers we get the neighbourhood relations. We are calling them "right" and "left". They are connections building up a part of the application structure and they are between configured objects. The derived names are "con_right" and "con_left". The other part of the application's links are the references between each philosopher and the two reachable forks. The names of these references are "agg_LFork" and "agg_RFork". The prefixes are declaring the references to be of additional structural relevance. Looking at such annotational references, the locations the informations for the introspective facilities of the configured objects and logical nodes inherited by the appropriate meta super types can be found.

5.2 Setting the Model of the Model to Work

The modelled objects have to be set to work. This task and subsequent reconfigurations are called configuration programming. It is purely structural and done by the following type module.

```
1   TYPE_MODULE Initial_configuration
2   OPERATION create(Mytype)
3     META
4     IS
5     BEGIN
6       VAR t:Integer   := 0;
7       VAR number:Integer := 4;
8       VAR names:VECTOR[STRING]:=VECTOR[STRING]'{"Bloch","Sartre",
9         "Kant","Russell","Nietsche","Platon","Skinner","Postman",
10        "Jaspers","Eratostenes","Aristoteles","Descartes",
11        "Sokrates","Schopenhauer","Wolff","Xenophanes",
12        "Baumgarten","Heidegger","Brunner"};
13      VAR p:VECTOR[Philosopher]:= create(VECTOR[Philosopher],number);
14      VAR g:VECTOR[Fork]:= create(VECTOR[Fork],number);

15        check(Physical_node, "e1");
16        create(Tisch,"t1",{});
17        migrate(Tisch["t1"], Physical_node["e1"]);

18        FOR j:INTEGER IN RANGE (1, number) DO
19          BEGIN
20            p[j] := create(Philosopher, names[j],{});
21            g[j] := create(Fork,"f"&string_form(Fork.all.high+1),{j});
22          END;
23        END FOR;
```

```
24          FOR j:INTEGER IN RANGE (1, number) DO
25            BEGIN
26              migrate(p[j],Logical_node["t1"]);
27              migrate(g[j],Logical_node["t1"]);
28            END;
29          END FOR;

30          FOR j:INTEGER IN RANGE (1,number) DO
31            BEGIN
32              connect(p[j],"right",p[(j mod number)+1]);
33              connect(p[j],"left",p[((j-2) mod number)+1]);
34              put_aggregation(p[j],"LFork",g[j]);
35              put_aggregation(p[j],"RFork",g[(j mod number) + 1]);
36            END;
37          END FOR;
38    END
39  END TYPE_MODULE;
```

In line 6 up to line 14 we are initializing some data structures. In line 15 we are checking whether the desired machine is available. If it is available we are going on in creating a logical node. Afterwards we migrate the table "t1" to the physical node "e1". In line 18 up to line 23 we are creating the philosophers and forks. In line 24 up to line 29 we are migrating these instances to the table "t1". The lines 30 until 37 are interconnecting the application instances.

A part of the resulting configurations is shown in picture 5. Administration tools can easily take advantage of the features given to the objects. E.g. the annotation of aggregations can be used to get a small snapshot of the configuration. Figure 6 shows the forks reachable by Mr. Kant and Mr. Sartre.

5.3   Optimization Mechanisms of the Objects

Now we will explain some requirements met for the philosopher. They give her/him the facilities to contemplate in the most suitable environment. We will use some facilities mentioned above like the *name service* and the reference to the *physical location*.

```
1  operation isolate_myself (me)
2        returns (boolean)
3        private
4        is
5        begin
6          not(hungry(me)) cand
7          (var all_tables: set[tisch] :=
8                            convert(set[tisch],tisch.all);
9          var all_locations: set[tisch] := create(set[tisch]);

10         for p: philosopher in elements(mytype.all) do
11              all_locations := union_1(all_locations,get_location(p));
12         end for;
```

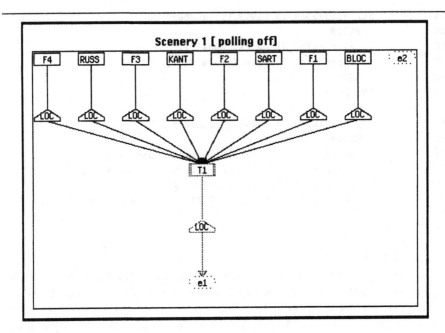

Fig. 5. The table "t1" located on the machine "e1" and its distinguished dining-party shown by the configuration administration tool "CAT".

```
13        all_locations := difference(all_tables, all_locations);
14        migrate(me, all_locations.an_element);
15        except on empty do
16          return false;   ! do not migrate

17        me.agg_RFork := nil;
18        me.con_right.con_left := me.con_left;
19        me.con_left.con_right := me.con_right;
20        me.con_left := me;
21        me.con_right := me;
22        return true;
23        ); ! if I'm hungry I'll stay. Need two forks
24      return false;
25    end
```

The operation listed first is a method of the class "philosopher". It should be called whenever the instance has eaten enough and the next contemplation process will take a large amount of CPU power.[2] In line 6 we test whether the philosopher is still hungry. If s/he is not hungry we try to migrate her/him. In the following lines 7 up to 12 we assemble the distribution situation of the

---

[2] we get this information by looking at the component me.philosophy.

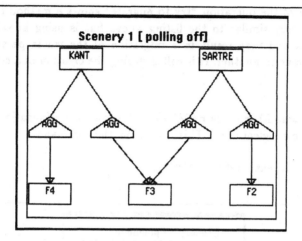

Fig. 6. Some aggregations of the configuration.

philosophers. Here we use the informations held by the name service (table.all, mytype.all). In the case of finding a table which is not used by a philosopher (line 13) we migrate her/him to this target (line 14). Otherwise we give up (lines 15 and 16). The rest of the operation is used to correct the connections and aggregations.

The logical node "table" has also been given the facilities to decide whether it should migrate or not.

```
1   operation try_to_migrate (me)
2       private
3       is
4       begin
5           var all_locations: set[physical_node] :=
6           create(set[physical_node]);
7           var all_nodes: set[physical_node] :=
8                       convert(set[physical_node],physical_node.all);

9           for t: tisch in elements(mytype.all) do
10              all_locations := union_1(all_locations,get_location(t));
11          end for;

12          all_locations := difference(all_nodes, all_locations);
13          migrate(me, all_locations.an_element);
14          except on empty do
15              ;  ! do not migrate
16      end;
```

The listing of the operation "try_to_migrate" shows a method of the object "table". It is very similar to the listing above but is using knowledge about physical nodes and may result in a migration of the whole party of a table from one machine to another. It is called during the creation of a corresponding instance.

How Does these Mechanisms Work? To show the optimization working we will create a new logical node. This is done by the command:

```
1              create(table, "t2",{})
```

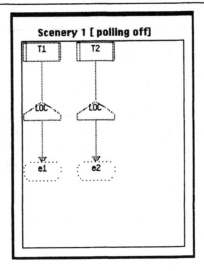

Fig. 7. The table "t2" migrated to the physical node "e2" after creation.

The "table" will be created at any physical node and will migrate to a still unoccupied one according to the operation "try_to_migrate". The picture 7 shows the resulting configuration. If a philosopher is not hungry anymore, s/he migrates to the table "t2". Picture 8 depicts the new situation. One fork automatically migrates with its user. We have not explained how dynamic type modification by objects is done. This would show the full abilities of our reflective concept. But this is what we currently are working on.

6 Future Work

The next step to improve the quality of this environment will be the integration of incremental and distributed compilation which is still a pretentious task, due to the need for synchronization and data consistency in a distributed environment.

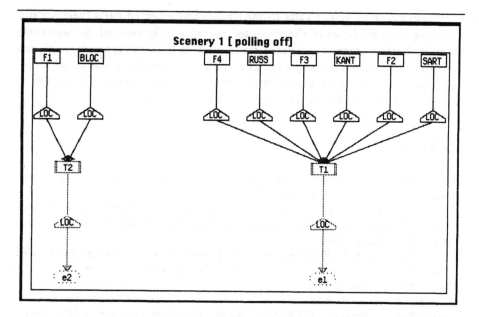

Fig. 8. Another snapshot made by CAT shows Mr. Bloch sitting on the table "t2".

At the moment we are investigating some ideas on necessities and possibilities of dynamic type manipulation within a distributed environment. In parallel we try to elaborate the abilities which are already offered by DOWL, which we have to implement and which cannot be implemented in DOWL. We are also looking for an adequate way to integrate more operational reflection into a distributed environment, so that versioning, type exchange and type modifications on runtime would be enabled. Furthermore, supplying more intelligent and pragmatic workbenches, based on the structural and operational reflection, are intended. Some target functionality is refined monitoring, more efficient debugging and error handling.

7   Summary

In this paper we have presented a concept for integrated configuration programming. Our approach is object-oriented and enables structural and operational programming within one programming paradigm in contrast to other approaches which always use one configuration and one programming language. This is done by extension of the object-oriented paradigm with a meta level in which reflective language components are available by means of a configuration library. Together with the introduction of categories and annotations a powerful object-oriented environment is supplied, which combines structural and operational programming in a uniform way. We are validating our concepts in a distributed object-oriented workspace language (DOWL), but also any general purpose object-oriented language could be extended by these features.

Though earning good results by the already implemented parts there are still encouraging possibilities of the presented concepts to be realized. So we expect to make further progress in related tasks, such as dynamic type exchange and distributed incremental compiling. The ability of integrating additional structural aspects to the environment by programming meta functionality is another important feature to be prepared for future requirements.

References

[Achauer 93] Bruno Achauer. The DOWL distributed object-oriented language. *Communications of the ACM*, 36(9):48–55, Sept. 1993.

[Ahamad 90] M. Ahamad, P. Dasgupta, R.J. LeBlanc, D.T. Wilkes. Fault Tolerant Atomic Computing in an Object-Based Distributed System. *Distributed Computing*, pages 69–80, April 1990.

[Bal 92] H.E. Bal, M.F. Kaashoek, A.S. Tanenbaum. Orca: A Language For Parallel Programming of Distributed Systems. *IEEE Transactions on Software Engineering*, 18(3):190–205, March 1992.

[Black 87] A. Black, N. Hitchinson, E. Jul, H. Levy, L. Carter. Distribution and Abstract Types in Emerald. *IEEE Transactions on Software Engineering*, 13(1):65–75, Jan. 1987.

[Borghoff 92] U.M. Borghoff. *Catalogue of Distributed File/Operation Systems*. Springer-Verlag, 1992.

[Caseau 88] Y. Caseau. A Model for a Reflective Object-Oriented Language. *SIGPLAN Notices*, 24(4):22–24, April 1988.

[Christian 91] F. Christian. Understanding Fault-Tolerant Distributed Systems. *Comm. of the ACM*, 34(2):56–78, Jan. 1991.

[Dasqupta 90] P. Dasqupta, R.C. Chen, S. Menon, M. Pearson, R. Ananthanarayanan, U. Ramachandran, M. Ahamad, R. LeBlanc Jr., W. Applebe, J.M. Bernabeu-Auban, P.W. Hutto, M.Y.A. Khalidi, C.J. Wilkenloc. The Design and Implementation of the Clauds Distributed Operation System. In *Computing Systems Journal*, volume 3. USENIX, 1990.

[Foote 92] B. Foote. Objects, Reflection and Open Languages. In *ECOOP'92 Workshop on Reflection*, June 1992.

[Haban 90] D. Haban, D. Wybranietz. A Hybrid Monitor for Behavior and Performance Analysis of Distributed systems. *IEEE Transactions on Software Engineering*, 16(2):197–211, Feb. 1990.

[Ichisugi 92] Y. Ichisugi, S. Matsuoka, A. Yonezawa. Rbcl: A reflective concurrent language without a run-time kernel. In *ECOOP'92 Workshop on Reflection*, 1992.

[Kramer 91] J. Kramer, J. Magee, M. Sloman, N. Dulay, SC. Cheung, S. Crane, K. Twidle. An Introduction to Distributed Programming in REX. In *ESPRIT Conference'91, Project Nr. 2080*, Brussels, Nov. 1991.

[Magee 89] J. Magee, J. Kramer, M. Sloman. Constructing Distributed Systems in CONIC. *Transactions on Software Engineering*, 15(6):663–675, June 1989.

[Magee 90] J. Magee, J. Kramer, M. Sloman, N. Dulay. An Overview of the REX Software Architecture. In *Second IEEE Workshop on Fututre Trends of Distributed Computing Systems*, pages 396–402, Cairo, Agypt, Sept. 1990.

[Marzullo 91] K. Marzullo, R. Cooper, M.D. Wood, K.P. Birman. Tools for Distributed Application Management. *IEEE Computer*, 24(8):42–51, Aug. 1991.

[Masuhara 92] H. Masuhara, S. Matsuoka, T. Watanabe, A. Yonezawa. Object-Oriented Concurrent Reflective Languages can be Implemented Efficiently. *ACM SIGPLAN Notices*, 27(10):127–144, Oct. 1992.

[Moffett 92] J.D. Moffett, M.S. Sloman. Policy Hierarchies for Distributed Systems Management. Technical report, Imperial College of Science, Technology and Medicine, Departement of Computing, 180 Queen's Gate, London SW7 2BZ, June 1992.

[OMG 92] OMG. The omg object model. Technical report, Object Management Group, Framingham Corporate Center, 492 Old Connecticut Path, Framingham, MA 01701-4568, U.S.A., March 1992. DRAFT.

[Segal 93] M.E. Segal. On-The-Fly Program Modification: System For Dynamic Updating. *IEEE Software*, pages 53–65, March 1993.

[Turek 92] J. Turek, D. Shasha. The Many Faces of Consensus in Distributed Systems. *IEEE Computer*, 25(6):8–17, June 1992.

[Zeidler 90] Ch. Zeidler, W. Gerteis, L. Heuser, M. Mühlhäuser. DOCASE: A Development Environment and a Design Language for Distributed Object-Oriented Applications. In *Proc. Tools Pacific '90*, pages 298–312, Sydney, Australia, Nov. 1990.

[Zeidler 92] Ch. Zeidler, W. Gerteis. Distribution: Another Milestone of Application Management Issues. In G. Heeg, B. Magnusson, B. Meyer, editors, *Proc. of TOOLS EUROPE'92*, pages 87–99, Dortmund, Germany, March 1992.

[Zeidler 93] Ch. Zeidler, J. Seitz. Intergrational configuration management. In *Second Workshop on Networked Systems Management*, Aachen, Germany, April 1993.

Concurrency and Communication: Choices in Implementing the Coordination Language *LO*

Marc Bourgois, Jean-Marc Andreoli and Remo Pareschi

European Computer-Industry Research Centre

Abstract. By means of an illustrative application, we discuss the implementation choices of the rule-based coordination language *LO*.

Distributed applications written in *LO* manifest two levels of granularity, each with their specific communication paradigm. At the finer level, individual objects are composed into agents and communicate through blackboards. At the coarser level, these agents interact through broadcasts.

This dichotomy determines implementation choices: Concurrency among agents naturally maps onto distributed processes (with e.g. RPC), whereas concurrency among objects maps onto threads (in shared memory). These four abstractions (objects, blackboards, agents, and broadcasts) together with *LO*'s basic computation paradigm (rules) are implemented as a class-based run-time library, thereby enriching classical object-oriented platforms.

Finally we stress the fact that the resulting run-time library is polymorphic: The run-time can manipulate any independently defined application object, provided its class respects a minimal protocol. Run-time polymorphism has turned out to be the key to composition-based reuse.

1 Introduction

Formal presentations of the operational semantics of *LO* have been given elsewhere [2]; a short summary is provided in the Appendix. In this paper we will focus on implementation issues. We do not look at *LO* as a new programming language, but rather as a set of coordination primitives which should be integrated into industrial-strength general-purpose languages, and especially traditional object-oriented programming platforms. We want to enrich those platforms with the four coordination primitives of *LO*: *rules*, *agents*, *blackboards*, and *broadcasts*. But most importantly, we want to enable easy reuse of application *objects* within these augmented platforms. In the remainder of this introduction we motivate these concepts in more detail.

Objects. Foremost we advocate a development methodology where fine-grained objects are composed into agents (gluing them intimately together with blackboards), and those coarse-grained agents in turn compose the full-fledged application (gluing them loosely together with broadcasts). The specification of the application objects is not part of the coordination language *LO* itself. We will therefore offer ways to reuse any legacy object written in languages which are accessible from within the implementation platform for *LO*.

Agents encapsulate sizable chunks of the state of an application. They are on the borderline between the shared and distributed dataspace programming models. Concurrency within agents centers around competition for data on shared blackboards; concurrency among agents relies on broadcasting copies of the tuples. Although shared memory and distributed memory are dual techniques (one can embed the other and vice versa), tightly-coupled fine-grained components of an application are more easily modeled by shared memory, whereas distributed memory models naturally fit loosely-coupled coarse-grained components.

Many other distributed programming systems offer language constructs that relate application components of sufficiently large granularity to physical distribution. Additionally, our own experience [4] with multi-user diary managers and distributed knowledge retrieval systems indicates the appropriateness of the two-layered model.

Blackboards offer a shared memory programming model and correspond to the internal view of an individual agent. They contain all tuples shared by the concurrent activities within an agent. Those concurrent activities are programmed by rules which describe (potentially concurrent and competing) transitions on the shared data set.

Blackboards are a basic communication paradigm in artificial intelligence and for many concurrent programming languages. Since *LO* blackboards model local, data sharing components of an application, we will not consider physical distribution at this level.

Broadcasts offer a distributed memory programming model and correspond to the external view of the agents. Agents cooperate by sending other agents copies of tuples. Again, message broadcasting is specified by rules. This communication mode assures maximal asynchrony and independence, suiting autonomous subsystems.

Recently, many application studies in Computer Supported Cooperative Work have stressed the need for a communication paradigm based on broadcasts. Though on the hardware level broadcast is often the basic communication paradigm among physically distributed systems, as provided by ethernet or satellite communication, multiple layers of additional system software make this facility effectively unaccessible. Notable exceptions are [25].

LO blackboards and broadcasts stand for quite opposite (but complementary) programming models. Nevertheless, they also share important properties: communication is asynchronous (sender and receiver remain mutually independent), anonymous (sender and receiver remain mutually unknown), and associative (retrieval is through pattern matching).

Rules are the format for all *LO* computations. They describe the modularization, the communication and state transitions of the application objects.

Rules are a basic programming paradigm behind production systems, shared dataspace, and logic programming languages. Transferring their expressive power to object-oriented programming holds the promise of greatly enlarging their community of potential users.

We proceed as follows: In the next section we model an example using the four coordination primitives. Then we detail their implementation, discuss optimizations, and relate to other work.

2 An Example

For introducing the syntax and clarifying the operational semantics of *LO* we will use the example of the mastermind puzzle, which is a representative instance from the important class of search problems. The solution of this puzzle consists in finding a code word with a minimal number of guesses. After each guess, the number of bulls (number of characters at the same position in the guess and the code) and cows (number of characters common to guess and code, but appearing at different positions) is returned. For simplicity we will use words of width 4 and composed of digits (0..5), covering a search space of size 1296.

2.1 A single-agent program

A naive algorithm enumerates all possible words and uses them as individual guesses, neglecting the information known from replies to previous guesses. Such a generate and test strategy corresponds to the *rules* in Fig. 1.

---

r11 n(N) @ d(D) @ w(W) @ {gen(N,D,W,G)} <>- g(G) @ n(N+1) @ d(D) @ w(W).

r12 g(G) @ s(S) @ {test(G,S,true)} <>- a(G).

Fig. 1. Generate and Test Search

The rule *r11* generates possible combinations *g(_)*, using the depth *d(_)* and width *w(_)* of the code and a pointer *n(_)* for traversing the (linear) search space. Rule *r12* takes an individual guess and compares it with the solution *s(_)*, possibly resulting in the answer *a(_)*.

An individual *LO* agent, such as this generate and test agent, is modeled by a private *blackboard* which contains all its local data tuples. The rules for an agent describe the possible transitions on its blackboard: the left-hand side of a rule tells us which tuples will be replaced by the tuples in its right-hand side. Rules can also specify additional guard tests which should succeed before the transition applies. The {*gen(_)*} and {*test(_)*} functions illustrate this. Applying *r11* to an initial blackboard *s11*, we get the consecutive generation steps of Fig. 2.

2.2 Incorporating application objects

Here we should interrupt the construction of the algorithm to make an important remark concerning the application *objects*. The variables in *LO* rules always

s11	s12	s13	s14	s15	s16	s17	s18
d(6)	d(6)	d(6)	d(6)	d(6)	d(6)	d(6)	d(6)
w(4)	w(4)	w(4)	w(4)	w(4)	w(4)	w(4)	w(4)
n(0)	g([0,0,0,0])	g([0,0,0,0])	g([0,0,0,0])	g([0,0,0,0])	g([0,0,0,0])	g([0,0,0,0])	g([0,0,0,0])
	n(1)	g([0,0,0,1])	g([0,0,0,1])	g([0,0,0,1])	g([0,0,0,1])	g([0,0,0,1])	g([0,0,0,1])
		n(2)	g([0,0,0,2])	g([0,0,0,2])	g([0,0,0,2])	g([0,0,0,2])	g([0,0,0,2])
			n(3)	g([0,0,0,3])	g([0,0,0,3])	g([0,0,0,3])	g([0,0,0,3])
				n(4)	g([0,0,0,4])	g([0,0,0,4])	g([0,0,0,4])
					n(5)	g([0,0,0,5])	g([0,0,0,5])
						n(6)	g([0,0,1,0])
							n(7)

Fig. 2. Initial Snapshots

stand for application objects. However the rules do not manipulate these objects directly, but only through their guard tests. This approach respects encapsulation and allows us to deal, at the *LO* level, with object identifiers only. The mastermind programs mainly deal with *combinations*. The protocol of Fig. 3 specifies the *combinations* objects which represent both the guesses $g(\_)$ and the solution $s(\_)$.

    c15   *class* combinations
          defines gen: integers x integers x integers -> combinations
                valid: combinations x combinations lists -> booleans
                query: combinations x combinations -> integers x integers

Fig. 3. *combinations* Objects

Notice that the internal representation for *combinations* objects is not exported by this interface. In snapshots we will nevertheless represent *combinations* as lists to make our illustrations concrete.

2.3   Toward a realistic program

A more sophisticated algorithm was presented in [22]. The algorithm makes about the same number of guesses as a human player would.[1] The algorithm

---

[1] This is not to say that the strategies used by humans and by the algorithm are comparable.

will only query for a combination if it does not contradict the replies to previous queries. Intuitively, a new combination does not contradict a reply if that reply would have been the same if the new combination were the solution. In Fig. 4 we show the query history for the example data.[2]

	bulls	cows	(bulls+cows)
q11 [0,0,0,0]	0	0	(0)
q12 [1,1,1,1]	1	0	(1)
q13 [1,2,2,2]	0	1	(1)
q14 [3,1,3,3]	0	1	(1)
q15 [4,4,1,4]	3	0	(3)
q16 [4,4,1,5]	2	2	(4)
q17 [4,5,1,4]	4	0	(4)
q21 [2,1,1,1]	1	0	(1)
q22 [4,1,1,1]	2	0	(2)
q23 [3,1,3,3]	0	1	(1)
q24 [4,1,3,3]	1	1	(2)

Fig. 4. Sequence of Guesses

This algorithm will reach the solution *q17* by just 7 queries (instead of 1054). Where the naive strategy would have queried for each generated guess, we can now skip all combinations between *[0,0,0,0]* and *[1,1,1,1]* because they contain 0s, which is inconsistent with the 0 bulls and 0 cows reply in *q11*. Guess *[1,2,2,2]* is the next query, because it does not contains 0s (consistent with *q11*) and shares exactly one 1 with *q12*. Analogously, *q14* is the following legitimate query.

In writing the program for this strategy, we can keep the old generation rule but replace the test rule by *r22* and *r23* (Fig. 5). Rule *r23* checks the generated combination, using the replies *rs(_)* to previous queries. In case the verification succeeds ($V = true$), we compare that combination with the solution in *r23*.

Finally, rule *r24* detects an answer if the bulls in the reply equal the width of the code. If not, *r25* adds the reply to the list of previous replies, so that it will be used in future validations.

2.4 A multi-agent program

Let us now expand the example to illustrate the use of multiple *agents*, each with their own blackboard. A classical approach to speeding up large search problems consists in partitioning the search space and then exploring each subspace in parallel. Therefore we assign the different subspaces to different agents and locate

---

[2] The second halve of the table, from *q21* to *q24*, will be used later.

```
r11  n(N) @ d(D) @ w(W) @ {gen(N,D,W,G)} <>- g(G) @ n(N+1) @ d(D) @ w(W).

r22  g(G) @ rs(Rs) @ {valid(G,Rs,V)} <>- v(G,V) @ rs(Rs).

r23  v(G,true) @ s(S) @ {query(G,S,B,C)} <>- q(G,B,C) @ s(S).

r24  q(G,W,C) @ w(W) <>- #t.

r25  q(G,B,C) @ w(W) @ {diff(B,W)} @ rs(Rs) <>- w(W) @ rs([(G,B,C)|Rs]).
```

Fig. 5. Generate, Validate and Test Search

those agents on physically distributed processors. Thus we can achieve an almost linear speed-up with the number of agents (i.e. the size of the partition) created. *LO* has a cloning operator **&** for creating new agents from existing ones. Rule *r37* (Fig. 6) initializes the three agents with their disjunct parts of the search space.

Moreover, if we also use the *broadcast* communication, we can inform any agent of replies received by any other agent, thereby increasing the effectiveness of its validation procedure and thus speeding up its search. The super-linear speed-ups stemming from such a collaboration between agents that share partial results is well-known result [11]. Note that, in general, search algorithms need to be adapted to be able to usefully integrate partial results. Our example needs only minor modifications for one agent to benefit from the replies to another agent's queries (Fig. 6): Rule *r35* broadcasts an agent's reply ^ *r(_)* to all other agents. Rule *r36* inserts communicated replies *r(_)* in the local list *rs(_)*, which immediately increases the effectiveness of the local verification procedure *r22*.

```
r35  q(G,B,C) @ w(W) @ {diff(B,W)} @ rs(Rs) @ ^r(G,B,C)

       <>- w(W) @ rs([(G,B,C)|Rs]).

r36  r(G,B,C) @ rs(Rs) <>- rs([(G,B,C)|Rs]).

r37  clone <>- n(0) & n(432) & n(864).
```

Fig. 6. Distributed Search

The snapshots in Fig. 7 illustrate the distributed search. The complexity of these diagrams has dramatically increased compared to the earlier single agent example. This is partly due to the fact that not just one, but all the rules are considered concurrently; and partly because of the broadcasts between the three agents. Luckily, for what we are interested in, it suffices to concentrate on a subset of the tuples in the blackboards. We can also skip numerous intermediate transitions.

s21	s22	..s23	..s24	..s25	..s26	..s27
s(q17)	s(q17)	s(q17)	s(q17)	s(q17)	s(q17)	s(q17)
rs[]	rs[]	rs[]	rs[q11]	rs[q12,q11]	rs[q21,q12,q11]	rs[q23,q22,q21,q12,q11]
clone	n(0)	q11	-	-	-	-
	n(259)	q12	-	-	-	
		n(283)	n(283)	n(432)	-	

	s32	..s33	..s34	..s35	..s36	..s37
	s(q17)	s(q17)	s(q17)	s(q17)	s(q17)	s(q17)
	rs[]	rs[]	rs[q11]	rs[q12,q11]	rs[q21,q12,q11]	rs[q23,q22,q21,q12,q11]
	n(432)	n(432)	n(475)	q21	-	-
				n(705)	q23	-
					n(864)	-

	s42	..s43	..s44	..s45	..s46	..s47
	s(q17)	s(q17)	s(q17)	s(q17)	s(q17)	s(q17)
	rs[]	rs[]	rs[q11]	rs[q11]	rs[q22,q12,q21,q11]	rs[q24,q22,q12,q21,q11]
	n(864)	n(864)	n(907)	q22	-	-
				n(921)	q24	-
					n(1018)	q15
						q16
						q17

Fig. 7. Distributed Snapshots

The cloning rule *r37* creates three copies (*s22*, *s32*, *s42*) of the initial state *s21*. We do not show the *d(_)* and *w(_)* atoms which are also copied. Additionally, different initial values *n(_)* are written on the three blackboards. The first agent starts out and proposes consecutively *q11* and *q12*. Its next consistent guess would be *q13*, but by the time this agent wants to propose it (at *..s26* in Fig. 7), the query *q21* from the second agent has been added to its list, making *q13* inconsistent too. The first agent will find no further consistent guesses in its subspace.

Switching to the third agent, we see that it reaches the solution in only five steps (compared to seven for the single agent case). This was possible because the search space was reduced by the queries $q11$, $q12$ and $q21$ received from the other agents. Notice that broadcast messages are not necessarily received by each agent with the same delay: the second agent receives $q12$ at $..s35$ whereas the third agent has to wait till $..s46$. Looking at the contents of the $rs[\_]^3$ tuples, we note that interleavings of rule firings are quite different for different agents.

3 Implementation

The main goal of the implementation is to augment traditional object-oriented programming languages with the *LO* coordination model. This should allow developers to compose ever larger applications out of (reusable) fine-grained objects. True concurrency and physical distribution are the other implementation goals.

Although the implementation on which we base our presentation uses Modula-3 [20], its general principles can be transferred to any other object-oriented language equipped with facilities for implementing or simulating concurrent behavior (e.g. C++ [24] along with a threads package [13]). Languages which are not properly object-oriented but provide for encapsulation and have appropriate language extensions for concurrency (e.g. ML [17]) can be used as well.

The following subsection provides an overview of the run-time library which implements *LO*'s coordination primitives, stressing object-oriented aspects. Thereafter we detail the strategies underlying competitive, but fair, access to blackboards. In the third subsection we outline the distributed aspects. Drawing upon these explanations we can then discuss the code generated by our compiler for each *LO* rule.

3.1 Reuse of objects

The coordination primitives are implemented as a conservative extension to object-oriented programming platforms. By conservative extension we mean that all added facilities are provided by library functions only. Thus *rules, blackboards, broadcasts* and *agents* all have their class definitions. In Fig. 8 we give their specifications. As is visible from the inheritance relations among these classes, we rely on the existence of threads (for concurrency) and mutexes (for exclusive access to shared memory) within the implementation platform.

Note that these six (simplified) class definitions, which represent the kernel of the run-time library, do not make any assumption on the application-specific *objects*. All the run-time objects are concerned with, is the fact that they can *copy* those application objects and test them for *equality*. It is therefore sufficient to implement an *equal* and *copy* method for each object class in the application.

In order to seamlessly integrate pre-existing (or independently developed) applications, we will not touch their classes directly. Rather, a *wrapper* class *(c36)* is created for each application class (In Fig. 9 this is done for the *combinations* objects). This wrapper class inherits all functionality from the original

---

[3] For increased readability, we omitted the rounded brackets for the rs tuples.

c21   *class* variables *inherits from* identifiers
       defines match: variables x identifiers -> identifiers
              diff: variables x variables -> booleans

c22   *class* tuples *inherits from* identifiers

c23   *class* rules *inherits from* threads
       defines fork: rules x tuples lists -> rules x rules

c24   *class* blackboards *inherits from* mutexes
       defines write: blackboards x tuples -> blackboards
              read: blackboards x integers -> tuples
              wipe: blackboards x integers -> blackboards

c25 .   *class* broadcasts *inherits from* blackboards
       defines send: broadcasts x identifiers -> broadcasts

c26   *class* agents
       defines clone: agents -> agents x agents
              terminate: agents ->

Fig. 8. Simplified Run-Time Kernel

application *(c15)*, and moreover provides concrete methods for the *equal* and *copy* messages in the (abstract) *identifiers* class *(c31)*. This way the original functionality of the objects is preserved whereas, simultaneously, the wrapped objects can be manipulated by the run-time.

This double class hierarchy, one for run-time objects and one for wrapped application objects, realizes a clean separation of concerns. Note that some *identifiers* classes *(c32,c33,c34)*, such as *booleans*, *integers* and *lists*, are useful to multiple applications and thus play the role primitive types have in other programming languages.

3.2   A shared memory implementation for blackboards

Previously we clarified the concept of *blackboard* by means of snapshots. Instead of concentrating on the states, we will now concentrate on the transitions to describe the implementation. Given the single-agent program and some blackboard state along the computation path (as indicated in the header of Fig. 10), we now concentrate on potentially parallel transitions.

State transitions are implemented by threads. Threads are lightweight processes with private memory and stack, and governed by a preemptive scheduling policy. The private memory is used for storing the variable bindings generated by successful matches. The stack, in turn, makes the cascaded message calls of

---

c31 *class* identifiers
      defines equal: identifiers x identifiers -> booleans
            copy: identifiers -> identifiers

c32 *class* booleans *inherits from* identifiers

c33 *class* integers *inherits from* identifiers
      defines add: integers x integers -> booleans

c34 *class* a lists *inherits from* identifiers
      defines "|": a lists x a -> a lists

c15 *class* combinations
      defines gen: integers x integers x integers -> combinations
            validate: combinations x combinations lists -> booleans
            query: combinations x combinations -> integers x integers

c36 *class* wrappers *inherits from* identifiers *and* combinations

Fig. 9. Reusing Objects through Inheritance

---

the object-oriented implementation possible. The preemptive scheduling policy implies some non-determinism and some notion of fairness.[4] The function of the threads is to scan the blackboard for the next matching tuple.

The transitions *t111* through *t114* correspond to *r11*, *t221* through *t225* to *r22* and so forth. For each individual rule we examine all possible alternative sets of matching tuples in parallel. As a result there is one thread for each matching set. Thus *t223* considers the set consisting of *rs(_)* and *g[3,4,4,2]*, where *t225* considers *rs(_)* and the alternative *g[3,4,4,4]*. Since these two transitions compete for the some common tuple *rs(_)*, only one will actually fire its rule. This choice is made non-deterministically. When transitions do not share tuples, such as *t114* and *t225*, they can fire their rules concurrently.

We implemented a concurrent thread forking policy which embodies a run-time optimization of the matching process in rule evaluation. It trades computation (repeated matches) for memory (threads): Initially, each agent starts up one thread for each rule. Thus *t111* will start scanning for a tuple in the blackboard that matches *d(D)*, the first head of *r11*. If such a match exists, this thread forks another one that will look for the second head. Concretely, *t111* finds *d(6)* and will fork *t112* which in turn will look for *w(W)*. The original thread *t111* will continue to look for alternative matches, i.e. other data tuples *d(_)*. Once *t112* finds a match, it will fork another thread. This goes on till some thread finds

---

[4] For our purposes, fairness can be thought of as a policy which assures that no rule, or its corresponding threads, can be starved.

	d(6)	w(4)	s[4,5,1,4]	n(840)	g[3,4,4,2]	g[3,4,4,4]	v([3,4,4,3],false)	q[3,1,3,3]	rs[q11,q12,q13]	?next tuple
t111	-	-	-	-	-	-	-	-	-	?d
t112	x	-	-	-	-	-	-	-	-	?w
t113	x	x	-	-	-	-	-	-	-	?n
t114	x	x	-	x	-	-	-	-	-	-
t221	-	-	-	-	-	-	-	-	-	?g
t222	-	-	-	-	x	-	-	-	-	?rs
t223	-	-	-	-	x	-	-	-	x	-
t224	-	-	-	-	-	x	-	-	-	?rs
t225	-	-	-	-	-	x	-	-	x	-
t231	-	-	-	-	-	-	-	-	-	?s
t232	-	-	x	-	-	-	-	-	-	?v
t233	-	-	x	-	-	-	x	-	-	-
t241	-	-	-	-	-	-	-	-	-	?w
t242	-	x	-	-	-	-	-	-	-	?q
t243	-	x	-	-	-	-	-	x	-	-
t251	-	-	-	-	-	-	-	-	-	?w
t252	-	x	-	-	-	-	-	-	-	?q
t253	-	x	-	-	-	-	-	x	-	-

Fig. 10. Concurrent Threads

matches for all heads of a rule. At that point, the thread removes the matching tuples from the blackboard and tuples corresponding to the body of the rule are put on the blackboard. Threads that are looking for a matching tuple, but cannot find it yet, suspend till new tuples arrive.

The last column of the table (Fig. 10) indicates which tuple a suspended thread is looking for next. All threads that have a "-" in this column, matched all the heads of their corresponding rules and are triggered. All threads that are triggered and do not share any tuple, i.e. have no **x** in the same column, can fire concurrently. The competition for tuples in the blackboard is implemented with the mutual exclusion primitives of the threads package.

Finally there are two ways threads die. First, they can die because they fire their rules. Second, they can die because the tuples they rely upon have been removed from the blackboard by some other thread which fired. Threads lazily detect the latter situation, since each time they acquire read access on the blackboard (before scanning for more matches) they check whether all tuples they rely upon are still available.

The specification of the *blackboards* class is given by *(c24)* in Fig. 8. The *read* message is sent when threads are scanning the blackboard, a *wipe* message to remove tuples when a rule fires, and a *write* message to add the tuples from the body. The implementations of these messages enforce a multiple-read-single-write locking policy on the contents of the blackboard.

3.3   Towards a distributed memory implementation for broadcasts

We will now outline how the concurrency between agents can be implemented. It is also at this level that physical distribution comes into play. The *LO* agents can be distributed on different nodes, enabling applications which are inherently distributed or which rely on multiple processors to speed up the overall computation.

Communication in *LO* is equivalent to storing in and retrieving from associative memories. Broadcasts differ from blackboards in their storage strategy, which is non-competitive, but have equivalent matching strategies. Therefore all broadcast implementations rely on additional objects to memorize the messages, but matching is defered till the message is copied in the appropriate blackboard, for which the matching strategy is already implemented. This copying is done by one dedicated thread per blackboard which works concurrently with the threads that perform the matching on the blackboard.

We are experimenting with different implementation strategies for the broadcast buffer. All schemes share the property that they store their broadcasts in a linear message buffer. This does however not mean that all agents process those messages in the same order, since this depends on their local threads scheduling sequence. In short, the sequentiality of the buffer does not bias the asynchrony of message processing.

Our latest experiments with physical distribution use message passing platforms such as Remote Procedure Calls [21]. In the first scheme, the buffer is encapsulated by one object whose address is known by all agents. Broadcasting is achieved by sending messages to the buffer. These messages are then dispatched to the agents, either lazily upon demand or eagerly upon reception. Since a centralized broadcast memory imposes too many synchronization restrictions, we started experimenting with a second scheme in which the buffer is distributed over the agents. Our practical experience is still limited, but a clear operational semantics for these latter experiments has been given in [1].

A third scheme, for which we have a stable implementation, uses a shared memory approach for the buffer. This implementation resembles very much the blackboard implementation, in fact so much so that it is implemented by subclassing blackboards (while eliminating the wipe method, see *c25* in Fig. 8). Since the shared memory implementation of blackboards relies on threads, the broadcasts are also confined to one address space. With the advent of Virtual Shared Memory on distributed memory machines, this scheme might in fact usable for true physical distribution. This model should also be straightforwardly portable to multiprocessors using truly parallel system threads, though the memory locking policy might need some tuning.

3.4 Compilation of rules

We have implemented a compiler which automatically generates code for the concurrent thread forking strategy. As an illustration, all threads corresponding to *rule r35* will execute the program in Fig. 11. This fragment is written in a simplified fragment of Modula-3. It relies on the class definitions for the run-time objects (Fig. 8). The rule objects *(c23)* inherit from *threads*. In fact, rules correspond to those initial threads (with no **x** in any column of Fig. 10) from which all other threads are (indirectly) forked.

The broadcast buffer is globally accessible, since all threads might send messages. The compiler defines a new record structure for each rule, containing all the variables in the rule. The fields in this record will gradually be filled with bindings as more heads are matched.

Each thread executes the (infinite) loop corresponding to the head it tries to match. Thus the thread looking for a match for *w(W)*, the second head in this rule, will execute the loop with *while H.equal(2) do*. Scanning of the blackboard starts at position $N = 1$. Before a match with the next tuple is tried, the variables are copied. This is needed because *match* might generate additional bindings which should be passed, when it succeeds, to the forked thread only. Whether matching with the current tuple in the blackboard succeeds or not, the forking thread continues scanning for alternative matches (by incrementing the scan pointer N).

The call to *match* might suspend in case the end of the blackboard is reached. This thread will then be woken up when new tuples are written to the blackboard. The thread which has matched all heads, H will then have the value *5*, broadcasts *r(G,B,C)* and then completes by writing the tuples from the body to the blackboard.

4 Optimizations

The high-level coordination primitives of *LO* make it at first sight also a very expensive model to implement. However, much like Self has proved that pure object-oriented languages do not have to be more expensive than hybrids or procedural languages [26], static analysis can dramatically reduce *LO*'s implementation cost. For a detailed discussion we refer to [3]. The approach strongly relies on the formal operational semantics of *LO* based on Linear Logic [18]. The optimizations concentrate on two phenomena:

- *Non-determinism:* Rule matching against blackboards is intrinsically inefficient since, in general, it requires checking all possible combinations of tuples after each transition. Optimizations should reduce this *non-determinism:* Rules should be matched only when needed, and then only on those parts of the blackboard that are relevant.
- *Saturation:* Sending broadcasts is also intrinsically inefficient since, in general, it requires each agent to memorize all the messages it does not consume

```
global
  BC: broadcasts                    % the BC is globally accessible

type
  vars35 =                          % record structure for variables of r35
    G: combinations
    B,C,W: integers
    Rs: combinations lists

method m35(Vs: vars35; H: integers; BB: blackboards) =
local
  N : integers <- 1                 % try to match first tuple on BB first
  Cs : vars35                       % copy of (partly grounded) variables
  T: tuples
body
  while H.equal(1) do               % first head
    Cs <- Vs.copy
    T <- Tuples.new(q,Cs.G,Cs.B,Cs.C)
    if T.match(BB.read(N))          % read may suspend
    then m35(Cs,2,BB).fork          % new thread continues with next head
    N <- N.increment                % try next tuple on BB

  while H.equal(2) do               % second head
    Cs <- Vs.copy
    T <- Tuples.new(w,Cs.W)
    if T.match(BB.read(N))
    then m35(Cs,3,BB).fork
    N <- N.increment

  if H.equal(3) and not B.diff(W)   % test guard
  then exit                         % thread dies if test fails

  while H.equal(4) do               % fourth head
    Cs <- Vs.copy
    T <- Tuples.new(rs,Cs.Rs)
    if T.match(BB.read(N))
    then m35(Cs,5,BB).fork
    N <- N.increment

  if H.equal(5)                     % body
  then
    BC.send(Tuples.new(r,G,B,C))    % broadcast
    BB.write(Tuples.new(w,W))       % write first tuple from body
    BB.write(Tuples.new(rs,[(G,B,C)|Rs]))
end
```

Fig. 11. Compiled Rule

during its entire lifetime. Optimizations should reduce this *saturation*: Messages should only be received by agent that could make use of it, and they should only be kept for as long as they are relevant.

The static analysis approach deduces properties of abstract versions of *LO* programs in which guard functions, broadcasts, and parameters are abstracted away. This abstract program is then evaluated using a specific initial blackboard. The result is an *and-or* tree, with one *and* branch for each cloned blackboard, and one *or* branch for each triggered rule. An additional generalization step collapses this (possibly) infinite tree into a finite graph which represents all the possible concrete executions, and can be reasoned upon.

Although our example produces a rather degenerated graph[5], we can deduce some optimizations. For example, it can be shown that threads *t111*, *t112*, *t113*, *t222*, *t224*, *t231*, *t241* and *t251* from Fig. 10 can be actually eliminated. This amounts to almost 50% of the active threads. Furthermore, pattern matching in the remaining threads can be greatly optimized (sometimes even replaced by direct access to a precompiled address in memory)

The above compile-time optimizations can be synergetically combined with specialized run-time algorithms. Our threads-based architecture for rule matching, which embodies the fundamental principle of the RETE algorithm, namely the idea of memorizing partial matches of rules, serves as an illustration.

5   Related Work

We compare the *LO* implementation effort with published results from related models such as Gamma, Production Systems, Linda and Shared Prolog.

5.1   Gamma

Gamma is a model which describes computation in terms of reactions among molecules floating in a chemical solution. Such a computational model, based on the Chemical Abstract Machine metaphor, corresponds to a subset of *LO*: rules and only one blackboard. Although Gamma is viewed more as a specification language than a practical programming language, a parallel implementation has been pursued [12] on top of an architecture of pipelined processors. In contrast, we did not at all want to depend on a specific architecture. Therefore we chose to implement *LO*'s fine-grained concurrency using the shared memory model offered by the (rather standard) threads abstraction. This shared memory model has been implemented on both message-passing and shared memory multiprocessors. Next generation operating system software provides real parallel implementations for threads [14]; for the time being our experiments are limited to simulation.

---

[5] In this example there are no *and* branches, since we did not include any cloning rule.

5.2 Production Systems

Production Systems [6] are rule-based systems (rules are called productions) with a shared working memory (or blackboard). The RETE algorithm [15] is generally considered the best evaluation strategy. Since these systems have been a major topic in mainstream AI for over two decades, there exists a large body of relevant implementation work.

Our threads-based implementation of individual *LO* agents can be considered a parallel implementation of RETE, where the alfa and beta memories are spread out over all threads that share previous matches. The main merit of the threads solution lies in extremely simple removals. Whereas RETE needs to propagate negative elements through its network to remove elements from the memories (a process which heavily complicates the implementation), we have implemented a parallel technique that terminates all invalid threads lazily and need not precede (and thus need not be synchronized with) subsequent additions.

Most work on implementing/analyzing parallel execution of production systems is done on the basis of simulations [19]. Notable exceptions are the implementations targeted at specific architectures [23]. Nevertheless a comparison with an analysis of all possible sources for parallelism in RETE reveals that our threads-based solution exploits most:

- *Rule Parallelism:* each rule is executed in parallel, since each rule generates different control code, and thus different threads.
- *Node, Intra-Node and Data Parallelism:* all tests (also the ones generated for variable consistency) are executed in parallel, since different threads are dedicated to those tests.
- *Action Parallelism:* all actions in the body are executed in parallel. We do not exploit this source of parallelism in *LO* since threads which find matching tuples for all their heads, will sequentially broadcast and add atoms.

The main restriction of the threads-based implementation comes from the sequential investigation of the blackboard: When a partial instance wants to match the next head, it starts at the beginning of the blackboard and runs through it, forking off new threads at each successful match. Since thread abstractions do not provide parallel thread creation, we cannot fully avoid sequentiality. Once the threads have been created, they can match and test in parallel; this accounts for the data parallelism.

5.3 Linda

Linda [16] is a well-established concurrent programming language mainly used for scientific computations based on the blackboard model. The access patterns to the blackboard are however considerably simpler, since there is no equivalent for the multi-headed rules of *LO*: Individual matching tuples trigger transitions. We mention two implementations for Linda: First, the S/Net Linda Kernel [7] which is also linked to very specific hardware. Second, an implementation which addresses distribution (networked processors), an issue we do not intend to pursue for individual *LO* agents, since the possibility of modeling a problem using multiple agents results in considerably smaller individual blackboards for which the overhead entailed by distribution is not justified. Moreover, distributing the Linda blackboard is relatively easy since rules are single-headed, allowing a partitioning of the blackboard such that each rule affects only one partition [10].

5.4   Shared Prolog

Shared Prolog [5] extends the logic programming paradigm into the area of concurrency through the introduction of a blackboard abstraction. Multi-headed activation patterns are the equivalent of *LO* rules. The presence of multiheaded rules leads inevitably to stringent synchronization protocols for the distributed implementations [8].

Furthermore, a recent extension of this model, called Polyspaces [9], gives names to individual blackboards and offers one-to-one name-based communication between them. This can be seen as an alternative to the pattern-based broadcast communication in *LO*. Dynamic (re)configuration of the set of agents remains a distinct advantage of the *LO* model.

6   Summary

We have presented here the implementation principles of the language *LO*, a coordination language based on two levels of agents granularity. One level is concerned with tightly coupled processes communicating via a blackboard, whereas at the other level, loosely coupled activities communicate via broadcast messages. The first level is best suited for implementation on a shared memory architecture, whereas the second level is more adapted to message passing architectures on a network.

Our implementation aims at augmenting in a conservative way a traditional object-oriented platform (here Modula-3) with the coordination primitives of our language. Existing legacy objects written on such platforms need only be wrapped into application objects used by the runtime library. Application objects provide, in addition to the operations of the legacy objects they encapsulate, two basic operations needed by the runtime: *copying* and testing for *equality*.

Coordination in *LO* is achieved via rules reminiscent of production rules. We have implemented them using an adaptation of the classical RETE algorithm for production rules. Each *LO* rule is compiled into a piece of Modula-3 code which defines the behavior of a thread. This thread searches for all the heads of the *LO* rule and spawns a new thread each time a matching tuple is found. Threads compete for resources over a linear blackboard and die when one of their resources is deleted from the blackboard by another thread. Deletion occurs when the tread commits, i.e. when all the heads have been found.

7 Acknowledgments

The authors thank Alexander Herold and the anonymous referees for their careful comments.

References

1. J-M. Andreoli, L. Leth, R. Pareschi, and B. Thomsen. True concurrency semantics for a linear logic programming language with broadcast communication. In *Proc. of TAPSOFT'93*, Orsay (France), 1992.

2. J-M. Andreoli and R. Pareschi. Communication as fair distribution of knowledge. In *Proc. of OOPSLA'91*, Phoenix, Az, U.S.A., 1991.

3. J-M. Andreoli, R. Pareschi, and T. Castagnetti. Abstract interpretation of linear logic programs. In *Proc. of the 1993 International Logic Programming Symposium*, Vancouver (Canada), 1993.

4. M. Bourgois, J-M. Andreoli, and R. Pareschi. Extending objects with rules, composition and concurrency: the lo experience. In *Proc. of the OOPSLA'92 workshop on Object-Oriented Programming Languages — The Next Generation*, Vancouver, Canada, 1992.

5. A. Brogi and P. Ciancarini. The concurrent language shared prolog. *ACM Transactions on Programming Languages and Systems*, 13(1):99–123, 1991.

6. L. Brownston, R. Farrell, E. Kant, and N. Martin. *Programming Expert Systems in OPS-5*. Addison-Wesley, Reading, Massachussetts, 1985.

7. N. Carriero and D. Gelernter. The s/net linda kernel. *ACM Transactions on Computer Systems*, 4(2):110–129, 1986.

8. T. Castagnetti and P. Ciancarini. Static analysis of a parallel logic language based on the blackboard model. *Journal of Parallel and Distributed Computing*, 13(14):412–423, 1991.

9. P. Ciancarini. Polis (poli spaces): Programming with multiple tuple spaces. Technical report, Dept of Computer Science, Yale University, Hew Haven, Ct, U.S.A., 1991.

10. P. Ciancarini and D. Gelernter. A distributed programming environment based on logic tuple spaces. In *Proc. of FGCS'92*, Tokyo, Japan, 1992.

11. S.H. Clearwater, B.H. Huberman, and T. Hogg. Cooperative solution of constraint satisfaction problems. *Science*, 254, 11 1991.

12. C. Creveuil. Implementation of gamma on the connection machine. In *Proc. of the workshop: Research Direction in High-Level Parallel Programming Languages*, Mont Saint Michel, France, 1992.

13. Cooper E.C. and Draves R.P. C threads. Technical report, Dept. of Computer Science, Carnegie Mellon Univ., Pittsburgh, Pennsylvania, 1990.

14. J.E. Faust and H. Levy. The performance of an object oriented threads package. In *Proc. of OOPSLA/ECOOP'90*, Ottawa, Canada, 1990.

15. C.L. Forgy. Rete: a fast algorithm for the many pattern/many object pattern match problem. *Artificial Intelligence*, 19(1), 1982.

16. D. Gelernter. Generative communication in Linda. *ACM Transactions on Programming Languages and Systems*, 7(1):80–113, 1985.

17. A. Giacalone, F. Cosquer, A. Kramer, T. Kuo, L. Leth, S. Prasad, and B. Thomsen. Distribution made Facile. Technical report, ECRC, Munich, Germany, 1992.

18. J-Y. Girard. Linear logic. *Theoretical Computer Science*, 50:1–102, 1987.

19. A. Gupta, C. Forgy, and A. Newell. High-speed implementations of rule-based systems. *ACM Transactions on Computer Systems*, 7(2):119–146, 1989.

20. G. Nelson. *Systems Programming with Modula-3*. Prentice Hall, Englewood Cliffs, New Jersey, 1991.

21. Xerox PARC. Rpc library for modula. Provided with the modula-3 public release.

22. L. Sterling and E. Shapiro. *The Art of Prolog*. MIT, 1986.

23. S. Stolfo. Five parallel algorithms for production system execution on the DADO machine. In *Proc. of AAAI'84*, Austin, Tx, U.S.A., 1984.

24. B. Stroustrup. *The C++ Programming Language*. Addison-Wesley, Reading, Massachussetts, 1986.

25. A. Tannenbaum, M. Kaashoek, and H. Bal. Parallel programming using shared objects and broadcasting. *IEEE Computer*, August 1992.

26. D. Ungar and C. Chambers. Efficient implementation of object-oriented programming languages. In *Tutorial Notes, OOPSLA '92*, Vancouver, Canada, 1992.

A The *LO* Model

The *LO* model of computation is based on the notion of processes manipulating resources, syntactically denoted as atoms. The behavior of an *LO* system is specified by a set of *rules* which have the following syntax (formally defined in Fig. 12): an *LO* rule is composed of a head and a body, connected by the symbol <>- (BECOMES); the head is an expression built from atoms, possibly prefixed with the symbol ⁻ (BCAST), and the binary operator ℂ (PAR); the body is an expression built from atoms, the nullary operator #t (TOP) and the binary operators ℂ (PAR) and & (WITH).

Rule	=	*Head* BECOMES *Body*
Head	=	*Atom*
		BCAST *Atom*
		Head PAR *Head*
Body	=	*Atom*
		TOP
		Body PAR *Body*
		Body WITH *Body*
PAR	=	ℂ
WITH	=	&
TOP	=	#t
BECOMES	=	<>-
BCAST	=	⁻

Fig. 12. Formal Syntax of *LO* Methods

The trigger of an *LO* rule is the multiset of atoms which occur in its head but are not prefixed with the symbol ⌃. The message part of an *LO* rule is the multiset of atoms of its head prefixed with the symbol ⌃.

An *LO* system is composed of a set of concurrent agents. Each agent consists itself of a multiset of resources. The evolution of the system under a given program $\mathcal{P}$ (i.e. set of *LO* rules) is non deterministic, but obeys the following principle (called the Progression rule): If the state of an agent contains (in the sense of multiset inclusion) the trigger of a rule of the program, then it can perform a transition to a new state where the trigger of the method is removed (multiset subtraction), and replaced by the body of the rule, which is then immediately decomposed in the context of the remaining atoms. At the same time, the message part of the rule is broadcast to all the other agents, i.e. added to their states.

When the state of an agent contains bodies of program rules, these are decomposed according to the Decomposition rules below, which lead to zero, one or several new states. This provides the basic mechanism for dynamic termination, transformation and creation of agents in *LO*.

- *Transformation*: An agent in a state $B1@B2, \mathcal{C}$ performs a transition to a new state $B_1, B_2, \mathcal{C}$.
- *Creation*: An agent in a state $B_1 \& B_2, \mathcal{C}$ performs a transition to two new clone states, respectively $B_1, \mathcal{C}$ and $B_2, \mathcal{C}$.
- *Termination*: An agent in a state #t, $\mathcal{C}$ terminates.

The evolution of a system of agents can be represented as a tree structure, growing according to the Progression rule and the Decomposition rules (the latter being deterministic are in general not represented in the tree). The structure of such a tree has been given a clear formal characterization in the framework of Linear Logic (hence the name of the language, Linear Objects).

Toward Languages and Formal Systems for Distributed Computing [†]

Mario Tokoro [*] and Kazunori Takashio [**]

Department of Computer Science, Keio University
3-14-1, Hiyoshi, Kohoku-ku, Yokohama, 223, Japan
Tel: +81-45-560-1150   Fax: +81-45-560-1151

Abstract. In this paper, we attempt to reveal the most essential properties of distributed computations. We claim that the notions of asynchrony, real-time, and autonomy are vitally important to a widely distributed, open-ended, ever-changing environment. We then propose a programming language, called DROL, for asynchronous real-time computing. It supports self-contained active objects that have threads of control and a clock, and introduces the notion of timed invocation, that guarantees the survivability of each active object. We place DROL as a first step in constructing programming languages to realize the above three notions. We also classify distributed computation into four forms according to asynchrony and real-time properties, and try to develop formalisms for the four categories based on a process calculus. The formalisms allow us to describe and analyze both globally and locally temporal properties as well as the behavioral properties of distributed objects and the interactions among them. We discuss issues remaining to be solved and suggest some possibilities for future work.

1   Introduction

In the next decade, computing environments will become more widely distributed, open-ended, and ever-changing. In this paper, we attempt to extract the most essential problems to be solved in distributed computing, then propose some approaches for solving these problems by both practical and theoretical means.

The notion of *object* is a very convenient way of describing problems in any of sequential, concurrent, distributed, and open computing. Especially, the notion of *concurrent object* [12], real self-contained objects that each includes a processor or a virtual processor, releases the programmer from the complications of describing execution control in distributed environments. However, are concurrent objects enough for describing applications that are distributed and open? The answer is "No." Widely distributed open systems have the following characteristics:

[†] This is an revised and enhanced version of [10].

[*] Email: *mario@mt.cs.keio.ac.jp*, Also with Sony Computer Science Laboratory Inc. 3-14-13 Higashi-Gotanda, Shinagawa-ku, Tokyo, 141, Japan.

[**] Email: *takashio@mt.cs.keio.ac.jp*

- The objects are widely dispersed. They therefore have distance between them, which causes a delay in communication. This yields the property of *the lack of the unique global view* of the system. The state-space of the system as viewed from one place, and that viewed from another are different. We thus need the notion of time, that is *real-time*, since the system is connected with the real world.

- In such a system, services may move their positions, terminate, or change their contents. Also, new services may appear from time to time. This is due to the property of openness.

Therefore, each object that constitutes a distributed system has to support the following properties:

- It has to interface with humans, other objects, and the real world in real-time.

- It has to be autonomous in the sense that the entity is an individual, and guarantees survivability.

In this paper, we focus our discussions on the distribution of computational activity, and we reveal real-time and asynchrony properties in distributed computation. Taking a practical approach, we present the design and implementation of a programming language based on a new concurrent object model, called the *Distributed Real-time Object (DRO)* model, extended for use with the widely distributed environment. From the respect of formalisms, we also present a new formalism, called *DtCCS*.

The organization of the paper is as follows: Section 2 relates the notion of asynchrony, real-time, and autonomy with a high level abstract model for future distributed computing, called the *Computational Field Model*, and discusses the possibilities of formalizing the model. Section 3 proposes an object-oriented programming language for describing distributed real-time systems. The language provides temporal facilities for managing asynchronously interacting objects by using time constraints. Section 4 proposes a new formalism for reasoning about distributed real-time computing. We classify distributed real-time computing according to two criteria, communication and time, then try to develop formalisms for distributed systems according to these criteria.

2 Asynchrony, Real-Time, and Autonomy in Distributed Computing

First, we contrast the characteristics of distributed computing with concurrent computing. *Concurrent computing* is characterized by its having more than one activity (i.e., object) in computation and no transmission delay in communication. Communication without delay means that there is no notion of distance in concurrent computing. Thus, communication is synchronous, in the sense that one object gives information to another and the other receives it at the same time. It is impossible for one object to give information to another and the other not receive it. Consequently, a concurrent system has a *unique global view* of the system.

In contrast to this, *distributed computing* can be characterized by communication delay between activities (i.e., objects). Hence, communication is *asynchronous*, in the sense that one gives information to another, the other receiving it at a later time. It is even possible for one object to give information to another and the other not receive it. This delay prevents distributed objects from knowing the current status of other objects. Consequently, a distributed system has no *unique global view* of the system.

The lack of the unique global view is one of the most important characteristics of distributed computing, and is the major source of difficulty in designing and developing efficient distributed systems. In distributed systems, objects may not be able to escape from dead-lock situations. This is because they are forced to wait for messages that will never arrive. Objects and networks can be inactive and faulty. Since it is difficult to detect such situations by means of logical methods, objects often use timeout handling. That is to say, *time* is the last resort that an object can depend on in a distributed environment. Also, many distributed systems must often cooperate with the real world where the time is *real*. Thus, the necessity for the real-time properties in distributed computing is inevitably derived.

Open computing means that an object is forced to use (communicate with) other objects without having complete knowledge of them. Thus, they look like they are changing by themselves, and therefore, each object needs to discover the services it needs. Each entity of computation in such a widely distributed and open environment should behave autonomously by itself, that is, it should be an *individual unit*. This means that it is a unit of security that corresponds to the immune system of the body, and a unit of reliability and maintenance that corresponds to homeostasis. In other words, security, reliability, and maintenance has to be done on an individual basis, not for the whole system, and each individual entity should provide such abilities per se.

"Survival" is, especially, the most important goal of each object. The goal is, in fact, the result that only the objects with higher survivability survive. To survive, an object has to make its *best effort* to satisfy its users (or other objects) in terms of response time and functionality or the quality of services in general. For instance, restaurants with bad food or that make you wait one hour for "plat de jour" would never survive. Moreover, to survive, the object has to keep its losses to a minimum. This is called the *least suffering* strategy. In the restaurant example, if your order had not arrived after one hour, you would have to decide whether to wait longer or move to a different restaurant. We have to monitor the situation and decide when to "time-out."

We noted that communication delay is the most essential characteristic of distributed systems. The delay is manifested in the function of geographical distance, communication bandwidth, other communication overhead and so on. Whether the delay (distance) can be transparent depends on the level of abstraction. For some applications, it is easy to hide the delay (distance) because they employ high-speed communication systems. For some other applications, it is difficult and inefficient to hide the delay (distance) because they employ slow communication systems and very widely distributed systems, and because they can utilize their computational resources concurrently with communication. It is clear, therefore, that whether the delay is transparent depends on the level of abstraction. That is to say, if the delay is modelled as transparent, the system can be modelled as a concurrent system. Otherwise, it is modelled as a distributed system.

One of the authors has proposed a model of distributed computing called the *Computational Field Model* [8] [9]. This is designed as a high-level abstraction of distributed computation for the near future. In this model, objects are floating in the continuous field of computation. Some forces, borrowing the idea from the theory of dynamics, such as *gravitational force, repulsive force, friction,* and *inertia* based on the *mass* and *distance* of objects are introduced, so that objects migrate as users move, objects form groups, objects balance the load, and objects avoid faults. This model provides a method of computing by maximally utilizing objects and determining the optimal locations of objects at the next timing, taking the cost and effect of migration into consideration.

The metaphor of this model is based on physical phenomena which essentially contain timed factors, such as acceleration and speed. A formal model and a programming language for the Computational Field Model need to manage the temporal properties. The formalisms and language presented in this paper can explicitly deal with properties and thus can provide a practical and theoretical contribution for the model.

3 DROL: A Programming Language for Distributed Real-Time Systems

We have been thinking about what kind of programming languages for distributed systems should be provided. To achieve software modularity, we decided to use the notion of objects. And, to describe concurrent activities, we decided to use *concurrent objects* [12]. However, these notions are in themselves not sufficient to describe safe and efficient distributed systems. We need to incorporate the notion of autonomy in programming languages. As a first step, such languages need to provide real-time facilities to manage time-critical responses and detect failures.

3.1 DROL and its Features

DROL [6] was proposed by the authors as such a language for describing distributed systems. In contrast to previously proposed real-time programming languages, every object has a clock and real-time properties. DROL is based on the maxim of *best effort and least suffering*. In distributed computing, objects receive request messages and also send request messages. That is, an object acts as a server and as a client at the same time. As a server, an object should try its best to achieve the requested operation within the limited time. This corresponds to the notion of *best effort*. Moreover, as a client, an object should return from a situation where unexpected delay (including deadlock) occurs to enable its survival This is the notion of *least suffering*.

DROL is implemented as an extension of C++ with the capability of describing temporal constraints, running on a distributed real-time operating system, called the ARTS kernel [11]. The syntax of DROL is an extension of RTC++ [2], the useful real-time notations of which DROL inherits. The DROL compiler translates a program written in DROL into C++ codes including interfaces for the ARTS kernel. DROL has the following features:

- In addition to C++ objects, DROL can define active objects that are multiple threaded objects and which are defined with timing information such as the timing constraints for each method. This notion of active object is as same as that of RTC++ proposed by Ishikawa in [2].

- It supports two types of *timed invocation* to realize the property of *least suffering*. One is *synchronous timed invocation*, and the other is *asynchronous timed invocation*.

- To realize the property of *best effort*, it introduces a new notion, called *timing polymorphism*, which allows the server object to dynamically select one execution body (a method) that can be executed within the timing constraint at that time. This is achieved by the scheduling facility at the server (callee) side.

3.2 Communication Protocols

DROL provides three types of communication protocols between active objects as the default.

- *AOI: Active Object Invocation*
  The semantics of this protocol are the same as those of RPC. A caller object (sender) that sends a request message will be blocked until it receives a reply message. A callee object (receiver) that receives the request message invokes a corresponding method, then returns a reply message to the caller. What has to be noticed is that this protocol does not manage the time-out on the caller object.

- *TimedAOI: Timed Active Object Invocation*
  This protocol provides the facility of time-out on the caller object to realize the *least suffering* property. In the same way as the AOI protocol, a caller object is blocked while awaiting the arrival of a reply message. If it does not receive a reply message within a specified timing constraint, a time-out occurs immediately on the caller side, which then sends a time-out message to a callee object, and executes a specified time-out routine. On the other hand, the callee object becomes aware that a time-out has occurred on the caller object by the reception of the time-out message.[1]

---

[1] We call this type of communication a *follow-up type communication protocol*.

- *AsyncTimedAOI: Asynchronous Timed Active Object Invocation*
  This is an asynchronous communication protocol between active objects which features the time-out facility on the caller side. A callee object receives a request message, then immediately returns a acknowledgement (request_ack) to the caller object. When the caller object receives this acknowledgement, it can resume its execution without having to await for a reply message. Reply messages that arrive while the caller is executing another operation are enqueued into a reply message queue for each object. The caller checks whether it has received a reply message from the callee object at the time when it needs the reply. If the caller has not yet obtained a reply message, and if the specified timing constraint has already passed, a time-out will occur. The behavior of the caller is equivalent to the synchronous timed AOI protocol. If the timing constraint has not yet passed at this time, the caller will be blocked until it receives the reply message or a time-out occurs. In this case, also, the caller has the same time-out semantics as the synchronous timed AOI protocol.

DROL provides these protocols as C++ objects called *protocol objects*. Each protocol object has unified interfaces, and behaves as a kind of meta-level object that gives semantics to each active object invocation. A caller object creates a protocol object at every active object invocation, then entrusts it with the control of the communication handling. On the other hand, a callee object creates a specified protocol object upon the reception of a request message. This facility enables the callee to dynamically deal with the protocol requested by the caller.

3.3 Timing Polymorphism

In a widely distributed environment, an object cannot know the current status of other objects. Therefore, a client object cannot predict the time actually allowed for execution in a server object. Depending on the case, the server object may reject its execution. Consequently, a significant problem may occur. To avoid this situation and to guarantee the *best effort* property, DROL provides a mechanism whereby when an invocation is issued by the client object, multiple execution bodies are associated with the invocation. Then, the server object dynamically selects one execution body (a method) that can be executed within the timing constraints at that time. We call this mechanism *timing polymorphism*. We can classify the definition of the behavior of timing polymorphism into two types: *receiver-initiated timing polymorphism* and *sender-initiated timing polymorphism*.

The *receiver-initiated timing polymorphism* has the following features. We define a method, called the *time virtual method*, which has no execution body but which has pointer entries to methods defined with different timing constraints as real execution bodies. At run time, a client object invokes the server object, specifying the time virtual method. Then, a method that satisfies the timing constraint required by the sender object is selected and executed dynamically in the server object. That is, the receiver of the request message has the initiative to decide which method body should be selected. Therefore, we call this type of timing polymorphism *receiver-initiated*. The time virtual method on the server object is defined with the following n+1 tuples.

$$< N_{M_{virtual}}, \{B_{exec,i} \mid i = 1, \ldots, n\} >$$

$N_{M_{virtual}}$ expresses the name of the time virtual method. The second part is the list of n *real execution bodies*. Each execution body has a timing constraint for its execution. When this method is invoked, an execution body that meets its deadline and which has the longest execution time is selected and actually invoked.

Unlike the *receiver-initiated*, in the *sender-initiated timing polymorphism*, when a client object publishes an invocation, it specifies different services according to the remaining time in a server object. This invocation involves n *message tuples*, formally expressed as 2 tuples, as follows:

$$T_{M_{req},i} = < C_{rm,i}, M_{req,i} >$$

Each message tuple $T_{M_{req}}$, is composed of *remaining time condition* C_{rm} and *requested method* M_{req}, means "if the remaining time on the server object T_{rm} is greater than C_{rm}, then the method M_{req} will be selected and invoked". So, we can write an invocation such that, for example, if there are 50 milliseconds left at the server then do method A or, if there are 30 milliseconds left at the server then do method B, otherwise do method C.

Although both the receiver-initiated and the sender-initiated timing polymorphism have common behavior, the method actually selected is dependent upon the capacity of the server object at that time. Both types of timing polymorphism differ in the behavior of the object that issues the invocation. The invocation based on the sender-initiated timing polymorphism specifies all the methods that can be executed by the server object, while the invocation based on the receiver-initiated timing polymorphism describes only one method, a time virtual method, at one invocation. Regarding this point, the receiver-initiated timing polymorphism can make a much simpler language construct and implementation than the sender-initiated timing polymorphism. On the other hand, the sender-initiated timing polymorphism enables the user to describe systems that predict the server's behavior. For these reasons, we adopt the sender-initiated timing polymorphism as the semantics of our timing polymorphism.

3.4 Programming Example

To illustrate the expressive power of DROL we take the example of a distributed real-time system: an air traffic control system. Two distributed real-time objects appear in this example: the *airplane object* and the *controlTower object*. The airplane object moves in the sky at high speed and thus the time it has to control itself is strictly limited. For the airplane object that provides services with strict timing constraints, a timing constraint for the communication with controlTower takes an important position to satisfy an entire timing constraint.

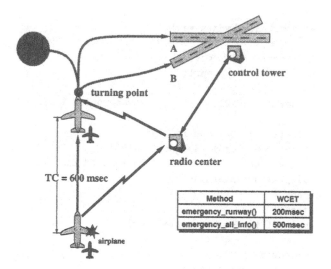

Fig. 1. Air Traffic Control System

```
 1 active class ControlTower {
 2   protected:
 3     ...
 4   public:
 5     EmData        emergency_runway()
 6        within(0t200ms) timeout(recover);
 7     EmData        emergency_info();
 8        within(0t500ms) timeout(recover);
 9     ...
10   activity:
11     protocol      ProtAOI, ProtTAOI, ProtATAOI;
12     slave[5]      emergency_runway(), emergency_info();
13 };
```

Fig. 2. Definition of Class ControlTower

We suppose the situation shown in Figure 1. The airplane suffers a malfunction in flight. Then, immediately, the airplane object calls a method **emergency()**. In **emergency()**, the airplane tries to access the controlTower object, and sends a request to obtain information on the airport. The airport has two runways A and B. And, the controlTower supports the method **emergency_info()**, that returns the name of the runway that is currently available for landing safely. The worst case execution time for this method is 500 milliseconds. The timing constraint up to the turning point is 600 milliseconds. If it misses the turning point, the airplane cannot land at this airport. So, the airplane has to decide on which runway it should land before this time.

Figure 2 depicts part of the definition of the controlTower object in the

```
 1 ComStatus
 2 Airplane::emergency(Emdata *ed)
 3 {
 4     ControlTower      *ct;
 5     Protocol          *prt;
 6
 7     prt = new ProtATAOI;          // Asynchronous Timed AOI
 8
 9     ct = query (narita) ControlTower;
10     ct -> (prt, 0t600ms) emergency_info();
11     within(0t500ms) {             // Background Execution
12         displayCurrentStatus();
13     } except {
14       timeout:
15         printf("timeout occurred!!\n");
16     }
17     *ed = receive(prt);
18     switch (prt->comm_status) {
19       case NORMAL:
20         return COM_SUCCESS;
21       case TIMEOUT:
22         ct = query (haneda) ControlTower;
23         ct -> (prt, 0t600ms) emergency_info();
24         within(0t500ms) {
25             displayCurrentStatus();
26         } except {
27           timeout:
28             printf("timeout occurred!!\n");
29         }
30         *ed = receive(prt);
31         switch (prt->comm_status) {
32           case NORMAL:
33             return COM_SUCCESS;
34           case TIMEOUT:
35             return COM_FAILURE;
36         }
37     }
38 }
```

Fig. 3. Definition of Method `Airplane::emergency()`

example of the air traffic control system. Distributed real-time objects are defined by adding the keyword **active** before the C++ **class** keyword. DROL defines methods [2] with timing constraints, where the user can specify the worst case execution time and exceptions. In this class, all methods are declared with timing constraints. For example, execution of the **emergency_info()** method takes 500 milliseconds.

---

[2] Member function in C++ terminology.

The **emergency()** method of the airplane object is defined as shown in Figure 3. In this method, Asynchronous Timed AOI (ATAOI) is used as the communication protocol (see line 7). First, this method obtains a controlTower object at the "narita" airport (where the airplane wants to land) by using a **query** operator. At line 10, the method **emergency_info()** of the controlTower object is invoked with a timing constraint of 600 milliseconds. Then, owing to the use of the ATAOI protocol, the airplane object can resume and execute the function **displayCurrentStatus()** immediately. Here, the execution of this method is limited to 500 milliseconds. A reply from the controlTower object is received at line 17 by using the **receive** operator. This statement (from line 17 to 33) means that if the airplane object cannot obtain a reply within 600 milliseconds, it abandons the request and attempts to access another control tower object (in this case, "haneda" airport is specified).

4 Formal Systems for Asynchronous Real-Time Computing

In this section, we present the possibilities of formalizing distributed computation. As we noted in section 2, asynchrony and real-time are characteristic properties of distributed computation. We first classify the computation systems according to two criteria: whether communication is *synchronous* or *asynchronous*, and whether the objects measure time by the *same clock* or *different clocks*. The former means whether the instants of time sent by the sender object and received by the receiver object are the same. The latter means whether the time basis of each object is valid for the whole system or only within each object. We show four combinations, classified according to criteria as follows:

- The first combination is a system featuring synchronous communication using the same clock. This corresponds to a *concurrent* real-time system. In this system, objects can interact with one another following the same global time.

- The second combination is a system with synchronous communication using different clocks. This corresponds to a system where objects following different local clocks interact with one another by using synchronous communications.

- The third combination is a system with asynchronous communication using the same clock. This is a system where objects are distributed and have the same clock. This models a system where distributed objects can share a global clock, such as a world-wide system using a satellite-synchronized clock.

- The fourth is a system with asynchronous communication using different clocks. This corresponds to a system where objects are distributed and have different clocks. This is the general model for widely distributed systems based on high-speed computers.

The correctness of programs for distributed computation depends not only on the logical results of the computation, but also on the time at which the results are produced. Therefore, the construction of its programs is more complex and difficult, especially when we have to consider asynchrony in interactions. Consequently, we need the support of formal models for reasoning about asynchrony and real-time properties in computation. Hereafter, we investigate formalisms for the above combinations. The formalisms presented in this section are based on Milner's CCS [3] and draws on its high expressive power of interactions between concurrent objects.

4.1 RtCCS: Formalizing Real-Time Concurrent Objects

In [4], Satoh and one of the authors investigated a formal model for the first combination, i.e., concurrent real-time systems, by extending CCS to represent temporal properties in real-time computing. In the extension, the model represents temporal properties by using two aspects: the passage of time and timed behavior. It also introduced two temporal primitives.

- *The passage of time* is modeled as a special action. The tick action is a synchronous message, broadcast to all objects, and corresponds to the passage of one unit of global time. It is described as $\sqrt{}$. The advance of time can be represented as a sequence of tick actions and is viewed as discrete time.

- *Timed behavior* is modeled as a special binary operator that has the semantics of timeout handling, written as $\langle\ ,\ \rangle_t$, and which is called the *timeout operator*. $\langle P, Q \rangle_t$ denotes an object that, after t time units, becomes Q, unless P performs any actions prior to that. Intuitively $\langle P, Q \rangle_t$ behaves as object P if P can execute an initial transition within t units of time, whereas $\langle P, Q \rangle_t$ behaves as object Q if P does not perform any action within t units of time.

The definition of RtCCS is given as follows. For details of the syntax and semantics, refer to [4].

Let $a, b, \ldots$ be communication action names and $\overline{a}, \overline{b}, \ldots$ be the complementary action of $a, b, \ldots$ respectively. Let τ denote an internal action, $\sqrt{}$ a tick action, and $\mathcal{L}$ be the set of action names and complementary action names, ranged over by $\ell, \ell', \ldots$. Let $Act \equiv \mathcal{L} \cup \{\tau\}$ be the set of behavior actions, ranged over by $\alpha, \beta, \ldots$. The set $\mathcal{E}$ of RtCCS expressions, ranged over by $E, E_1, E_2, \ldots$ is defined recursively by the following abstract syntax.

$$
\begin{array}{lll}
E ::= & \mathbf{0} & \text{(Terminated Object)} \\
\ \mid & X & \text{(Process Variable)} \\
\ \mid & \alpha.E & \text{(Action Prefix)} \\
\ \mid & E_1 + E_2 & \text{(Summation)} \\
\ \mid & E_1 | E_2 & \text{(Composition)} \\
\ \mid & E[f] & \text{(Relabeling)} \\
\ \mid & E \setminus L & \text{(Restriction)} \\
\ \mid & \mathbf{rec}\, X : E & \text{(Recursion)} \\
\ \mid & \langle E_1, E_2 \rangle_t & \text{(Timeout)}
\end{array}
$$

The syntax of RtCCS is essentially the same as that of CCS, except for the newly introduced tick action $\checkmark$ and timeout operator. Intuitively, the meanings of object constructions are as follows: 0 represents a terminated object; $\alpha.E$ performs an action α and then behaves like E; $E_1 + E_2$ is an object that may behave as E_1 or E_2; $E_1|E_2$ represents processes E_1 and E_2 executing concurrently; $E[f]$ behaves like E but with the actions relabeled by function f; $E \setminus L$ behaves like E but with actions in $L \cup \bar{L}$ prohibited ($L \subset \mathcal{L}$); $\mathbf{rec}\, X : E$ binds the free occurrences of X in E but we often use the more readable notation $X \overset{\text{def}}{=} E$ instead.

$$\alpha.E \xrightarrow{\alpha} E$$

$E_1 \xrightarrow{\alpha} E_1'$	implies $E_1 + E_2 \xrightarrow{\alpha} E_1',\ E_2 + E_1 \xrightarrow{\alpha} E_1'$
$E_1 \xrightarrow{\alpha} E_1'$	implies $E_1|E_2 \xrightarrow{\alpha} E_1'|E_2,\ E_2|E_1 \xrightarrow{\alpha} E_2|E_1'$
$E_1 \xrightarrow{a} E_1',\ E_2 \xrightarrow{\bar{a}} E_2'$	implies $E_1|E_2 \xrightarrow{\tau} E_1'|E_2'$
$P \xrightarrow{\alpha} P'$	implies $P[f] \xrightarrow{f(\alpha)} P'[f]$
$P \xrightarrow{\alpha} P',\ \alpha \notin L \cup \bar{L}$	implies $P \setminus L \xrightarrow{\alpha} P' \setminus L$
$P\{\mathbf{rec}\, X : P/X\} \xrightarrow{\alpha} P'$	implies $\mathbf{rec}\, X : P \xrightarrow{\alpha} P'$
$E_1 \xrightarrow{\alpha} E_1'\ ,\ t > 0$	implies $\langle E_1, E_2 \rangle_t \xrightarrow{\alpha} E_1'$
$E_2 \xrightarrow{\alpha} E_2'$	implies $\langle E_1, E_2 \rangle_0 \xrightarrow{\alpha} E_2'$

Fig. 4. Operational Rules on Global Time

$$0 \xrightarrow{\checkmark} 0$$
$$\ell.E \xrightarrow{\checkmark} \ell.E$$

$E_1 \xrightarrow{\checkmark} E_1',\ E_2 \xrightarrow{\checkmark} E_2'$	implies $E_1 + E_2 \xrightarrow{\checkmark} E_1' + E_2'$
$E_1 \xrightarrow{\checkmark} E_1',\ E_2 \xrightarrow{\checkmark} E_2',\ E_1|E_2 \not\xrightarrow{\tau}$ implies $E_1|E_2 \xrightarrow{\checkmark} E_1'|E_2'$	
$P \xrightarrow{\checkmark} P'$	implies $P[f] \xrightarrow{\checkmark} P'[f]$
$P \xrightarrow{\checkmark} P'$	implies $P \setminus L \xrightarrow{\checkmark} P' \setminus L$
$P\{\mathbf{rec}\, X : P/X\} \xrightarrow{\checkmark} P'$	implies $\mathbf{rec}\, X : P \xrightarrow{\checkmark} P'$
$E_1 \xrightarrow{\checkmark} E_1'\ ,\ t > 0$	implies $\langle E_1, E_2 \rangle_t \xrightarrow{\checkmark} \langle E_1', E_2 \rangle_{t-1}$
$E_2 \xrightarrow{\checkmark} E_2'$	implies $\langle E_1, E_2 \rangle_0 \xrightarrow{\checkmark} E_2'$

Fig. 5. Temporal Rules on Global Time

The operational semantics of RtCCS are given as a labeled transition system $\langle\, \mathcal{E},\ Act \cup \{\checkmark\}\rangle,\ \{\ \xrightarrow{\mu}\ |\ \mu \in Act \cup \{\checkmark\}\ \}\,\rangle$ where $\xrightarrow{\mu}$ is a transition relation ($\xrightarrow{\mu}\,\subseteq \mathcal{E} \times \mathcal{E}$). The definition of the semantics is structurally given in two steps. The first step defines the relations $\xrightarrow{\alpha}$ for each $\alpha \in Act$. The inference rules determining $\xrightarrow{\alpha}$ are shown in Figure 4. This is based on the standard operational semantics for CCS except for the addition of the timeout operator. The second step defines the relation $\xrightarrow{\checkmark}$ by inference shown in Figure 5. The new action $\checkmark$ does not effect the rules of CCS.

We now illustrate how to describe real-time objects in RtCCS. Suppose an interaction between a client object and a server object: the client object (*Client*) sends a request message ($\overline{req}$), then waits for a return message (*ret*). If the return message is not received within 6 time units, it sends the request message again; upon reception of a request message (*req*), the server object (*Server*) sends a return message ($\overline{ret}$) after an internal execution of 5 time units. These objects are denoted as follows:

$$Client \stackrel{\text{def}}{=} \overline{req}.\langle ret.0, \, Client \rangle_6$$
$$Server \stackrel{\text{def}}{=} req.\langle 0, \overline{ret}.Server \rangle_5$$

RtCCS can formally describe the time dependent aspect in real-time systems and enjoys many of the advantages of CCS. As proof techniques, we have introduced some timed equivalences that can verify whether two objects are indistinguishable in their time properties, as well as in their functional behavior. The details of the equivalences are given in [4].

4.2 DtCCS: Formalizing Real-Time Objects with Clocks

Here, we present the possibility of formalizing the second combination, i.e., real-time computing with different clocks. It is well-known that the clocks on different processors can never run at the same rate. The differences between clocks may cause interactions between objects to fail. Therefore, we need a formalism for reasoning about such locally temporal properties in distributed real-time programs. Satoh and one of the authors proposed such a formalism, called DtCCS, an extension of RtCCS [5]. Here, we will give an overview of it.

Before giving an exposition of DtCCS, we first present assumptions on the modeling of local time. If the relative motion of all processors is negligible, Einstein's Theory of Relativity tells us that the passage of physical *time* in every processor elapses at the same rate. On the other hand, each actual local clock reads its own current time by translating the passage of global time into its own time coordinates according to its own measurement rate. Clock rates differ from each other and these rates may vary within certain bounds. Therefore local times, as measured by different clocks, may differ from one another, although the clocks share the same global time.

To represent local time properties in distributed computation, we introduce a temporal primitive: *local clock*. In the definition of our formalism, local clocks are introduced as mappings that translate all occurrences of any instant times on local times into instant times in global time, according to the time units of the local clocks. Mappings may be non-deterministic to represent inaccurate clocks with drifting time units. Giving the lower and upper bound of the interval of one time unit on a clock, δ_{min} and δ_{max}, respectively, the mapping is defined as follows:

$$\theta(t) \stackrel{\text{def}}{=} \begin{cases} 0 & \text{if } t = 0 \\ \theta(t-1) + \delta & \text{if } t > 0 \end{cases} \text{ where } \delta \in \{\, d \in \mathcal{T}_G \mid \delta_{min} \leq d \leq \delta_{max} \}$$

where $\mathcal{T}_G$ is the global time domain that is the finest and absolute reference time basis for all local times. Note that, the global time does not imply an actual global clock but only provides the time that each local clock may measure. The extensions, except for local clock, are essentially equivalent to those of RtCCS.

The syntax of DtCCS is shown below. In the following definition, expressions S, ranged over by $S, S_1, S_2, \ldots$, represent objects on a processor (or a node) with a local clock, and expressions P, ranged over by $P, P_1, P_2, \ldots$, represent interactions between distributed objects following different clocks.

$$
\begin{array}{lll}
S ::= & \mathbf{0} & (\textit{Terminated Object}) \\
& \mid\ X & (\textit{Process Variable}) \\
& \mid\ \alpha.S & (\textit{Sequential Execution}) \\
& \mid\ S_1 + S_2 & (\textit{Alternative Choice}) \\
& \mid\ \mathbf{rec}\, X : S & (\textit{Recursive Definition}) \\
& \mid\ \langle S_1, S_2 \rangle_t & (\textit{Timeout}) \\
\end{array}
$$

$$
\begin{array}{lll}
P ::= & [\![S]\!]_\theta & (\textit{Local Object}) \\
& \mid\ P_1 | P_2 & (\textit{Parallel Composition}) \\
& \mid\ P[f] & (\textit{Relabeling}) \\
& \mid\ P \setminus L & (\textit{Encapsulation}) \\
\end{array}
$$

$[\![S]\!]_\theta$ means a sequential expression S, executed on a processor with a local clock θ.

In the interpretation of DtCCS, expressions describing concurrent objects with respect to local times are translated into those in the global time, using the translation rules shown below. Then, the expressions are interpreted as expressions based on global time. The basic idea of the rules is to map time values in descriptions with respect to local time into values with respect to the global time by using the clock mapping. The deadline of each timeout operator corresponds to the time value.

$$
\begin{aligned}
[\![\mathbf{0}]\!]_\theta &\longrightarrow \mathbf{0} \\
[\![X]\!]_\theta &\longrightarrow X \\
[\![\alpha.S]\!]_\theta &\longrightarrow \alpha.[\![S]\!]_{\theta'} \\
[\![S_1 + S_2]\!]_\theta &\longrightarrow [\![S_1]\!]_{\theta'} + [\![S_2]\!]_{\theta'} \\
[\![\mathbf{rec}\, X : S]\!]_\theta &\longrightarrow \mathbf{rec}\, X : [\![S]\!]_{\theta'} \\
[\![\langle S_1, S_2 \rangle_t]\!]_\theta &\longrightarrow \langle [\![S_1]\!]_{\theta'}, [\![S_2]\!]_{\theta''} \rangle_{\theta'(t)}
\end{aligned}
$$

where $\theta', \theta'' \stackrel{\text{def}}{=} \theta$ such that for all t_ℓ, $\theta'(t_\ell) = \theta(t_\ell)$, and $\theta''(t_\ell) + \theta(t) = \theta(t_\ell + t)$.

We briefly explain the intuitive meanings of the main rules. The third rule translates an unpredictable synchronization time for waiting for α into an unpredictable time on the global time domain. The fourth rule shows that all alternative subsequences in a processor share the same clock. The last rule means that deadline t on local clock θ is mapped into deadline $\theta'(t)$ on the global time. The clock translation rules can completely eliminate $[\![\cdot]\!]_\theta$ from any expressions in $\mathcal{P}$. Therefore, the syntax of the expressions translated into global time are equivalent to those of RtCCS and are interpreted using RtCCS's inference rules, presented in Figure 4 and 5.

We now illustrate how to describe a distributed object in DtCCS. Suppose that the previously presented client and server objects are allocated to different processors. By means of the mapping rules, we map the client and the server onto the global time domain, as shown below.

$$[\![Client]\!]_{\theta_c} \longrightarrow \cdots \longrightarrow \overline{req}.\langle ret.0, [\![Client]\!]_{\theta_c}\rangle_{\theta_c}(6)$$
$$[\![Server]\!]_{\theta_s} \longrightarrow \cdots \longrightarrow req.\langle 0, \overline{ret}.[\![Server]\!]_{\theta_s}\rangle_{\theta_s}(5)$$

where we assume θ_c to be the clock of the client and θ_s to be that of the server. The interaction between the objects is described as $([\![Client]\!]_{\theta_c} | [\![Server]\!]_{\theta_s}) \setminus L$, where $L \stackrel{\text{def}}{=} \{req, ret\}$. L makes internal communications encapsulated from the environment. The result of the interaction depends on the evaluated values of $\theta_c(6)$ and $\theta_s(5)$. Here we show the possible results:

(1) For $\theta_c(6) > \theta_s(5)$:

$$([\![Client]\!]_{\theta_c} | [\![Server]\!]_{\theta_s}) \setminus L$$
$$\xrightarrow{\tau(req)} ((\langle ret.0, [\![Client]\!]_{\theta_c}\rangle_{\theta_c}(6) | \langle 0, \overline{ret}.[\![Server]\!]_{\theta_s}\rangle_{\theta_s}(5)) \setminus L$$
$$(\xrightarrow{\checkmark})^{\theta_s(5)}((\langle ret.0, [\![Client]\!]_{\theta_c}\rangle_{\theta_c}(6) - \theta_s(5)|\overline{ret}.[\![Server]\!]_{\theta_s}) \setminus L$$
$$\xrightarrow{\tau(ret)} (0|[\![Server]\!]_{\theta_s}) \setminus L$$
$$(success)$$

In this case, the client can always receive a return message before it goes to timeout.

(2) For $\theta_c(6) \leq \theta_s(5)$:

$$([\![Client]\!]_{\theta_c} | [\![Server]\!]_{\theta_s}) \setminus \{req, ret\}$$
$$\xrightarrow{\tau(req)} ((\langle ret.0, [\![Client]\!]_{\theta_c}\rangle_{\theta_c}(6) | \langle 0, \overline{ret}.[\![Server]\!]_{\theta_s}\rangle_{\theta_s}(5)) \setminus L$$
$$(\xrightarrow{\checkmark})^{\theta_c(5)} ([\![Client]\!]_{\theta_c} | \langle 0, \overline{ret}.[\![Server]\!]_{\theta_s}\rangle_{\theta_c}(6) - \theta_s(5)) \setminus L$$
$$(\xrightarrow{\checkmark})^{\theta_s(6)-\theta_c(5)}([\![Client]\!]_{\theta_c} | \overline{ret}.[\![Server]\!]_{\theta_s}) \setminus L$$
$$(failure)$$

In this case, the client timeouts before receiving a return message ret. Thus, the objects go into timing failure.

DtCCS allows us to explicitly analyze how differences between local clocks affect the results of interactions in distributed computing.

Based on DtCCS, some timed equivalences are developed by extending CCS's bisimulation. These equivalences can equate two objects whose functional behaviors completely match and whose timings differ within a given bound. They are appropriate and practical for verifying distributed objects with temporal uncertainties and real-time objects with non-strict time constraints. For details of the equivalences, refer to [5].

4.3 Toward Formalizing Asynchronous Real-Time Systems

We here attempt to formalize the third and fourth combinations. From the temporal viewpoint, asynchronous communication corresponds to a communication where temporal distance between the occurrences of sending and receiving cannot be ignored. Thus, time is essential in the modeling of asynchronous communication. Also, as mentioned previously, asynchronous communication with time constraints, such as timeout handling, provides a practical method of detecting failures. Consequently, formalisms for reasoning about asynchronous communications need the ability to model such distance and time constraints. We are currently extending RtCCS and DtCCS to asynchronous real-time systems. The key idea of the extensions is to express asynchronous communication in terms of synchronous communication and a messenger creation, i.e. asynchronous message sending is represented by creating a process that can engage only in an input action having the same name as the message. We are also investigating the possibility of extending ν-calculus [1]. An account of the research into these is being left to our future papers.

5 Conclusions

In this paper, we attempted to extract the essential properties of distributed computing. Currently, we can isolate the properties of asynchrony, real-time and autonomy.

We then proposed a programming language, called DROL, that enables the description of asynchronous distributed systems, in which objects provide the properties of *best effort* and *least suffering* with respect to time and functionality. Fundamental language constructs were shown to give a feeling of how we describe such properties in programs. DROL defines active objects as self-contained computational activity, and supports the following two types of active object invocation:

- *synchronous timed invocation*, and
- *asynchronous timed invocation*.

In both of the invocations, an active object can monitor a communication situation and make a decision for *time-out* based on a specified timing constraint.

Therefore, an object can guarantee its *survivability* under circumstances where the objects cannot have a unique global view. Moreover, it introduces the notion of *timing polymorphism* that allows a server object to dynamically select one execution body (a method) that can be executed within the specified timing constraint. DROL is the first step toward a programming language that incorporates the notion of *object autonomy*. For details, refer to [6] and [7]. Especially, we discussed the realization of the *best effort* property in [7]. We plan to implement it on the Apertos Operating System [13] in the near future.

We also presented the possibility of formalizing distributed computation. We note particularly the following two criteria:

- whether communication is synchronous or asynchronous, and
- whether objects refer to the same clock or different clocks.

Based on these criteria, we classified distributed computation into four forms. As a first step, we proposed two formal models for concurrent real-time computations and real-time computations with different clocks. These models are extensions of CCS with the notion of global and local time, and thus can provide a powerful means of reasoning about globally and locally temporal properties and behavioral properties in the computations. We presented some approaches for describing asynchronous real-time computing.

It is important to note that the synchronous real-time property of a DROL program can be validated by using RtCCS and DtCCS. We are also developing a static verification framework for DROL based on RtCCS and DtCCS. Particularly, since DtCCS can analyze locally temporal properties, it provides a very powerful method of verifying DROL's applications for distributed systems where objects cannot share the same global clock, thus must follow different clocks. A short remark was also given to relate the notion of asynchrony and real-time with a higher level abstraction of distributed computing called the Computational Field Model. We feel that we have just come to the starting point for investigating distributed objects.

Acknowledgement

We would like to thank our co-researcher, Ichiro Satoh, for his valuable comments on this manuscript.

References

1. Honda, K., and Tokoro, M., *An Object Calculus for Asynchronous Communication*, Proceedings of ECOOP'91, LNCS 512, p133-147, June, 1991.
2. Ishikawa, Y., Tokuda, H. and Mercer, C. W., *Object-Oriented Real-Time Language Design: Constructs for Timing Constraints*, Proceedings of ECOOP/OOPSLA'90, October, p289-298, 1990.
3. Milner, R., *Communication and Concurrency*, Prentice Hall, 1989.

4. Satoh, I., and Tokoro, M., *A Formalism for Real-Time Concurrent Object-Oriented Computing*, Proceedings of ACM OOPSLA'92, p315-326, October, 1992.

5. Satoh, I., and Tokoro, M., *A Timed Calculus for Distributed Objects with Clocks*, Proceedings of ECOOP'93, July, 1993.

6. Takashio, K., and Tokoro, M., *DROL: An Object-Oriented Programming Language for Distributed Real-time Systems*, Proceedings of ACM OOPSLA'92, p276-294, October, 1992.

7. Takashio, K., and Tokoro, M., *Time Polymorphic Invocation: A Real-Time Communication Model for Distributed Systems*, Proceedings of IEEE WPDRTS'93, p79-88, April, 1992.

8. Tokoro, M., *Computational Field Model: Toward a New Computing Model/-Methodology for Open Distributed Environment*, Proceedings of IEEE Workshop on Future Trends of Distributed Computing Systems, September, 1990.

9. Tokoro, M., *Toward Computing Systems for the 2000's*, Proceedings of Operating Systems in 1990's and Beyond, LNCS 563, December, 1991.

10. Tokoro, M. and Satoh, I., *Asynchrony and Real-Time in Distributed Systems*, Proceedings of Parallel Symbolic Computing: Language, Systems, and Applications, October, 1992.

11. Tokuda, H., and Mercer, C. W., *ARTS: A Distributed Real-Time Kernel*, ACM Operating System Review, Vol.23, No.3, 1989.

12. Yonezawa, A., and Tokoro, M., editors, *Object-Oriented Concurrent Programming*, MIT Press, 1987.

13. Yokote, Y., *The Apertos Reflective Operating System: The Concept and its Implementation*, Proceedings of ACM OOPSLA'92, p397-413, October, 1992.

Decomposing and Recomposing Transactional Concepts

Jeannette M. Wing [1]
School of Computer Science
Carnegie Mellon University
Pittsburgh, PA 15213

1 Revisiting Transactions

Distributed systems are different from concurrent (and parallel) systems because they need to deal with failures, not just concurrency. Transactions are a way of masking the distributed nature of a computation at the programming language level by transforming all failures into aborted transactions. If a communication link goes down or a node crashes, the transaction simply aborts. Users may try again later to rerun their computation, but they are at least guaranteed that the system is left in some consistent state.

Transactions are a well-known and fundamental control abstraction that arose out of the database community. They have three properties that distinguish them from normal sequential processes: (1) A transaction is a sequence of operations that is performed *atomically* ("all-or-nothing"). If it completes successfully, it *commits*; otherwise, it *aborts*; (2) concurrent transactions are *serializable* (appear to occur one-at-a-time), supporting the principle of isolation; and (3) effects of committed transactions are *persistent* (survive failures).

1.1 Separation of concerns

Systems like Tabs [8] and Camelot [3] demonstrate the viability of layering a general-purpose transactional facility on top of an operating system. Languages such as Argus [4] and Avalon/C++ [2] go one step further by providing linguistic support for transactions in the context of a general-purpose programming language. In principle programmers can now use transactions as a unit of encapsulation to structure an application program without regard for how they are implemented at the operating system level.

---

[1] This research is sponsored by the Wright Laboratory, Aeronautical Systems Center, Air Force Materiel Command, USAF, and the Advanced Research Projects Agency (ARPA) under grant number F33615-93-1-1330.

The views and conclusions contained in this document are those of the authors and should not be interpreted as necessarily representing the official policies or endorsements, either expressed or implied, of Wright Laboratory or the U. S. Government.

The U. S. Government is authorized to reproduce and distribute reprints for Government purposes notwithstanding any copyright notation thereon. This manuscript is submitted for publication with the understanding that the U. S. Government is authorized to reproduce and distribute reprints for Governmental purposes.

In practice, however, transactions have yet to be shown useful in general-purpose applications programming. One problem is that state-of-the-art transactional facilities are so tightly integrated that application builders must buy into a facility *in toto*, even if they need only one of its services. For example, the Coda file system [7] was originally built on top of Camelot, which supports distributed, concurrent, nested transactions. Coda needs transactions for storing "metadata" (e.g., inodes) about files and directories. Coda is structured such that updates to metadata are guaranteed to occur by only one thread executing at a single-site within a single top-level transaction. Hence Coda needs only single-site, single-threaded, non-nested transactions, but by using Camelot was forced to pay the performance overhead for Camelot's other features.

The Venari Project at CMU is revisiting support for transactions by adopting a "pick-and-choose" approach rather than a "kit-and-kaboodle" approach [10]. Ideally, we want to provide separable components to support transactional semantics for different settings, e.g., in the absence or presence of concurrency and/or distribution. Programmers are then free to compose those components supporting only those features of transactions they need for their application. Our approach also enables programmers to code some applications that cannot be done without an explicit separation of concerns.

We want to support this approach at the programming language level. The current status of the Venari Project is that we can support concurrent, multi-threaded, nested transactions in the context of Standard ML. Our implementation, however, does not yet run in a distributed environment.

1.2 Why SML?

To explore the feasibility of designing a language to support orthogonal transactional concepts, we chose not to design a brand new language from scratch. Instead, we decided we would target an existing language as a basis for extension; we chose Standard ML, and in particular the New Jersey implementation.

SML is not the obvious choice for building a transaction-based programming language, even less so for building an object-oriented distributed language. SML's heart is in functional (stateless) programming and transactions are very much a state-oriented concept. SML has no notion of subtype or inheritance and no direct support for concurrency, distribution, or persistence.

However, SML does give a good starting point. In the design and implementation of our extensions, we gained leverage from SML's high-level language features including strong typing, exceptions, first-class functions, and modules. SML makes a type distinction between immutable and mutable values (**refs** and **arrays**); we rely on strong typing to let the runtime system safely operate on addresses (without the programmer's knowledge). SML's support for first-class functions (closures) allow us to make transactions first-class. We use signatures to separate interface information from implementation and functors to compose parameterized modules. SML's modules facility enables us to support our "pick-and-choose" approach at the language level.

2 The Application Programmer's View of Venari/ML Transactions

If f is a function applied to some argument a, then to execute:

```
f a
```

in a transaction, programmers can write:

```
(transact f) a
```

or more probably,

```
((transact f) a ) handle Foo => [some work]
```

where Foo is a user-defined exception. Here f might be multi-threaded. Informally, the meaning of calling f with transact is the same as that of just calling f with the following additional side effects: If f returns normally, then the transaction commits, and if it is a top-level transaction, its effects are saved to persistent memory (i.e., written to disk). If f terminates by raising any uncaught exception, e.g., Foo, then the transaction aborts and all of f's effects are undone. Through SML's exception-handling, in the case of an aborted transaction, the programmer has control of what to do such as clean-up and/or retrying the transaction.

As a more compelling (and the canonical) example, suppose we want to transfer money from one bank account to another. This would involve withdrawing money from one account and depositing it in the other. We need to make sure that either both the withdrawal and the deposit succeed, or that neither of them occur. If only the withdrawal happened, the money would be lost, and we would be very unhappy. If only the deposit happened, the money would be "duplicated," and the bank would be very unhappy. So, we use a transaction to effect the desired behavior.

```
fun transfer (account_1, account_2, amount) =
    let fun do_transfer () =
        (withdraw (account_1, amount);
         deposit (account_2, amount))
    in
        transact do_transfer ()
    end
```

The function transfer transfers money from account_1 to account_2 with the guarantee that a partial transfer will not occur. The transfer itself occurs in the function do_transfer, which withdraws the money from account_1 and deposits it into account_2. The functions withdraw and deposit are expected to raise an exception if something goes wrong, e.g., if account_1 has insufficient funds or the bank's computer goes down. We wrap a transaction around the call to do_transfer so that if anything goes wrong, the whole transfer will be aborted. If the transfer is aborted, we reraise the exception that caused the abort.

We could make the transfer transaction multi-threaded by having one thread do the withdrawal while another does the deposit. All we would need to do is to replace the two-line definition of **do_transfer** with the starred lines below:

```
fun transfer (account_1, account_2, amount) =
    let fun do_transfer () =
        (fork (fn () => withdraw (account_1, amount));   *
                        deposit (account_2, amount))     *
    in
        transact do_transfer ()
    end
```

3 The Venari/ML Interfaces

In our design, we teased apart the usual atomicity, serializability, and persistence properties rolled into transactions, and added the ability for transactions to be multi-threaded. In particular, we provide support for the following features, each as a separable component—the name of the Venari/ML signature is given in parentheses.

- Persistence (**PERS**)
- Undoability (**UNDO**)
- Reader-writer locks (**RW_LOCK**)
- Threads (**THREADS**)
- Skeins (**SKEINS**)

The basic idea is that we want the individual pieces to compose in a seamless way to give us transactions. Persistence ensures permanence of effects of top-level transactions. Undoability allows us to handle aborted transactions. Reader-writer locks provide isolation of changes to the store, and hence ensure transaction serializability of concurrent transactions. Skeins let us group a collection of threads together, giving us the ability to make multi-threaded transactions.

Putting all these pieces together into a single ML module culminates in our main **VENARI** interface shown below. It provides a way for application programmers to create and manipulate concurrent multi-threaded transactions. What distinguishes our model from the more standard model of concurrent, nested transactions is our ability to identify multiple threads of control (not just one thread) with a single transaction.

```
signature VENARI =
    sig
        val transact : ('a -> '_b) -> 'a -> '_b

        structure Threads : THREADS
        structure Skeins : SKEINS
        structure RW_Lock : RW_LOCK
        structure Undo : UNDO
        structure Pers : PERS
    end
```

Roughly speaking, a transaction is a *locking skein* of *threads* whose effects are *undone* if the transaction aborts or made *persistent* if it terminates. (In SML 'a is a polymorphic type variable.)

By having separated transactional concepts from one another, we also provide the ability to put some pieces together, ignoring others. This separation of concerns enables direct support for different non-transactional models of computation. Here are some of the more interesting combinations:

– Multi-threaded persistence (threads + persistence = persistent skeins)
– Multi-threaded undo (threads + undo = undo skeins)
– Locking threads (threads + r/w locks = locking skeins)
– Concurrent persistence (threads + r/w locks + persistence = locking persistent skeins)
– Concurrent multi-threaded transactions
  (persistence + undo + r/w locks + threads = transactional skeins)
  As seen, the VENARI interface above supports this particular combination directly.

All skeins can be nested, hence each combination above can be nested. Permanence of a nested persistent skein's effects is relative to its parent. All mixes are possible. For example, a transaction can have an undo skein or locking skein within it, and vice versa. A skein can have nested within it concurrent skeins of different flavors. Finally, the single-threaded case of any of these is just a special case in which a skein has just one thread; Venari/ML does not explicitly provide interfaces for the single-threaded cases.

In previously published papers, we have already reported on various aspects of the Venari/ML interfaces. Details of the design and implementation of the Threads interface are reported in [1]; of the separation between persistence and undoability for single-threaded nested transactions, in [6]. An early design of concurrent multi-threaded transactions appears in [11]. The remainder of this paper focuses on the details of the synchronization primitives provided for our model of computation.

4 Synchronizing Concurrent Multi-threaded Transactions

Our generalized model of transactions requires a generalization of Moss's (traditional) locking rules used for nested transactions [5]. Between transactions we must of course guarantee isolation; but within a transaction, threads may freely execute and need not be serialized with respect to each other. Our model also allows parents and children to execute simultaneously; parents are not suspended. To deal with some of the semantic complexity of this model, we provide a notion of *safe state* for users and we implement certain runtime checks that guarantee the principle of isolation for transactions. We can make this guarantee only under the assumption that users access only safe state. Thus, we begin by describing safe state and then describe the transaction guarantees that we have implemented.

4.1 Safe State

As seen, we not only allow transactions to run concurrently and we also allow each transaction to be multi-threaded. What implications does this model of computation have on access to shared data? It requires a means to synchronize concurrent threads and a means to synchronize concurrent transactions. These two different requirements suggest having two different grains of locks for synchronizing access to shared mutable data.

First, as typical for multi-threaded programs, we rely on *mutex locks*; second, as typical for concurrent transactions, we rely on *reader-writer locks*. Mutex locks allow threads within a transaction to synchronize, in particular, to enforce mutual exclusion; reader-writer locks allow concurrent transactions to synchronize, in particular, to enforce isolation (i.e., serializability). Without transactions, a thread need only acquire a mutex lock before accessing shared data, but with multi-threaded transactions, it must acquire a reader-writer lock.

To provide programming language support for this model we were easily in Standard ML to provide *safe state* [9]: mutable data that is guaranteed to be always accessed by a thread that has acquired the right kind of lock. What is "safe" about safe state are the correctness guarantees it provides: mutual exclusion between threads and isolation between transactions. Disciplined programmers, those who use only safe state, will be assured that their concurrent multi-threaded transactions are serializable.

Let's look in some detail at the abstractions needed. First, we need two types of locks, `mutex` locks and `rw_locks`, respectively defined in `Threads` and `RW_Lock` modules. In particular, the `Threads` module declares (among others) the following type and function values:

```
type mutex
val mutex     : unit -> mutex
val acquire   : mutex -> unit
val release   : mutex -> unit
val owner     : mutex -> bool
val with_mutex: mutex -> (unit -> 'a) -> 'a
```

Evaluation of the function call **mutex()** creates a new mutex value. The function **acquire** attempts to lock a mutex and blocks the calling thread until it succeeds; **release** unlocks a mutex, giving other threads a chance to acquire it; **owner** returns true if and only if the mutex is currently held by the current thread. The evaluation of **with_mutex m f** acquires the mutex **m**, applies the function **f**, and then releases **m**.

The **RW_Lock** module includes (among others) the following type and function values:

```
type rw_lock
val create   : unit -> rw_lock
val read     : rw_lock -> ('a -> 'b) -> 'a -> 'b
val write    : rw_lock -> ('a -> 'b) -> 'a -> 'b
```

The **read** and **write** functions take a lock, a function, and its argument, and apply the function to the argument with the guarantee that the lock is held in the appropriate read or write mode during the execution of the function. In particular, no other *thread* may use the lock in read or write mode while the function executes. If some thread within a transaction calls **read** or **write** without holding the lock in the appropriate mode, we raise an exception; otherwise, **read** and **write** will block until the condition is satisfied.

Second, we exploit the fact that SML makes a type distinction between immutable and mutable values. In SML, only **refs** and **arrays** are mutable. Thus, only refs and arrays need to be protected by any kind of lock. (Since refs and arrays are treated similarly, we will talk about just refs for the remainder of this paper.) Below are the two relevant functions on **ref** types:

```
val !  : 'a ref -> 'a
val := : 'a ref * 'a -> unit
```

If **x** is of type **int ref** then **x := 5** assigns the integer 5 to **x**; subsequent evaluation of **!x** is 5.

Now, we can build *mutex refs*, safe state for multi-threaded programs. An **m_ref** is a regular (unsafe) ref protected by a mutex lock. The relevant functions that we can perform on mutex refs are akin to their unsafe counterparts:

```
val m_get:  'a m_ref -> 'a
val m_set:  'a m_ref -> 'a -> unit
```

But, what is so elegantly expressible in SML are their definitions (implementations):

```
datatype 'a m_ref = M_Ref of ('a ref * Threads.mutex)

fun m_get (M_Ref (uref,l)) =
    if Threads.owner l then (!uref) else raise NotOwner
fun m_set (M_Ref (uref,l)) v =
    if Threads.owner l then uref := v else raise NotOwner
```

Here we see explicitly how an **m_ref** is implemented—as a pair of a regular ref and a mutex lock. A call to **m_get** checks to see that the caller owns the associated lock 1 before performing the access (!) on the ref **uref** itself. If the check fails, an exception is raised. Similarly for **m_set**.

Finally, we can play the same game of making transactionally safe state by building *reader-writer refs*. As for mutex refs, we can perform get and set functions on reader-writer refs:

```
val rw_get:   'a rw_ref -> 'a
val rw_set:   'a rw_ref -> 'a -> unit
```

where again by looking at their definitions, we can see how we enforce safe access:

```
datatype 'a rw_ref = RW_Ref of ('a ref * RW_Lock.rw_lock)

fun rw_get (RW_Ref (r,l)) =
    RW_Lock.read l !r
fun rw_set (RW_Ref (r,l)) v =
    RW_Lock.write l (fn () => r:=v) ()
```

Since a **rw_ref** is a regular ref protected by a reader-writer lock, a call to **rw_get** guarantees safe access to the ref because it acquires the lock 1 in read mode before returning the value stored in the ref **r**. Similarly for **rw_set**.

To show a simple use of mutex refs (reader-writer refs would be similar), consider a multi-threaded application that uses a logical clock to establish the order of events. Here's an SML signature for such a clock:

```
signature CLOCK = sig
    val get_time : unit -> int
end
```

It exports only the one function, **get_time**, which increments the clock and returns a new, unique time. We can implement the clock and its **get_time** function as:

```
val time = m_ref (0, Threads.mutex())

fun get_time () =
    with_m_ref time (fn () => (m_inc time; m_get time))
```

where the mutex ref **time** stores the logical time, **with_m_ref** is the mutex ref counterpart to **with_mutex**, and **m_inc** increments the integer value of the clock by 1 (defined in the obvious way in terms of the increment function on **int** refs.). **Time** must be protected by a mutex to avoid the following incorrect sequence of events in which two threads would be given the same time:

thread A	thread B
inc time	
	inc time
!time	
	!time

To ensure that each caller is given a unique time, the function get_time wraps with_m_ref around the calls to increment and read time.

To summarize, we guarantee the principle of isolation for transactions by making use of *safe state*. In the context of just threads, a normal SML ref is unsafe, while a ref protected by a mutex is a safe ref. In the context of transactions, a ref protected by only a mutex is an unsafe ref, while a ref protected by a reader-writer lock is a safe ref. A read or write of a safe ref will fail unless the thread (transaction) holds the mutex (reader-writer lock) of the ref. Thus, it is impossible to violate the isolation principle if the programmer uses only safe state.

4.2 Transaction Guarantees

Given that within a (multi-threaded) transaction only safe state is accessed, we generalize traditional rules for managing nested transactions.

If the body thread or any sub-thread raises an uncaught exception, the transaction *aborts*. If the body evaluates successfully, the transaction *commits*.

When a transaction aborts,

- all changes to the persistent and volatile stores made by the transaction and its descendants are undone; and
- all reader-writer locks held by the transaction and its descendants are released.

When a transaction commits,

- if this is a top-level transaction (i.e., no ancestor skein is persistent, undoable, or a transaction), and the persistent store is initialized, any changes to the persistent store are committed to disk; and
- all reader-writer locks are handed to the nearest locking ancestor skein.

If the functions executed within transactions have no effects except through the use of the safe state, then we can make certain guarantees regarding the interaction of those transactions. Let T be a transaction, and let S and S' be any locking skeins (thus S and S' may be transactions as well). (T, S, and S' are all different from one another.) The following guarantees hold:

- If neither S nor T is a descendant of the other, then
  - if T aborts, S observes no effects of T or T's descendants;
  - the effects of T and its descendants appear atomic to S (i.e., S sees either all of their effects or none of their effects); and
  - the effects of S and T are serializable from the viewpoint of any other locking skein S'.
- If T is a descendant of S, then
  - the effects of T and its descendants appear atomic to S; and
  - the state which T observes will reflect a "snapshot" of S's effects (taken at the instant after T acquires its last reader-writer lock); and
  - if S's effects before and after the "snapshot" point are denoted E_S^{before} and E_S^{after}, and the effects of T and its descendants are denoted E_T, then these effects will appear to S' to take place in the order $(E_S^{before}, E_T, E_S^{after})$.
- The image of the persistent store on disk will always be *consistent* (partial effects of a transaction will never appear on disk).

One should consider a transaction T_2 which is a child of transaction T_1 to be doing work "on behalf of" T_1. The guarantees above hold even if non-transactional skeins or threads are invoked within the transactions involved.

5   Summary and Future Work

Unlike other transaction-based high-level programming languages such as Argus and Avalon, Venari/ML is the first to support multi-threaded transactions, where each transaction may have multiple threads of control executing within its scope. This generalization of the standard transactional model led to our support for concurrent multi-threaded transactions and some novel abstractions like skeins and safe state. Moreover, our model required rethinking the synchronization rules for nested transactions, leading to the transaction guarantees described in Section 4.2.

The Venari/ML interfaces are cast in terms of SML's modules facility. Our modules support a separation of concerns, e.g., persistence from undoability, that are often tightly integrated in other transactional systems. We also make extensive use of closures in SML, allowing us at runtime to compose different functions, each of which supports a different feature of transactions. E.g., the argument to the function transact is a closure.

There are two main directions that we would like to pursue in the future. First, our effort to support a "pick-and-choose" approach for transactions has the advantage of providing us with a way to take performance measurements on different combinations of our separable modules. The Venari Project expects to do some careful performance analysis of our implemented features. Second, we hope to build a non-trivial and non-traditional application using our interfaces. Existing transactional facilities have been designed primarily for applications like electronic banking and airline reservations. We are more interested in applications like cooperative work environments and engineering design systems where the objects of interest are irregular in structure and the computations may span hours or even days.

6 Acknowledgments

This paper could not have been written without Greg Morrisett's work on the Threads package for SML/NL, Scott Nettles's work on persistence and undoability, Darrell Kindred's work on locks, and Nick Haines's work on putting it all together. Portions of this paper are from the technical report [10] that we jointly wrote.

References

1. E.C. Cooper and J. Gregory Morrisett. Adding threads to Standard ML. Technical Report CMU-CS-90-186, Carnegie Mellon School of Computer Science, December 1990.
2. D. L. Detlefs, M. P. Herlihy, and J. M. Wing. Inheritance of synchronization and recovery properties in Avalon/C++. *IEEE Computer*, pages 57–69, December 1988.
3. J. Eppinger, L. Mummert, and A. Spector. *Camelot and Avalon: A Distributed Transaction Facility*. Morgan Kaufmann Publishers, Inc., 1991.
4. B. Liskov and R. Scheifler. Guardians and actions: Linguistic support for robust, distributed programs. *ACM Transactions on Programming Language and Systems*, 5(3):382–404, July 1983.
5. J.E.B. Moss. Nested transactions: An approach to reliable distributed computing. Technical Report MIT/LCS/TR-260, Laboratory for Computer Science, April 1981.
6. Scott M. Nettles and J.M. Wing. Persistence + Undoability = Transactions. In *Proc. of HICSS-25*, January 1992. Also CMU-CS-91-173, August 1991.
7. M. Satyanarayanan et al. Coda: A highly available file system for a distributed workstation environment. *IEEE Trans. Computers*, 39(4):447–459, April 1990.
8. A.Z. Spector et al. Support for distributed transactions in the TABS prototype. *IEEE Transactions on Software Engineering*, 11(6):520–530, June 1985.
9. A.P. Tolmach and A.W. Appel. Debugging Standard ML without reverse engineering. In *Proceedings of the ACM Lisp and Functional Programming Conference*, pages 1–12, 1990.
10. J.M. Wing and et al. Venari/ML interfaces and examples. Technical Report CMU-CS-93-123, CMU School of Computer Science, March 1993.
11. J.M. Wing, M. Faehndrich, J.G. Morrisett, and S.M. Nettles. Extensions to Standard ML to support transactions. In *ACM SIGPLAN Workshop on ML and its Applications*, June 1992. Also CMU-CS-92-132, April 1992.

DPL to Express a Concurrency Control Using Transaction and Object Semantics

Rakotonirainy Andry[1]

INRIA Rocquencourt - Domaine du Voluceau BP 105 - 78153 Le Chesnay Cedex
France. Email: Andry.Rakotonirainy@inria.fr

Abstract. There is a currently considerable interest in advanced transaction processing. Most proposals weaken serializability. The concurrency of transactions executing on shared objects can be enhanced with the use of semantic information about operations type or through user defined semantics called transaction semantic. This paper attempts to unify the two approaches; we present an extended model which exploits both transaction and object semantics to increase concurrency. The approach we adopt is similar to the one used in [Lynch83,Molina83,FO89]. However, our mechanism for specifying allowable interleavings is based on predicate over step types and synchronization operators. It supports concurrent execution of steps and synchronization amongst them. We will integrate this distributed concurrency control policy into a high level language to hide low-level details such as locks, timestamps management and concurrent activities synchronization inside the implementation of the language constructs. We use ANSA computational language DPL (Distributed Programming Language) as a basic language construct. We propose a few DPL extensions to support our model. This model is suitable to express a wide range of synchronization constraints between concurrent activities.

1 Overview

This paper is organized as follows. Section 1 gives a taxonomy of existing concurrency control and gives motivating examples to clarify our model. Section 2 exposes our model through examples. In section 3 we present a concurrency control expressed with DPL and propose a few extensions to support our model. In section 4 we propose a possible implementation of our model by describing an algorithm based on lock mechanisms. Section 5 addresses recovery issues. Finally, we summarize the higlights of this paper and discuss related and future work.

A top level transaction can be considered as an ACID unit [GR92]. ACID means that a transaction must have the following properties: Atomicity: transaction is indivisible (all or nothing). Consistency: states change correctly (do not violate consistency constraints). Isolation: even though transactions execute concurrently, they must

---

1. This research was sponsored by «Ministère de la Recherche et de la Technologie Française» under MRE contract.

behave as if they execute serially. Durability: final states of a completed transaction survive failures. Each property cannot be waived without affecting the others. Relaxing Isolation means that we show intermediate (uncommitted) states to others transactions. These intermediate states may affect Consistency and imply a more complicated recovery mechanism. A concurrency control algorithm ensures ACI properties. The Atomicity we deal with is an atomicity that encompasses correctness and recoverability. The well-known two phases commit (2PC) ensures atomicity properties and has no common aspect with correctness criteria, but the main concern of 2PC is to provide atomicity in a distributed environment confronted with failures. We express atomicity as an equivalence to a correct execution under the (implicit) assumption that no failures occur.

The problem of controlling accesses to shared data by transactions has been solved by concurrency control algorithms. Several models have been proposed. Each one makes different assumptions, described in different terminology and uses different mechanisms to achieve consistency. All those approaches can be summarized in three classes. Let us define a few formal notations and terminologies to compare the three approaches.

Let $\mathcal{T}$ denote the set of transactions T_i of a distributed database $\mathcal{D}$ and O denote all objects o_i involved in $\mathcal{T}$. The value of each object $o_i \in O$ determines the state of the database $\mathcal{D}$. These states are manipulated by the set of transaction $T_i \in \mathcal{T}$ Explicit input/output predicates over $\mathcal{D}$ are associated with transactions. The input predicate is a pre_condition of transaction execution and must hold at the beginning of the transaction. The output condition is a post-condition that the transaction guarantees on the state of $\mathcal{D}$ at the end of the transaction provided that there is no concurrency and that the state of $\mathcal{D}$ satisfies a pre-condition. Let $\mathcal{H}(\mathcal{T})$ denote the execution history of a set of a transaction $\mathcal{T}$. Transactions are always specified as a piece of program that begins with pre_cond and leaves $\mathcal{D}$ in post_cond state.

$$\text{post\_cond} = \mathcal{T}(\text{pre\_cond}). \textbf{(Eq1)}$$

The criterion we use to classify a concurrency control mechanism is based on the equation (Eq1), $\mathcal{H}(\mathcal{T})$, post/pres_cond and operations types of O. Note that (Eq1) remains true even if one or more transactions abort. In concurrency control, two properties of transactions must be clarified: consistency and correctness. Consistent means that an execution satisfies database consistency constraints noted Co. Correctness means that an execution satisfies transaction consistency constraints noted Ct.

The first approach is related to traditional concurrency control. Traditional concurrency control theory has developed several classes of correct executions for distributed transaction systems. The common aspect of these classes is serializability (view serializability, epsilon-serializability, strict-serializability etc...). Transactions contain only read/write operations. If $\mathcal{T}$ is an isolated transaction or a set of serializable transactions then (Eq1) implies that post-condition and pre-condition are consistent states for $\mathcal{D}$ and correct for each $T_i \in \mathcal{T}$ Post/pre-condition tuples may be used to express consistency constraints Co on objects. Co is an invariant of the object system, this constraint is not violated if the history of execution is serializable and transactions are well-formed. If $\mathcal{H}(\mathcal{T})$ is serializable then (pre_cond, post_cond) $\in Co$ and (pre_cond, post_cond) $\in Ct$. This first approach is used in flat and nested transactions[Moss81].

The second approach places more structure on operations to exploit type specific properties of each $o_i \in O$ while keeping serializability as a basis for consistency criteria. The operations are more complex than those used in the first approach. Object oriented models present an opportunity to provide more concurrency than traditional approaches do because the object knows more about the operations that are being performed. Conflicts between operations are defined by users in a commutativity matrix. Commutativity of operations is exploited to avoid conflicts. Commutativity may depend on input/output parameters of each operations[Weihl88]. A dependency graph G is constructed from the compatibility matrix and $\mathcal{H}(\mathcal{T})$. If G contains no cycle then $\mathcal{H}(\mathcal{T})$ is semantically serializable. Semantically serializable means that $\mathcal{H}(\mathcal{T})$ may be non serializable but semantically acceptable (consistent) for each $o_i \in O$. In this case (pre_cond, post_cond) $\in Co$. This approach still respects serializability theory by redefining the notion of conflict. It is used in multi-level transactions [Weikum91].

The third approach exploits the semantics of transactions. A transaction shall have the correctness constraints Ct. Ct is different from Co because Ct is related to an application semantics but Co concerns object semantics. As an example, consider a banking transaction T_c that consults n accounts. Each consulted account $(o_1 ... o_n) \in O$ may have a global Co expressing the following conditions: Σ account$_i$ = Cte. An accurate consultation transaction must return Cte as a final value. The consultation operation doesn't commute with the transfer operation. Let us assume that T_c may tolerate an approximate result expressed by Ct. Ct information implies that T_c can freely interleave with concurrent transfer operations. Here, T_c is a non-accurate (non-sensible) transaction that can be processed without waiting for termination (abort/commit) of transfer transactions. In this approach, users can specify arbitrary allowable interleavings between concurrent transactions depending on semantic computation knowledge. It means that a transaction may decide to reveal intermediate states to others transactions. These intermediate states become pre_cond of others transactions. Revealed intermediates states may violate Co but this may be acceptable for Ct. Each $T_i \in \mathcal{H}(\mathcal{T})$ may be semantically correct even if (pre_cond$_i$, post_cond$_i$) $\notin$ Co but each post_cond$_i$ $T_i \in \mathcal{H}(\mathcal{T})$ must verify Ct.

Post and pre_conditions of the first approach verify Co and Ct. The second and the third approaches alleviate Ct or Co to increase concurrency. Table 1 shows which pre or post_conditions states are verified in each of the three approaches. An empty entry mean that pre or post-conditions may violate the associated constraint. Transaction semantics allow for more concurrency compared to object semantics and serializability theory.

Table 1 shows that transaction semantics schedules include all permissible schedules of the two others approach: Serializability $\subset$ Object Semantic $\subset$ Transaction Semantic. We'll use this fundamental result to model our algorithm. The algorithmic consequence of the presented principles is that the decision to schedule a step based on interleaving information is allowed even if it is forbidden by commutativity rules. This implies that interleaving rules are stronger than commutativity rules.

TABLE 1. Comparisons

$\in$	Co consistency	Ct correctness
Basic serializability	pre_cond; post_cond	pre_cond; post_cond
Oject semantics	pre_cond; post_cond	post_cond
Transaction semantics	-	post_cond

1.1   Related work

Concurrency control based on serializability theory is too restrictive for a broad range of new emerging applications such as CAD or long lived transactions [KKB88]. As we stated above, serializability theory is not the only correctness criterion in concurrency control. The limited concurrency offered by serializability theory has prompted researchers to investigate non-serializable concurrency control providing equivalent correctness. [Molina83] proposed the concept of *semantically consistent* schedules. In this model, transactions are classified by the user into classes (semantic types). A transaction is divided into a set of indivisible units called steps. Transactions are compatible if they belong to the same class. If two transactions are compatible, then their steps can interleave freely. Each step is associated with a *counterstep* that is used to possibly compensate the step. Countersteps are intended to handle situations where it is required to undo either committed or uncommitted steps without cascading abort effects on other transactions. Thus, when a counterstep c_i is executed, no effort is made to notify or abort transactions that might have seen the intermediate result before it was compensated for by c_i [GS87].

[Lynch83] has developed a concept called *multi-level atomicity* for the utilization of transaction semantics in concurrency control. Transactions are grouped into nested classes according to user semantic knowledge. Transactions which are closely related in the nesting structure will be allowed to interleave at a finer level of atomicity. Steps of a transaction can be interleaved with those of others when specified in breakpoints between transactions steps. The specification of breakpoints is relative to the classes of a transaction. Lynch has also developed a hierarchical form for specifying breakpoints. A schedule that satisfies such specification is said to be multi-level atomic.

1.2   Motivation

We do not address the way a transaction is partitioned into (atomic) steps. We assume that application programmers dispose of non ambiguous, clear and well-defined semantics about transaction computation to specify correct scheduling rules. Intuitively, a scheduling rule specifies how an indivisible step of a transaction may be interleaved with others. With only transaction syntactic information, the entire transaction must be taken as single atomic unit; serializability theory partitions each transaction in this way. Serializability theory is optimal under the condition that only syntactic information of transactions is used for scheduling [KP79]. We adopt an approach that enables the semantics of transactions and operations to be exploited. The traditional theory of serializability is weakened: a scheduling is said to be correct if it meets user specification constraints. Semantics knowledge allows a transaction to be partitioned into atomic steps and to specify allowable interleavings in breakpoints. Breakpoints are placed between steps of a transaction to specify allowable interleavings. Transaction steps may interleave at various points inside a transaction. The resulting scheduling may produce non-serializable, but semantically correct scheduling. In [Lynch83, FO89], breakpoints of a transaction T_i define a set of transaction types that may interleave with T_i at breakpoint. The set of transaction types of a breakpoint B_{ij} is denoted $ts(B_{ij})$. [FO89] imposes that a transaction T_i that is allowed to interleave with T_j at breakpoint $ts(B_{jl}) = \{T_i\}$ of T_j must proceed entirely before the beginning of the next step of T_j. Implicitly, it means that a transaction T_j may be interrupted by T_i, T_j will be suspended until the end of T_i. When T_j resumes processing after a breakpoint then it can continue its activities. The next step following the breakpoint must wait for the end of T_i.

Example:1
$T_i = \{S_{i1}, B_{i1}, S_{i2}, End_i\}$;
$T_j = \{S_{j1}, B_{j1}, S_{j2}, B_{j2}, End_j\}$.
Let $ts(B_{i1}) = \{T_j\}$ and $ts(B_{j1}) = ts(B_{j2}) = \varnothing$.
We have only three types of correct schedule:
$H1 = \{S_{i1}, S_{j1}, S_{j2}, End_j, S_{i2}, End_i\}$
T_j's steps must run after S_{i1} and before the beginning of S_{i2}
$H2 = \{S_{i1}, S_{i2}, End_i\}$ case where T_j did not run and
$H3 = \{T_i; T_j\}$ or $\{T_j; T_i\}$ serial execution

Let us assume that semantic knowledge allows the first step of T_j to interleave at B_{i1} and the second step S_{j2} is forbidden to interleave anywhere in T_i. This means that we allow the following schedules: $H_4 = (S_{i1}, S_{j1}, S_{i2}, End_i)$.

Specifying this kind of interleavings in existing models is impossible since the breakpoint set (ts) contains only whole transactions.

Our model provides breakpoints of finer granularity. We use a set of *steps types* instead of a set of transaction types. Breakpoints use predicates and DPL operators to have a richer and simpler tool for specifying all the user requirements. DPL includes serial, concurrent, sequence and serial synchronization operators. The sole purpose of predicates and operators is to specify and handle complex synchronizations and conditions under which several transactions may proceed. These kind of synchronizations cannot be described by existing models. This finer granularity has the advantage that it allows more parallelism than allowed by [Lynch83, FO89] models, thus finer partitions lead to a larger set of permissible schedules and a higher degree of concurrency.

2   Model

We illustrate our model by describing a bank account example, defining some types of steps, describing the allowable interleavings and commutativity rules between operations. We use two types of transaction namely T-Balance and T-Transfert, as shown in Figure 1 .T-Balance is a transaction used to provide an approximate total amount over a set of account. T-Transfert transfers an amount X from account a to b.

FIGURE 1.   Bank account

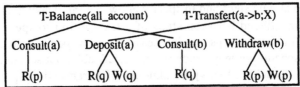

The above scenario shows the concurrent execution of two transactions, involving operations on two different levels of abstraction. The scheduling is not serializable at any level because read/write operations conflicts at page level and Consult/Deposit and Consult/Withdraw don't commute so that each level has a cycle in its conflict graph. Let us assume that T-Balance is allowed to return an approximate value. We suppose that this approximation is unbounded for the sake of simplicity (see [WA92]). The execution in Figure 1 produces a semantically correct execution and achieves higher concurrency at the expense of consistency. The concurrency control mechanism for this kind of scheduling requires model using rules beyond the commutativity and serializability.

Our model is similar to the one used in [Molina83, Lynch83, FO89]. We use breakpoints and steps to delimit allowable interleavings. Transactions contain steps type (S), Breakpoints (Bs) and transaction's terminations (End). Transaction's steps are abstracts operations semantically richer than traditional read/write primitives. We assume that a step accesses only one individual object. A step can be an operation associated with predicates, it is a method in an object oriented fashion. All of our predicates are formed by step and synchronization operators: S_{ij} op S_{kl} with op $\in$ {parallel, serial, choice} operators. A step may be invoked by concurrent transactions.

In the next sections, we will define and explain the mechanism through examples that are used in our model. These requirements are not exhaustives.

In Figure 2 , each arrow starts from a breakpoint and ends on a step. These arrows mean that pointed steps are allowed to interrupt an associated breakpoint. Transactions T_1, T_2 and T_3 have a serial specification, breakpoints are used for concurrent specifications. The steps of T_1 are S_{11} and S_{12}, its breakpoint is Bs_{11}.

T_1:S_{11};Bs_{11};S_{12},End_1. with $ss(Bs_{11}) = S_{21}$
T_2:S_{21};Bs_{21};S_{22};End_2. with $ss(Bs_{21}) = \{S_{11},S_{31}\}$
T_3:S_{31};Bs_{31};S_{32};Bs_{32};S_{33};End_3 with $ss(Bs_{31}) = S_{22}$ $ss(Bs_{32}) = \varnothing$

FIGURE 2.   Basic Model

T_1 = Begin()	T_2 = Begin()	T_3 = Begin()
S_{11}	S_{21}	S_{31}
Bs_{11}	Bs_{21}	Bs_{31}
S_{12}	S_{22}	S_{32}
End_trans	End_trans	Bs_{32}
		S_{33}
		End_trans

We associate with each breakpoint Bs_{ij} of a transaction T_i a set of step types noted $ss(Bs_{ij})$. Breakpoints may contain predicates and composition operators. Transaction T_2 in Figure 2 includes breakpoint Bs_{21}. S_{11} or S_{31} or both of them can interrupt arbitrarily T_2 at breakpoint Bs_{21}. An application may wish to impose an interleaving order. We can do it using DPL operators. For example, let us assume that T_2 allows S_{11} and S_{31} to interrupt at Bs_{21} with the condition that S_{11} must precede S_{31}. The breakpoint specification will look like this:

$ss(Bs_{21}) = \{S_{11};S_{31}\}$

«;» is a DPL sequential operator. If transaction S_{31} of T_3 asks to proceed at breakpoint Bs_{21} of T_2 then it must be blocked until S_{11} is finished. In this case, S_{11} is an event predicate. These ordering constraints are valid only during Bs_{21} execution. T_2 can control the allowable interleavings only during this active phase. If T_2 ends, then other concurrent transactions are free to execute and control their own steps.

The specification of $ss(Bs_{21})$ did not make any assumption about the identity of the activity that invoked steps in breakpoints. We must take care of this information in concurrency control. A transactional activity is uniquely identified by a Transactional Identifier Tid. S_{11} and S_{31} are types of steps but not instances of types. They can be invoked either from two different Tids or from the same Tid. Two or more steps of a breakpoint Bs_{ij} associated with operators may be invoked either from the same thread (instance of a transaction) or from different threads of control (different instance of transaction). In the first case, an activity must respect an ordering constraint within an activity. In the second case, it does not matter who invoked the steps since they respect the object ordering constraints. Our model allows both of the above possibilities. We use the following notation to express the above constraints.

$ss(Bs_{12}) = \{[S_{11};S_{31}]\}$. Brackets are used to restrict the ordering execution within the same Tid. If brackets are omitted then steps may be executed in an arbitrary order by any activity.

Another advantage of our model is the possibility to include predicates and if_then_else statements in breakpoints.

Example:2. Let us define a breakpoint

$ss(Bs_{11}) = \{(S_{32};S_{11})$ or (if $(S_{45} \parallel S_{67})$ then $(S_{28};S_{29}))\}$. $ss(Bs_{11})$ contains a conditional statement where each step S_{ij} is the sequence of a program and $(S_{45} \parallel S_{67})$ forms a predicate. $(S_{45} \parallel S_{67})$ is a predicate because it is evaluated by «if» and the evaluation will return true or false.

This statement means that we have an exclusive choice between the execution of the right part of «or» and the left one. If an occurrence of S_{32} terminates then the next allowable step is S_{11}. S_{11} must wait until the end of S_{32} before proceeding. Otherwise if S_{45} and S_{67} are active concurrently then the next allowable schedule is a sequential execution of S_{28} and S_{29}. Note that we use parallel ($\parallel$) and sequential (;) operators applied to a conditional 'if then else' statement.

We introduce a notation to allow a transaction T_i to interleave with steps of T_j and the associated breakpoint *by transitivity*.

Example:3

Consider two transactions T_i and T_j:

$T_i: S_{i1},Bs_{i1},End_i;$ $ss(Bs_{i1}): \{S_{kl}\}$

$T_j: S_{j1},Bs_{j1},End_j;$ $ss(Bs_{j1}) = \{S_{i1}+\}$

$S_{i1}+$ means that we allow the following scheduling:

H: $S_{j1};S_{i1};S_{kl};End_j$.

In the case where $ss(Bs_{j1})=\{S_{i1}\}$ then S_{kl} is forbidden to interleave with $S_{j1};S_{i1}$.

We introduce a concept of *dynamic multi-view* to allow a transaction to give different views of atomicity to one or more transactions. Dynamic means that we can add or remove steps dynamically from the breakpoint set.

Example:4

Consider a transaction T_i that allows a set of interleaving under real time constraints.

$T_i: S_{i1},Bs_{i1},End_i;$ $ss(Bs_{i1}): \{S_{kj}\}$.

Suppose that during run-time, T_i detects that the deadline is very close and that some actions must be taken to avoid T_i to abort. One of several actions that T_i may adopt is to forbid dynamically one or more concurrent steps to interrupt T_i at a breakpoint. In our example, T_i must remove S_{kj} from $ss(Bs_{i1})$ to have a greater probability to terminate. In the opposite case, steps may be added dynamically in a breakpoint if T_i has enough time to be interrupted or T_i must cooperate with concurrent steps of other transactions. Triggers may update breakpoints .

The transaction T_k will see two types of transactions T_i that give different views of atomicity depending on time. Sometimes T_k sees T_i as a single atomic entity, sometimes it sees T_i as two atomic entities. Our model allows or forbids interleavings dynamically under complex conditions based on predicates. Allowing interleavings implicitly means that we externalize the private states of a transaction.

Concerning existing models, we do not restrict the breakpoint set ss(Bs) to contain statically all steps of a given transaction[FO89], nor do we require that allowable interleavings be hierarchical [Lynch83]. Breakpoint set (ss) is evaluated by the concurrency manager before allowing interleavings. Finer step granularity allows more parallelism. Predicates are used to specify precise conditions under which interleavings are allowed.

[Lynch83,FO89] allow pre_conditions of transactions specified in breakpoint to be inconsistent, but the post_condition of these transactions must be semantically correct because a transaction must leave a post_condition semantically correct as shown in Table 1. Our model allows pre_conditions and post_conditions of steps to be inconsistent but imposes that the post_conditions of the last step must be correct to meet a degree of correctness. As far as our model reveals intermediate states to concurrent transactions, there is no guarantee that these intermediate states which are input states to others transaction preserve consistency constraints. We can avoid this lack by specifying complex conditions under which intermediate states may be revealed.

2.1   Correct schedule

We use execution-history to verify that a schedule meets the specification. Users specify dependencies between steps. These dependencies express the order in which steps must be executed. The basic serializability theorem qualifies a history $\mathcal{H}$ to be correct if there are no cycles in the relations describing dependencies among transactions. Intuitively, «cycle» means that a transaction appears to both precede and follow another transaction. In our model, dependencies appear if steps are semantically in conflict. The scope of semantic conflicts ranges from traditional read/write conflicts [GR92] to application dependent conflicts [FO89] through abstract data types commutativity [Weihl88].Two steps conflict if the execution order matter. A conflict is a dynamic dependencies. A history is correct if semantic conflict contains no cycle. Semantic conflicts are less strict than traditional read/write conflicts and must be specified by application programmers. Two sets of steps S_1 and S_2 are equivalent (noted '≈') if Dependency Graph (DG in S_1 are preserved in S_2 and vice versa. We assume that the breakpoint specification is well formed, i.e. conforms to the transaction's internal order, otherwise predicates will never be satisfied. We require the following conditions to guarantee a semantically correct scheduling:

- $\mathcal{H}$ is stepwise serial [Molina83]; each step in $\mathcal{H}$ appears without interleavings.

- the internal order of steps within a transaction must be preserved in $\mathcal{H}$.
  Formally, let T'_i be the specification of T_i without breakpoints. (no permissible interleavings)
  $T'_i = T_i\backslash_{\{Bs\}}$. (read hide ss in T_i).
  DG is applied to $\mathcal{H}$ and T to extract dependency structure. The above sentence is formalized as followed:
  For each T_i : $DG(\mathcal{H}) \cap DG(T'_i) \approx DG(T'_i)$.

- The first step S_{kl} between two consecutive S_{ij} and S_{ij+1} must be in $ss(Bs_{ij})$. All steps S_{xy} between S_{kl} and S_{ij+1} are obtained by transitivity.

- If a step is allowed to interleave then synchronization constraints and predicates specified in breakpoint must be preserved in $\mathcal{H}$.
  Formally, for each breakpoint Bs_{ij} of all transaction T_i:
  If $ss(Bs_{ij})$ occurs then $DG(Bs_{ij}) \in (\mathcal{H})$.

- There must be no cycle in $DG(\mathcal{H})$. (similar to serializability theory)
  Formally, for any two conflicting steps $S_i, S_j \in \mathcal{H}$, either $S_i < S_j$ or $S_j < S_i$. «<« is an execution order symbol on $\mathcal{H}$.

3   DPL (Distributed Programming Language)

DPL is an object based language used by the ANSA [ANSA91] computational model. The ANSA concurrency control model is based upon Extended Open Path Predicate Expressions (EOPPE). EOPPE is a high level language that provides a mechanism whereby a list of operations can be subjected to ordering constraints. The supporting infrastructure called engineering model provides guarantees enabling the scheduling to meet EOPPE specifications. EOPPEs are attributes of interfaces since they control operations at the interface level. The concurrency control manager determines, upon evaluation of EOPPE, whether an activity requesting an invocation may proceed immediately or if some other action must be taken. A single path expression controls the shared use of an interface, each client expects the behaviour of the service to be governed by the semantics of the service. EOPPE is the entity that is evaluated concurrently within the same object to ensure a degree of consistency.

ANSA provides a mechanism called *concurrency guard* to control parallel, choice and sequential operators at interface level. Each operation of an EOPPE interface is associated with *event counters* cardinals.

```
eoppe = type (
            req():(Integer)
            act():(Integer)
            term():(Integer)
            )
```

Each of the three operations returns the current value of a counter representing the number of requested, actived and terminated operations. Each of the three events can be considered to occur at the interface of the service provider and so can be considered to give a uniform view to different observers. Figure 3 which was taken from [ANSA91] gives an example where serial operator (ser) and event counters cardinals are used. Writers have a priority such that only a single writer can be active at any time and, only if no writers are requested can readers become active, although more than one reader can be active in parallel.

FIGURE 3.   Strong writer preference in DPL

```
eoppe(« %start of eoppe attribute
        dpl ( % definition block in dpl
            i=interface
            (delayed_writers():(Integer)
                    [write.req().minus(writers.act())]
            )
        )
        ser (%path expression %
            *:ser(
                *:ind(
                [i.delayed_writers().equal(0)]read)
                )
                write
            )
        )
        «)> % end attribute
```

We use these invocation constraints to enforce properties such as temporal or causal ordering that hold when invoking an object is used in a transaction. EOPPE is a language support for the expression of object coordination.

Coordination patterns are specified abstractly, independently of the underline protocol. Existing languages used to express coordination of activities are very close to implement aspect (e.g. 2 phase commit or 2 phase locking), so it is difficult to change the coordination without re-organizing the implementation. As EOPPE is expressed at interface level, it leads to a clean separation between coordination design and object functionality. The separation enables system design with a larger potential of reuse. The synchronization constraints are expressed in the form of boolean predicates. These booleans involve the invocation history of invoking operation.

3.1 Proposed extensions

DPL may be extended to provide an adequate treatment of distributed transactional operations using semantic knowledge. EOPPE is suitable to express both transaction and operation semantics. Breakpoints can be specified at the interface level to allow easy evaluation of predicates. Operation commutativity can be easily derived from path predicate. This extension has to support dynamic insertion or alteration of steps and utilization of remote methods within an interface.

The main drawback of EOPPE concerns the scope of an operation. Operations and associated predicates are in the same local object. They don't address distributed predicates. A predicate may require remote S_{ij} to be evaluated by a transaction T_k at breakpoint. We must take care of this distributed unstable predicate evaluation in a failure prone asynchronous system [HPR92]. Re-use of EOPPE code in concurrent OO languages is difficult due to inheritance anomaly.

The way we specify commutativity and interleaving is very similar. Example: two steps S_1 and S_2 that commute or can interleave are specified as followed in EOPPE: ind(S_1 S_2) ind is a parallel operator indicating that S_1 and S_2 can interleave freely.

The above list of operators is not exhaustive, other synchronization operators will be defined to express a recovery mechanism, but this is out of the scope of this paper.

4 Concurrency Control

In this section we present a locking mechanism that supports the core of our model. Note that our model is generic enough to run on top of other synchronization mechanisms. Locking is a special instance of our model. In order to simplify our presentation, we will take some strong assumptions and we will ignore some implementations details. (refer to [ANSA91] for EOPPE implementation based on a finite state machine)].

Object semantics captures the effects of transactions on objects. Transactional semantics captures the effect of a transaction on other transactions. Our mechanism captures both of them. Breakpoints provide a convenient way to specify and reason about the behaviour of concurrent transactions. A transaction can see the effect of another transaction on objects while they are executing. The ability to externalize uncommitted states is due to interleavings and commutativity rules. External visibility induced by breakpoints occurs at a point in time depending on breakpoint execution. The visibility induced by commutativity depends on commutativity matrix with respect to uncommitted operations.

4.1 Dependencies

Dependencies between transactions may thus be the result of the dynamic interactions of transactions over shared objects [BHG87]or the result of the user defined static structure properties of its steps [CR92]. The second type of dependencies is known as conflict. A transaction can perform a step on a shared or non-shared object without conflicting with another transaction if it is allowed to proceed by breakpoint specification or by commutativity rules. Roughly speaking, two steps conflict if their «semantic effects» on the state of an object or a transaction are not independent of their execution order. If operations conflict, then the order of the access to object implies dynamic dependencies between operations. Dependencies can express inter- (intra)-relationship structure between steps of (a) transaction(s). Intra-relationship can be a causal order of steps within a transaction [CR92] (Ex: the parent - child - siblings dependencies in a nested transaction). Dependencies can also provide a convenient way to specify and reason about the behaviour of concurrent transactions (inter-relationship). These two kinds of dependencies may be complicated but all kind of conflicts can be expressed in our model.

We assume that if two steps do not commute or cannot interleave, then the second operation must wait for the commit/abort of the first one before proceeding. It implicitly means that each object must understand Begin, Commit, Abort verbs.

We assume that we use DPL facilities that offer a mechanism which schedules operations upon EOPPE specifications. EOPPE specifications allow to express commutativity operations; our extension allows EOOPE to control both transactions semantics and object semantics. We do not address the way interleaving informations and commutativity are composed to form an EOOPE specification. EOPPE implementation remains transparent to our model. We assume that EOOPE is a black box performing the evaluation of the predicates and insertion/alteration of step within EOPPE sentences.

Roughly speaking, if a transactional operation (step) is issued, local concurrency manager (CM) intercepts all operations and schedules upon evaluation of EOPPE statements. The EOPPE is tested against requested, activated and terminated operations. EOPPE states change automatically if one of these actions occurs. The test may be covered by a short duration exclusive mode lock. This lock is released as soon as the predicate is tested and then made available to other evaluations. CM knows each objects' EOPPE in the local node. If a request is allowed to proceed, then it is sent to the object. A request is associated with the type of the request (step type) and the transaction Identity.

TABLE 2. Lock Compatibility

Granted Mode	Requested mode		
	unlock	locked	retained
unlock	+	+	+
locked	at the end of T	- ·	at the end of S
retained	at the end of T	+	-

We use three mode locks (see Table 2). If a lock is requested in one mode and granted to another step in a second mode, the lock request can be granted immediately if the two modes are compatible (+). If the modes are not compatible (-), then the new lock request must either wait for the first one to release its locks or wait for a given condition (ex: the end of T) to be true. «locked» mode is used to ensure indivisibility of steps; «retained» mode allows interleavings and commutative operations to be computed. A «retained» or «locked» mode lock becomes unlocked at the end of transaction execution; precisely after commit or abort. That is why unlock and retained/locked mode as shown in Table 1 are compatible only at the end of transactions execution. A «locked» mode becomes «retained» mode at the end of step execution. CM knows all steps state and associated EOPPE. EOPPE changes its states upon reception of req, act and term events of a step. If a step is allowed to proceed, then it is sent to the object which executes the operation as shown in Figure 4 .

FIGURE 4.   Concurrency Manager

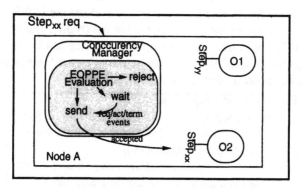

Each step is associated with a «status» structure described below.

---

status: <lock ;lock_type;Tid; EOPPE>

    lock: locked I unlocked I retained

    /* locked: a step has locked */

    /* retain: no step proceed but transaction have

                not yet finished */

    /* unlock: no step ask to proceed. */

    lock_type: Type (Step)

                /*a lock associate with the type of step */

    Tid: /*Transactions Id of invoker activity,

                transaction which retain a set of steps */.

    EOPPE: Path expression that express ordering constraints

based on commutativity and interleaving expressions.

When an operation (S_{xx}) is received by the CM, the CM executes the Test_to_proceed procedure. This procedure evaluates EOOPE in order to know if this (S_{xx}) operation can be performed. It answers by either processing the step, delaying it or advising to try later. A step can be executed even if a step is locked. This case could happen if a requested step commutes with another one that has not finished its step yet. In this case, S_{xx} must wait till the end of the current operation before proceeding. At the end of its execution the locked mode status is transformed into retained mode.

```
Procedure Test_to_proceed (Step;Tid)
   if (Test_eoppe (Step,Tid) == OK) then
      if (Step.status == <locked> then
      wait until Step.status == unlock or retained;
      step.status = <locked,Step,Tid,EOPPE>
      send Step;
      status = <retained,Step,Tid,EOPPE>;
   else test later;            /*NOK */
End Test_to_proceed
```

The Test_to_proceed function calls Test_eoppe to evaluate the EOPPE expression. It responds by either accepting the operation (OK) or not (NOK). The step is allowed to proceed in the following case: it has already used this step and left it in a «retained» mode. The step commutes (Co) with all the activity that used this step; the step can interleave with, due to breakpoint information (Ct).

```
Procedure Test_eoppe (Step,Tid)
   if ((Step.Status == <retained> and (Step.Tid == Tid ))
            /* transaction has already locked this Step */
      or ((Step,Tid) ∈ Ct(EOPPE))
               /* Step can interleave with ( ∈ breakpoint )*/
      or (Step.status == <retained> and (Step,Tid)
               ∈ Co(EOPPE) ) /*all retained Step commut */
   then return (OK)
   else return (NOK)
End Test_eoppe
```

Test_eoppe uses two functions Ct and Co that read the EOPPE specification. They return a path expressing allowed execution for a given step. Ct function tests if the current step can interleave with all active steps that have accessed the step. Ct represents the breakpoint test information expressed in EOPPE. Co function test if the current step can commute with all active steps that accessed the object. Co represents the commutativity test matrix expressed in EOPPE.

```
Procedure Ct(EOPPE;Step;Tid)
      return (interleaving control flow path allowed)
End Ct
```

```
Procedure Co(EOPPE;Step;Tid)
      return commutative control flow path allowed)
End Co
```

End_t performs the termination command of a transaction. It releases all locks retained by Tid.

```
Procedure End_T (Tid)
      Unlock all steps retained or locked by Tid
End End_T
```

When a CM receives a breakpoint, then CM composes the new path expression (EOPPE) with the older EOPPE specification. Note that a verification must be made during the composition of an EOPPE.

```
Procedure Breakpoint(Tid, {Path expressions})
    Step.status.I(EOPPE) = status.I(EOPPE) ∪ {Path expressions}
End Breakpoint
```

Note that we have discerned object semantics computation (Co(EOOPE)) and transaction semantics computation (Ct(EOPPE)) for the sake of simplicity.

Test_eoppe shows that if a step is «retained» by a transaction then an incoming step commuting with the owner of the lock may proceed. Commutativity can be implemented as a layered system architecture called multilevel transaction. Each layer of a multilevel transaction realizes a set of abstract operation, each represented by a set of lower level operations or states. Each layer sees operations or state transitions in the form of an atomic operation provided by the direct lower level. Synchronization may be achieved with two phases locking protocol applied to each layer to ensure serializability level by level (see [Weikum91] for more details). Specific typed locks are defined for each layer. The defined types capture the semantic of the step.

In Section 2 we assumed that steps must be executed atomically; the above algorithm locks the steps in a mutual exclusion manner when it is allowed to proceed. This assertion implies that our model behaves as a flat transaction. The above condition can be relaxed by using multi-level transactions. In fact a locked step may be composed of one ore more independent steps and there is no need to block all lower level steps to achieve atomicity to higher level steps.

In order to support multi-level transaction, the lock in «retained» mode must be associated with the type of the lock and the abstract level of the operation (Ex: Credit is at level 1 in Figure 1) in order to have a serializable execution level by level. A lock has the following structure.

retained	0 ... n	Credit
lock mode	Level	type lock

The field type lock is used to exploit compatibility matrix for expressing commutativity rules. Level and type lock are used to use multi-level mechanism.

5 Abort aspect

We use the recovery method for Multi-Level System (MLR) defined in [Lomet92] for tackling system failures within a top level transaction. Lomet uses compensation operation to «undo» the effect of an operation, the intra-transaction recovery is well-defined. As we said, each level uses a two phases locking protocol so that cascading abort is avoided in a multi-level system.

Interleaving rules may lead to cascading aborts. To avoid this effect we assume that the programmer can specify a backout sphere [Walter84] to limit the abort propagation among transactions. Dependencies formed by the interactions of transactions over a shared or non-shared object are determined by the objects' synchronization properties. These dependencies are expressed with path predicates.

Conclusion and future work

Our model is attractive because it allows to meet concurrency gained by exploiting transaction semantic while retaining the positive feature of exploiting operation commutativity. EOPPE is a synchronization tool that allows easy specification of common synchronization problems. The current version of DPL allows to control and restrict the set of correct schedule over a non distributed object. We are currently working on the following points: (1) A formal tool to prove that our model meets a given degree of correctness and avoid deadlocks. (2)A well formed algorithm to evaluate distributed unstable predicates. (3) An extension for DPL to support inheritance of path predicates.

The main drawbacks of our model are: (1) Evaluation of distributed predicates may be expensive. (There is a need to understand the performance implications of this specific point). (2) Insertion or alteration of steps or predicates within an interface may require a complete re-organization of EOPPE statements across objects involved in transaction.

It may be objected that our model is not realistic since it assumes that application programmers must know all step types and their associated conflicts that adhere to a transaction. It is realistic since steps may be considered as methods in an object-oriented model and all methods must be exported to a trader [ANSA91] to be used and composed by clients objects at will.

In this paper, we proposed a simple, flexible and powerful mechanism for specifying potential interleaving that may produce non serializable but semantically correct schedules. Another subtle implication of our model is that: giving rules about allowable steps interleavings at computation level implies no constraints on the way to schedules them. This is an advantage since we are free to use our favourite underlying concurrency control management (locking, timestamps, optimistic concurrency control etc...). Our model is suited to specify and control different degrees of semantic correctness at language level without re-organizing the supported infrastructure. Our correct schedule criterion contains a large number of schedules, including a set of serializable schedule. Full correctness (serializable) may be achieved by removing breakpoints in transaction specification. Our model also addresses temporal consistency since predicates may dynamically change over the time. New applications that need various styles of cooperations are not well supported by serializability theory. Serializability theory is specially designed to isolate concurrent activities rather than to make them cooperate. New emerging applications support more loosely defined correctness criteria requirements than they have in past. Our model is adapted to express these loose constraints. This observation has led to a new area of research, often based on object-oriented technology.

Acknowledgments.
I'm very grateful to S.Sedillot and F. Armand for their helpful comments.

References

[ANSA91]   «The ANSA Programmers' Manual» APM/RC.105.04 1991. «Concurrency Control» APM/RC.248.01 1991.

[BHG87]   A.Bernstein, V.Hadzilacos, N.Goodman «Concurrency Control and rRecovery in Database Systems».Addison-Wesley Publishing Co. 1987.

[CR92]   P.K.Chrysanthis, K.Ramamritham « ACTA: The SAGA Continues» in A.K Elmagarmid (Ed.) Database Transaction Models for Advanced Applications, Morgan Kaufmann 1992.

[FO89]   A.A.Farrag; M.T.Ozsu. «Using Semantic Knowledge of Transactions to Increase Concurrency,». ACM Transactions on Database Systems, Vol 14, No 4 December 1989.

[GR92]   J.Gray A.Reuter, "Transaction Processing, Concepts and Techniques" Morgan Kaufmann Edition. 1992.

[GS87]   Garcia-Molina, K. Salem «SAGAS» In Proceedings of ACM SIGMOD 1987 International Conference on Management of Data, San Francisco.

[HPR92]   M.Hurfin, N.Plouzeau, M.Raynal «Detecting Atomic Sequences of Predicates in Distributed Computations» TR 695 IRISA Rennes 1992.

[KKB88]   H.Korth, W.Kim, F. Bancilhon "On long Duration CAD Transactions. Information Science 1988.

[KP79]   H.T Kung, H.Papadimitrou. «An Optimal Theory of Concurrency Control for Databases». Proceedings of SIGMOD- ICMD - ACM 1979.

[KS88]   H.Korth, D.Speegle « Formal Model of Correctness Without Serializability» Proceedings ACM-SIGMOD 1988 International Conference on Management of Data - Chicago June 1988.

[Lomet91]   D.B Lomet. « MLR: A Recovery Method for Multi-level Systems». Technical Report CRL 91/7 Digital Cambridge Research Laboratory. July 1991.

[Lynch83]   N.Lynch «Multilevel Atomicity - A New Correctness Criterion for Database Concurrency Control». ACM Transactions on Database Systems, Vol 8 No 4 December 1983.

[Molina83]   H.Garcia-Molina «Using Semantic Knowledge for Transaction Processing in a Distributed Database». ACM Transactions on Database Systems, Vol 8 ,No2 December 1983.

[Moss81]   J. Moss. «Nested Transactions:An approach To Reliable Distributed Computing" MIT Laboratory for Computer Science, MIT/LCS/TR-260 1981.

[Walter84]   B. Walter «Nested Transaction with Multiple Commit Points: An Approach to the Structuring of Advanced Database Applications» Proceedings VLDB 84 Singapore 1984.

[Weihl88]   W. Weihl « Commutativity-Based Concurrency Control for Abstract Data Types». IEEE Transactions on Computers Vol37 No12 December 1988.

[Weikum91]   G. Weikum «Principles and Realization Strategies of Multilevel Transaction Management. ACM TODS Vol 16 No 1 1991.

[WA92]   M.H Wong, D.Agrawal « Tolerating Bounded Inconcistency for Increasing Concurrency in Database Systems». 11th Proc ACM SIGACT-SIGMOT-SIGART San Diego 1992.

A Reflective Invocation Scheme to Realise Advanced Object Management

Stijn Bijnens, Wouter Joosen and Pierre Verbaeten

Department of Computer Science
Celestijnenlaan 200A
B-3001 Leuven
Belgium

Abstract. The integration of the notion of distribution in an object-oriented language not only introduces a need for location independent object invocation but also has to cope with various object management operations. These meta-operations include object migration, object replication and granularity control. Additionally, in a multithreaded environment, the concurrency control specifications defined on an object by the application programmer must be realised correctly. Our object invocation scheme offers mechanisms for realising these management operations and concurrency control transparently. This scheme –based on reference objects– is generic in the sense that it can be extented to realise some additional object management operations currently not supported by our prototype. This prototype is realised in a C++ environment on various distributed memory platforms.

1 Introduction

This paper is a result of ongoing work in the XENOOPS project [BJMV91]. XENOOPS is an acronym for an 'eXecution ENvironment for Object-Oriented Parallel Software'. It is both a language and a system in the sense that it supports a uniform object model for developing applications on a distributed memory platform. The basic goal of the XENOOPS project is to develop an object-oriented environment which offers automatic support for load balancing and fault tolerance by means of reusable class libraries which incorporate different strategies [JBV93a, JBV93b]. Although XENOOPS focuses on parallel applications, the issues described in this paper are related to distribution and are applicable to distributed applications in the broad sense.

Object-oriented distributed programming requires an extension of the object-oriented paradigm with distribution and concurrency issues, which have to be combined with the notions of data abstraction, encapsulation, modularity and hierarchy [1] (e.g. as in inheritance).

This paper is structured as follows. First we will describe the application programming interface. In section three, we will introduce the advanced object

---

[1] Data abstraction, encapsulation, modularity and hierarchy are considered to be the major elements of the object model [Boo91] while distribution and concurrency are not essential for the object-oriented approach.

management operations currently supported by the environment and used by the load balancing and fault tolerance facility. Section four will describe the concepts behind our object invocation scheme. An invocation results in a reflective computation which transparently determines the actions required to perform the invocation in a distributed environment. In section five we will describe the internals of the invocation system and in section six we will indicate how it realises transparency and dynamic behaviour. Then, in section seven, we will describe the realisation of the concurrency control specifications. Finally, we will compare our work with related research projects.

2 The Application Programmers Interface (API)

The major characteristic of the API is the fact that it explicitly supports concurrency but hides distribution. The API offers a global object space and some *simple* object management operations. These meta-operations take care of object creation and object destruction. A global object space hides distribution by means of location independent object invocation. This concept offers to the application programmer the abstraction of a uniform transparent object universe and hides the idiosyncratics of the message passing primitives of the underlying distributed memory architecture.

Concurrency is introduced by active objects and by asynchronous object invocations. An active object has at least one own thread of control to realise some autonomous behaviour; it can take the *initiative* for sending messages to other objects (invoke operations). A C++ language extension is introduced for the realisation of asynchronous invocation (overloading of invocation operator) and for concurrency control specifications[BJP+93]. This paper will only focus on the *realisation* of the concurrency control and not on the formalism for specifying the concurrency control [2]. The ideal formalism has still got to be discovered due to the inheritance anomaly; this issue has been described extensively in [MY91].

3 Advanced Object Management

Our system offers automatic support for load balancing and fault tolerance. An application can be developed without knowing of the existence of these system facilities. Then, the application can be *plugged* into the framework (Figure 1).

The system offers a hierarchy of load balancing and fault tolerance policies [JBV93a, JBV93b]. These policies can be specialised by the advanced system programmer. The realisation of these policies is based on the availability of some advanced object management operations. Basically, *object migration* offers the opportunity to transfer objects between address spaces at run time in case of a work imbalance. In addition, another object management function –granularity control– is provided. *Granularity control* involves the splitting and joining of

[2] At the moment, Xenoops uses synchronisation counters[SMV+90] but we're looking at some alternatives.

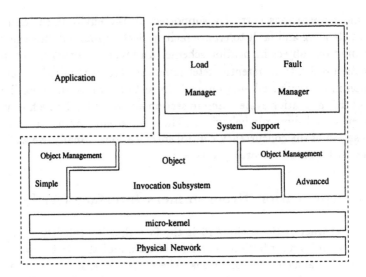

Fig. 1. Overview

objects that represent a particular amount of *work* [3] and can be used as a mechanism –in cooperation with object migration– for re-establishing the ideal work load distribution.

Object replication provides copies of objects on different nodes in the distributed system. The Replicate() meta-operation on an object will create replicas of that object on different nodes and increases the reliability of the system. Different policies for consistency between these replicas can be implemented in the fault tolerance facility. Exploiting active replication, an invocation on a replicated object will lead to the execution of the invoked operation on all the replicas. This technique can lead to strict consistency between replicas using appropriate invocation protocols (e.g. based on reliable broadcast). On the other hand, using passive replication, the invoked operation will only be executed on a single (active) replica. The other (passive) replicas need to be made consistent using some update protocol.

4   The Object Invocation Subsystem

The invocation system has to realise: (1) location transparency, (2) migration transparency, (3) granularity control transparency and (4) replication transparency. In addition, it must also realise the concurrency control specifications.

Messages between objects in the global object space will be reified using reference objects (Figure 2). Message reification is a powerful concept in object-orientation to be able to perform computations in a distributed environment. Every interaction between application objects will be transparently intercepted

---

[3] The application programmer must provide some *hints*: he must provide an operation *GetLoad()*.

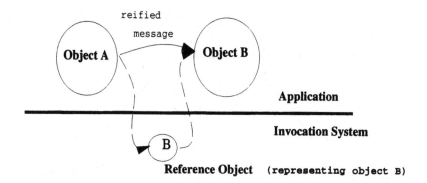

Fig. 2. Message Reification

by reference objects which reside in the object invocation subsystem. These reference objects perform computations on object invocations.

These reference objects realise the various kinds of transparency and concurrency control. For example, location independent object invocation can be realised by a reference object which acts as a proxy in the address space of the invoker.

Depending on the *kind of* object the reference object represents, it must take the appropriate action upon an invocation. The basic skeleton of the algorithm performed by a reference object upon intercepting an invocation is:

1. What 'kind of' object do I represent ? (reification)
2. What action do I have to perform knowing that I reference a particular *kind of* object ? (reflective computation)
3. Does the concurrency control specification allow the invocation on the object I represent ?
4. – If NO : wait.
   – If YES : delegate the invocation towards the object.

A reference object can change its behaviour via the *Become()* operation [4]. The behaviour of a reference object must change dynamically if the behaviour of the represented object changes. This happens if a management operation (meta-operation) is invoked on the object; e.g. migration, granularity control or replication.

5 Realisation

A polymorphic function call realises the dynamic behaviour of reference objects. For example, location transparency is achieved by applying the inheritance relationship to define the LocalReference and RemoteReference classes (Figure 3).

---

[4] Inspired by the Actor model [Agh]

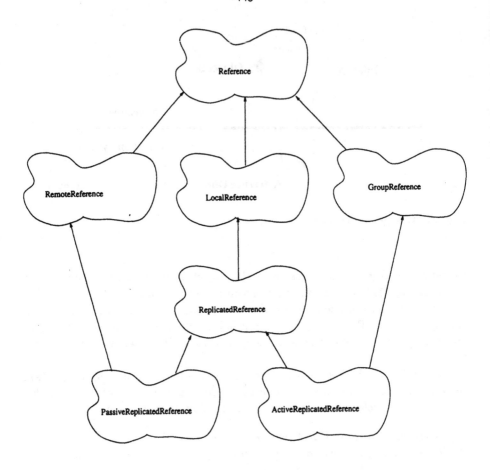

Fig. 3. Reference Class Hierarchy

These are both specialisations of the Reference class, with a different implementation of the operations. Remote references are objects that cause the use of OS kernel communication software to use the physical network. For a given object, the distinction between a local and remote peer object is transparent because they will both be addressed using the more general reference object. In Figure 4, the following scenario is represented:

1. Object A performs an invocation on object B. Object B resides at this moment in A's address space. This invocation will be reified by a reference object of type LocalReference.
2. This reference object will delegate the invocation –after satisfying the concurrency control specification– towards object B.
3. Object B invokes an operation on object C. Object C resides in another address space. This invocation will be reified by a RemoteReference object.

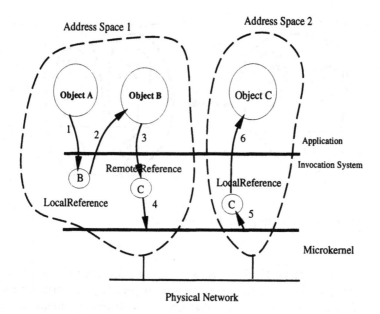

Fig. 4. An Example

4. This reference object will use kernel communication software to transfer the invocation to the address space of object C. A RemoteReference object knows the location of the address space of the application object it represents. Internally, remote address spaces are represented by *port* objects [5].

5. The invocation message will be delivered to a LocalReference object representing object C in C's address space.

6. This LocalReference object will delegate the invocation –after satisfying the concurrency control specification– towards object C.

The invocation system also supports transparent group invocation. A reference object instantiated from the GroupReference class can represent a group of objects. The application objects, which constitute the group, can be in the same address space or not. The action upon an invocation on a group will delegate the invocation towards the members of the group. Delegated invocations towards the member objects are again reified by reference objects. These reference objects can be of any type (RemoteReference, LocalReference,...). Thus, group invocation and remote invocation are two orthogonal concepts. Different kinds of group invocation protocols exist [BSS91]. These different protocols can be integrated within our framework by specialising the GroupReference class into different subclasses, each implementing a particular protocol (e.g reliable multicast, atomic multicast,...).

---

[5] Almost all micro-kernels offer a port based communication abstraction [BGJ+92, RAA+92].

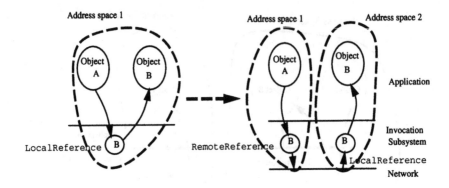

Fig. 5. Before and After migration of object B

In conclusion, one particular invocation can be forwarded by a *chain* of reference objects. In figure 4, the invocation on object C performed by object B will be reified by two reference objects; first by a RemoteReference object and then by a LocalReference object. In order to achieve the best performance, the invocation system has to keep this chain as short as possible.

Only a reference object instantiated from the LocalReference class (or its descendents) provides concurrency control, for a reference object of this type is always the last reference object in the invocation chain.

6 Advanced Object Management Revisited

The Reference class hierarchy and the ability of reference objects to change their behaviour dynamically, realises several object management operations. A reference object can change its behaviour via the *Become()* operation.

– Object migration will be fully transparent for the application developer: the Become(RemoteReference) will be invoked on the reference object at the old location and the Become(LocalReference) will be invoked on the reference object at the new location. In figure 5, object B migrates to another address space. Invocations performed by object A will transparently be forwarded to object B's new location. If, at a particular moment, object B migrates again, we have the situation illustrated in figure 6. At this moment, the invocation chain is not optimal (3 indirections). The RemoteReference object in object A's address space only knows the old location [6]. This reference object will only know the new location after object A has performed a new invocation on object B. This invocation will go via the RemoteReference object in address space 2. This reference object will detect the non optimal situation and will inform the reference object in object A's address space by sending the new location of object B. All future invocations will go via the shortest chain.

---

[6] For efficiency reasons, the invocation system uses a lazy location update protocol.

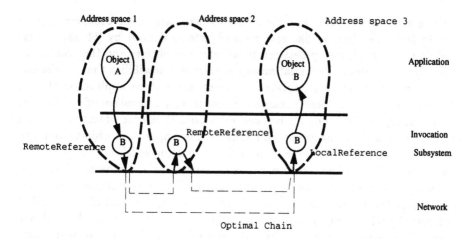

Fig. 6. Object B migrates again, the chain of reference objects has to be shortened

- Granularity control is made transparent by means of the group invocation facility: the Become(GroupReference) will be invoked on the LocalReference object that resides in the same address space as the application object that will be *split*. This reference objects will forward all invocations –which were meant to go to the original coarser grained object– to all finer-grained, newly created application objects.
- Replication is made transparent because invocations towards a replicated application object are reified by reference objects of descendents of type ReplicatedReference. A ReplicatedReference class is derived from a Local-Reference class because there is a need to provide concurrency control (section 7): a ReplicatedReference always has an application object in its address space –although it may be a replica. The two specialisations of the ReplicatedReference class offer opportunities to implement different replication policies. For example, if an application objects must be replicated, Become(ActiveReplicatedReference) will be invoked on the LocalReference object. A reference object of type ActiveReplicatedReference is also a GroupReference (multiple inheritance), this way an invocation will be forwarded to all replicas.

The Become() operation is atomic and is implemented as the creation of a new reference object of the appropriate type at the same memory location (*placed new* in C++).

7 Concurrency control

The most complex reference object is the LocalReference object (and its descendants) because they delegate the invocation towards the application objects in the global object space, and they have to take care of the concurrency control. In fact, they behave like real meta-objects as defined by [Mae87]. There exists a causal relationship between these reference objects and the application object they represent. This relationship enables the possibility that a reference object can observe and manipulate the internal state of the application objects. This way we can transparently realise the concurrency control specifications very easily and efficiently. Upon an invocation, a LocalReference object performs a pre-action, delegates the invocation towards the application object, and performs a post-action if the execution of the invocation finishes. The pre-action has to check whether the concurrency control specifications allow the delegation of the invocation towards the application object. To realise this, the pre-action will inspect the internal state [7] of the object. Thus, a LocalReference object performs the scheduling of method invocations for the application object it represents. The post-action will register the end of the invocation and will trigger the delegation of some blocked invocations. Only those invocations for which the concurrency control specifications are satisfied will be triggered.

8 Current Status

Currently, the prototype is implemented on:

- A cluster of DEC Alpha workstations on top of the Mach Microkernel [BGJ+92] (in an OSF/1 environment). Mach Kernel threads are used to realise active objects and asynchronous object invocation. Network communication happens via the NetMsgServer (user space).
- A Transputer system running helios. Both threads and network communication are realised within this port-based micro-kernel.
- A SUN4 cluster running SUNOS. Active object are realised with user-space threads, network communication happens via UDP-ports.

Applications prototyped within our project are in the area of computational fluid dynamics, molecular dynamics simulation and exhaustive search problems, like the Traveling Salesman Problem [MR88] and parallel chess. The performance evaluation of a parallel iterative Red/Black SOR (successive over-relaxation) solver with adaptive local grid refinement on top of the XENOOPS prototype has shown its applicability. Performance results are reported in [BJV94].

9 Related Work

Object-oriented approaches are applied to a variety of application domains in the computer science area. Although object-orientation has been identified as the most promising structuring paradigm for operating systems, little work has been done on execution environments in parallel computing systems. Our design

---

[7] This causal relation is implemented using the *friend* statement in C++.

of the execution environment will rely on experience with object-oriented distributed operating systems, object-oriented language systems and micro-kernel technology. This paragraph presents a survey of object-orientation in operating systems; we will emphasise object invocation and the offered object management functions (e.g. migration).

- SOS [SGH+89] is an object-oriented operating system. The system implements object migration; this mechanism is generic, but can be tailored to specific object semantics thanks to the prerequisite and upcall concepts. SOS supports Fragmented Objects (FOs). A Fragmented Object is a group of Elementary Objects which can be located in several contexts, on different sites; its representation is the union of the local *fragments*. A fragment acts as a proxy, i.e., a local interface to the FO. A proxy is a local representation of a remote object or server. SOS implements generic mechanisms for object management, such as migration, identification, location, storage, naming, and communication.

- Choices [CJR87] is a family of operating systems; it embodies the notion of a customised operating system that is tailored for particular hardware configurations and for particular applications. Choices views all entities in a system as objects that belong to a class hierarchy. The Choices programming interface is built using proxy objects. Proxy objects provide indirection and late run-time binding for objects that cannot be accessed directly from an application (e.g., remote or kernel objects). A method invocation on a proxy results in a corresponding method invocation on the object it represents. Choices object management functionality is rather conventional; there exists no support for object migration within the kernel.

- Emerald [RTL91] is a programming language as well as a run-time system that supports location-independent operations on objects. The Emerald compiler transforms the user-defined object representation: its first few bytes are a standard descriptor. Conceptually, all objects live in a single, network-wide address space. An object reference is global, but a local reference is optimised into a pointer. Emerald objects can move at any time, even while invocations are executing inside them. Emerald can be considered as one of the most advanced object-oriented distributed system since it offers advanced object management support within a uniform object model.

- COOL [HMA90] (the Chorus Object-Oriented Layer) uses the distributed virtual memory system in Chorus. COOL enables objects to be migrated between two machines. Although coupled with remote invocation, object migration is carried out by mapping and unmapping virtual memory segments on different machines.

- The Muse distributed operating system [YTM+91], and its successor Apertos [Yok92], provides an open and self-advancing dynamic environment. Muse provides reflective computing that presents facilities for self-modifying an object with its environment. Objects reside in the context of a collection of meta-objects to handle dynamic system behaviour and to provide an optimal execution environment for the object.

One of the advantages of our prototype is the fact that it does not need a compiler extension (like SOS) or a complete new compiler (like Emerald). This increases the portability as it only needs a C++ compiler. This is a prerequisite if one wants to run parallel applications on an idiosyncratic platform.

From the view point of efficiency one could argue that the reification of an invocation between two application objects in the same address space is inefficient because all invocations happen via an indirection (LocalReference object). In our opinion a LocalReference object is not inefficient; the indirection introduced by the LocalReference is needed anyway to realise the concurrency control specification.

The transparent interception of object invocations by the run-time environment has been reported in several research papers. Encapsulators [Pas86] are an extension of Smalltalk-80 to perform a pre-action and a post-action upon an invocation. This concept is extented by [GGM93] to incorporate distribution and replication. Composition filters, another mechanism for message reification, is proposed in [AWB+93]. In this approach, the basic object model is extented by introducing input and output composition filters that effect the received and sent invocations respectively. Meta-level (or reflective) techniques have been applied in various domains and they are still an active area of research. In CLOS MOP [GKB91] a meta-level technique is applied to a practical language: all specifications are modifiable. Another reflective language system is ABCL/R2. This language applies a meta-level technique to parallel computations.

10 Conclusion

An efficient and reliable global object space is realised by an advanced object invocation system. Message reification is used to intercept all object invocations transparently. This interception enables the run-time environment to forward all invocation to the appropriate application objects at the appropriate time (correct concurrency control). Message reification is implemented by universal reference objects. These objects offer full transparency of various advanced object management operations: object migration, object replication and granularity control.

The invocation system is part of XENOOPS; an environment to develop object oriented parallel applications on distributed memory machines. XENOOPS offers automatic support for load balancing and fault tolerance.

Acknowledgements

This text presents research results of the Belgian Incentive Program "Information Technology" - Computer Science of the future, initiated by the Belgian State - Prime Minister's Service - Science Policy Office. The scientific responsibility is assumed by its authors. Our research has also been sponsored by the ESPRIT Parallel Computing Action and N.F.W.O project S2/5 - CL.D709.

References

[Agh]   G. Agha. *ACTORS: A Model of Concurrent Computation in Distributed Systems.* The MIT Press series in artificial intelligence.

[AWB+93] M. Askit, K. Wakita, J. Bosch, L. Bergmans, and A. Yonezawa. Abstracting Object Interactions Using Composition Filters. In *Proceedings of the ECOOP'93 Workshop on Object BasedDistributed Programming*, July 1993.

[BGJ+92] David L. Black, David B. Golub, Daniel P. Julin, Richard F. Rashid, Richard P. Draves, Randall W. Dean, Allessandro Forin, Joseph Barrera, Hideyuki Tokuda, Gerald Malan, and David Bohman. Microkernel Operating system Architecture and Mach. In *Proceedings of the Usenix Workshop on Micro-kernels and Other Architectures*, pages 11–30. USENIX association, April 1992.

[BJMV91] Y. Berbers, W. Joosen, H. Moons, and P. Verbaeten. The XENOOPS Project. In *Proceedings of the 1991 International Workshop on Object-Orientation in Operating Systems*, pages 144–146, October 1991.

[BJP+93] Stijn Bijnens, Wouter Joosen, Jan Pollet, Yolande Berbers, and Pierre Verbaeten. Active Objects, Message Passing and Concurrency Control in XENOOPS. In *Proceedings of the TOOLS EUROPE'93 Workshop on Distributed Objects and Concurrency*, March 1993.

[BJV94]   Stijn Bijnens, Wouter Joosen, and Pierre Verbaeten. Observation of a Global Object Space on a Distributed Memory Machine. In *Proceedings of 27th Hawaii International Confererence on System Science.* IEEE, to be published, January 1994.

[Boo91]   Grady Booch. *Object-Oriented Design with Applications.* Benjamin/Cummings, 1991.

[BSS91]   Kenneth Birman, Andre Schiper, and Pat Stephenson. Lightweight causal and atomic group multicast. *ACM Transactions on Computer Systems*, 9(3):272–314, August 1991.

[CJR87]   R. Campbell, G. Johnston, and V. Russo. Choices (Class Hierarchical Open Interface for Custom Embedded Systems). *ACM Operating Systems Review*, 21:9–17, July 1987.

[GGM93]   B. Garbinato, R. Guerraoui, and K. Mazouni. Distributed Programming Using Two Orthogonal Object Levels. In *Proceedings of the ECOOP'93 Workshop on Object BasedDistributed Programming*, July 1993.

[GKB91]   J. des Rivieres G. Kiczales and D. G. Bobrow. *The Art of the Metaobject Protocol.* The MIT Press, 1991.

[HMA90]   Sabine Habert, Laurence Mosseri, and Vadim Abrossimov. COOL: Kernel support for object-oriented environments. *SIGPLAN Notices*, (25):269–277, 1990.

[JBV93a] Wouter Joosen, Stijn Bijnens, and Pierre Verbaeten. Reusable Load Balancing Software for Distributed Memory Applications. Technical report, Department of Computer Science, KULEUVEN, January 1993.

[JBV93b] Wouter Joosen, Stijn Bijnens, and Pierre Verbaeten. Reusable Load Balancing Software for Parallel Search Problems. *The Euromicro Journal*, 38:205–212, September 1993.

[Mae87]   P. Maes. Computational Reflection. Technical Report TR-87-2, Vrije Universiteit Brussel, 1987.

[MR88] E. Maehle and J. Rost. Implementation of a parallel branch-and-bound algorithm for the travelling salesman problem. In *CONPAR 88*. Cambridge University Press, 1988.

[MY91] Satochi Matsuoka and Akinori Yonezawa. Analysis of the Inheritance Anomaly in Object-Oriented Concurrent Programming. Technical report, Dept. of Information Science, University of Tokyo, 1991.

[Pas86] Geoffrey Pascoe. Encapsulators: A New Software Paradigm in Smalltalk-80. In *Proceedings of OOPSLA'86*, pages 341–346. ACM, September 1986.

[RAA+92] M. Rozier, V. Abbrossimov, F. Armand, I. Boule, M. Gien, M. Guillemont, F. Herrman, C. Kaiser, S. Langlois, P. Leonard, and W. Neuhauser. Overview of the Chorus Distributed Operating System. In *Proceedings of the Usenix Workshop on Micro-kernels and Other Architectures*, pages 39–69. USENIX association, April 1992.

[RTL91] Rajendra K. Ray, Ewan Tempero, and Henry M. Levy. Emerald: A General-Purpose Programming Language. *Software: Practice and Experience*, 21(1):91–92, January 1991.

[SGH+89] Marc Shapiro, Yvon Gourhant, Sabine Habert, Laurence Mosseri, Michel Ruffin, and Celine Valot. SOS: An Object-Oriented Operating System - Assessment and Perspectives. *Computing Systems*, 2(2):287–337, Fall 1989.

[SMV+90] S.Krakowiak, M.Meysembourg, H.Nguyen Van, M.Riveill, C.Roison, and X. Rousset de Pina. Design and Implementation of an Object-Oriented, Strongly Typed Language for Distributed Applications. *JOOP*, pages 11–21, October 1990.

[Yok92] Y. Yokoto. The Apertos Reflective Operating System: The Concept and Its Implementation. In *Proceedings of Object-Oriented Programming Systems, Languages and Applications.*, October 1992.

[YTM+91] Y. Yokote, F. Teraoka, A. Mitsuzawa, N. Fujinami, and M. Tokoro. The Muse Object Architecture: A New Operating System Structuring Concept. *ACM Operating System Review*, 25(2):22–46, April 1991.

Abstracting Object Interactions Using Composition Filters

Mehmet Aksit[1], Ken Wakita[2], Jan Bosch[1], Lodewijk Bergmans[1] and Akinori Yonezawa[3]

[1]TRESE project, Department of Computer Science, University of Twente, P.O. Box 217, 7500 AE Enschede, The Netherlands.
email: {aksit, bosch, bergmans}@cs.utwente.nl
[2]Department of Information Science, Tokyo Institute of Technology, 2-12-1 Oh-okayama, Meguro-ku, Tokyo, 152, Japan. email: wakita@is.titech.ac.jp
[3]Dept. of Information Science - Faculty of Science- University of Tokyo, Hongo, Bunkyo-ku, Tokyo 113 Japan. email: yonezawa@is.s.u-tokyo.ac.jp

Abstract

It is generally claimed that object-based models are very suitable for building distributed system architectures since object interactions follow the *client-server* model. To cope with the complexity of today's distributed systems, however, we think that high-level linguistic mechanisms are needed to effectively structure, abstract and reuse object interactions. For example, the conventional object-oriented model does not provide high-level language mechanisms to model layered system architectures. Moreover, we consider the message passing model of the conventional object-oriented model as being too low-level because it can only specify object interactions that involve two partner objects at a time and its semantics cannot be extended easily. This paper introduces *Abstract Communication Types* (ACTs), which are objects that abstract interactions among objects. ACTs make it easier to model layered communication architectures, to enforce the invariant behavior among objects, to reduce the complexity of programs by hiding the interaction details in separate modules and to improve reusability through the application of object-oriented principles to ACT classes. We illustrate the concept of ACTs using the composition filters model.

1. Introduction

The dynamic semantics of object-oriented languages are based on the *message passing* mechanism. A message is a request for an object to carry out one of the object's operations. Since objects can only communicate by sending messages, message passing is the basic means for creating executions in the system.

To cope with the complexity of today's distributed systems, we think that high-level linguistic mechanisms are needed to effectively structure, abstract and reuse object interactions.

Originating from the construction of operating systems, large distributed systems are structured in terms of vertical layers. Functionally, each layer communicates with its peer-level layer, although physical data exchange occurs with the adjacent layers. The conventional object-oriented model does not provide high-level language mechanisms to model layered system architectures. Moreover, we consider the message passing model of conventional object-oriented languages as being too low-level because it can only specify communications that involve two partner objects at a time and its semantics cannot be extended easily. Mechanisms like inheritance and delegation only support the construction and behavior of objects but not the abstraction of communication among objects. These mechanisms therefore fail in abstracting patterns of messages and larger scale synchronization among objects.

We have applied the *composition filters* model to abstract communications among objects. In this approach, the basic object model is extended *modularly* by introducing *input* and *output composition filters* that affect the received and sent messages respectively. This mechanism enables software engineers to abstract communications among objects into a first-class object called *abstract communication type*[1] (ACT). ACTs make it easier to model layered architectures, to enforce the invariant behavior among objects, to reduce the complexity of programs by hiding the interaction details and to improve reusability through the application of object-oriented principles to ACT classes.

This paper is organized as follows. The next section describes the problems in object-oriented modeling which form the motivation for abstracting inter-object communications. Section 3 studies the background and related work, including the composition filters model. Section 4 first gives a list of requirements to effectively integrate communication abstractions with the object-oriented model. It then introduces ACTs and explains how ACTs can be expressed using composition-filters. Section 5 presents examples in 3 categories: examples of inter-object invariant behavior, inter-object synchronization, and coordinated behavior. Section 6 evaluates the ACT concept as presented and gives conclusions.

2. The Problem Statement

The conventional object models lack support for abstracting object interactions. This reveals itself through a number of problems that are encountered in object oriented software development:

1. Lack of Support for Meta-levels and Reflection:

   Assume for example that object *A* sends a message to a remote object *B* by executing the message statement

   B.moveTo(X, Y);

---

[1] The term abstract communication type is derived from abstract data type and may refer to both objects and classes. Terms ACT object and ACT class will be used to refer to an object or class respectively.

For *A*, the details of this execution are abstracted. However, in reality, this message must be intercepted by the underlying layer to determine, for example, the physical location of the *receiver* of the message.

From the object-oriented modeling perspective, this requires reflection[2] of messages. In message reflection, the so-called *message reification* operation allows the meta-layer to process the explicit representation of the reified message [Barber 89].

Conventional object-oriented methods [Booch 90, Coad&Yourdon 91a, Coad&Yourdon 91b, Champeaux 91, Rumbaugh 91] do not provide support for reflective system development. Conventional object-oriented languages (such as C++) provide only a limited or ad-hoc reflection [Madany et al. 92].

2. *Complexity and Lack of Reusability*: The manageability of programs is affected by the complexity of interactions among modules. In object-oriented programs, the code for describing the interactions is distributed over the participating objects. This causes a mixture of functional and interaction related code, which affects both maintainability and extensibility.

Different classes may adopt identical patterns of communication and synchronization. Similarly, a single class might participate in various patterns of communication. Thus, hardcoding the interaction patterns in a class severely reduces the reusability (of the class itself, and of the interaction code). Especially reuse through extension (subclassing) is an important issue.

3. *Enforcing invariant behavior:* If the code that implements the invariant behavior is distributed over a number of objects, verifying the invariants is far from trivial. A single module that explicitly represents the interaction between objects is an attractive approach for ensuring the invariant behavior of this interaction.

---

[2] A reflective system is a system which incorporates models representing (aspects of) itself. This self representation is *casually connected* to the reflected entity, and therefore, makes it possible for the system to answer questions about itself and support actions on itself. Reflective computation is the behavior exhibited by a reflective system. The term reflection was introduced by [Smith 82] as a technique to structure and organize self-modifying procedures and functions. In [Maes 87] reflection was applied within the object-oriented framework. Recently a considerable amount of work has been done in object-oriented reflection, for example, in concurrent programming [Ichisugi et al. 92], operating system structuring [Yokote 92], compiler design [Lamping et al. 92] and real-time programming [Honda&Tokoro 92].

3. Background and Related Work

This section describes the background and related work for ACTs. It consists of two main sections: in the first section the related work in analysis and design, and programming models is described. In the second section the composition-filters model is explained. We will apply the composition-filters model for expressing and illustrating ACTs.

3.1. Related Work in Object Interactions

This section describes the work that has been done with respect to object interactions. We first describe the attention that object-oriented analysis and design methods pay to modeling object interactions, and then one specific modeling approach, *Contracts*. Then we discuss two programming models, respectively *Scripts* and reflective computation, how they can be applied for abstracting object interactions.

Object-Oriented Analysis and Design Methods

Most object-oriented analysis and design methods model interactions among objects, usually after identifying *inheritance* and *part-of relations*. Different terms are used to express object interactions such as *object diagrams* [Booch 90], *process model* [Champeaux 91], *message connections* [Coad&Yourdon 91a], *data-flow diagrams* [Rumbaugh 91] and *collaboration graphs* [Wirfs-Brock et al. 90]. The Demeter system [Lieberherr et al. 91] is a Computer-Aided Software Engineering (CASE) environment which provides a tool to generate repeated operations called *propagation patterns*. In addition, the Demeter system incorporates a design rule for minimizing interactions between objects [Lieberherr&Holland 89][3]. Object-Oriented Design by Coad and Yourdon [Coad&Yourdon 91b] introduces a *task management* component which aims at defining object interactions.

Object-oriented analysis and design methods model interactions among objects in a way similar to object-oriented languages. Basically, they define graph structures that represent execution threads and therefore these methods have the same limitations as programming languages. The *task management* component [Coad&Yourdon 91b] can be considered as a module to model object interactions. In this method, however, there is no emphasis on using these constructs for this purpose. Moreover, it does not provide solutions to the problems as presented in section 2.1.

---

[3]   *Contracts* were developed as a part of the research activities related to the Demeter system.

Contracts

In the area of object-oriented modeling, the idea of specifying object interactions as an explicit module is applied by *contracts*[4] [Helm et al. 90, Holland 92]. Contracts are used to specify the *contractual obligations* that a set of *participants* must satisfy. It is possible to *refine* a contract in order to make it more specific and it is possible to *include* existing contracts in a new contract. In its first version [Helm et al. 90] a declarative language was introduced to define contractual obligations. In the second version [Holland 92], however, a procedural language was adopted instead of a declarative one. In the following we refer only to the second version of contracts.

A contract specification includes the specification of the participating objects, the contractual obligations of all participants, the invariants to be maintained by the participants and the method which instantiates a contract.

A contract can be seen as an *abstract class*, defining both abstract and concrete methods for its participants. The abstract methods must be provided by the participants themselves. The concrete methods of the contract (or its refinement) override the concrete implementations of the participants. A contract may also define variables that are shared by all the participants. In order to put a contract to use, a conformance declaration must be made which initializes the contract with actual participants. Obviously, these participants have to satisfy the contractual obligations of the contract. An object may participate in several contracts. Contracts offer two alternatives: either the methods are implemented at the contract specification, or they are distributed over the participating classes.

Contracts are primarily targeted as a design tool. Contracts are quite useful for the implementation of coordinated behavior and the abstraction of object interactions but are unable to reflect upon the actual message interactions between objects for purposes such as monitoring and manipulating messages. Contracts are treated differently from normal classes. Contracts also do not address concurrency and synchronization issues.

Scripts

A language construct called *scripts* [Francez 86] was introduced to abstract patterns of messages into a module. A script is a parameterized program section in which processes *enrol* in order to participate. The concept of *enrolment* is similar to the subroutine call mechanism whereby the execution of the role in a given script instance is a logical continuation of the enrolling process. A script consists of formal process parameters called *roles*, data parameters and a concurrent program section called the *body*. Processes can enrol in scripts by means of *enrol in* statements.

Scripts are program modules and do not provide mechanisms for object-oriented computing. Scripts, for example, do not allow users of the system to create several

---

4   Apart from the object-oriented language Sina.

instances belonging to the same communication module. Inheritance or delegation mechanisms are also not defined for scripts thereby resulting in a less systematic reuse of communication abstractions.

Reflective Computation

In principle, languages that provide full reflection are able to represent object interactions. However, full reflective languages have complicated semantics and may bring unnecessary additional complexity. One particular example of a restricted reflective language is MAUD [Agha et al. 92]. Each object in MAUD owns three meta-objects called a *dispatcher*, a *mail queue* and *acquaintances*. The sent and received messages are handled by the dispatcher and mail queue objects respectively. The acquaintances object contains a list of objects that may be addressed by its owner object. In the MAUD language, one can implement coordinated behavior by replacing the meta-objects with the objects implementing the required protocol. To install a protocol for an object the original mail queue and dispatcher must be replaced by a pair implementing the required protocol.

In MAUD, a shared protocol among objects is implemented by mail queues and dispatchers. Coordinated behavior is distributed among mail queue and dispatcher objects which are added to all participating objects. Therefore designers cannot define and reuse coordinated behavior as a single entity.

Apertos is an object-oriented reflective operating system [Yokote 92] designed for open and mobile computing environments. Apertos introduces object/metaobject separation in the operating system design. An object is associated with a group of metaobjects and a metaobject defines the semantics of its object. An object can change its metaobject (or group of metaobjects) by migration. Although Apertos provides a general reflective system framework, it does not emphasize abstraction and reuse of interactions among objects.

3.2. The Composition Filters Model

We will first briefly introduce the components of the composition-filters object model and then present them in greater detail later. This computation model is adopted by the Sina language[5]. In Sina, operations and local variables are called *methods* and *instance variables*, respectively. As illustrated by Figure 1, a composition-filter object consists of two parts: an *interface* and an *implementation* part. The interface part deals with incoming and outgoing messages. It consists of one or more *input*

---

[5] The early version of the Sina language was published in [Aksit&Tripathi 88, Tripathi&Aksit 88, Aksit et al. 91]. This version introduced only a simple filter mechanism which was then called *predicates*. The recent version of the language was published [Aksit et al. 92, Bergmans et al. 92]. These publications did not address the issues related to abstract communication types. The preliminary version of ACTs was first published in [Aksit 89a].

and *output filters*, optional *internal* and *external* objects and *method header* declarations.

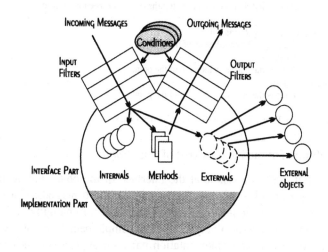

Figure 1. The interface components of the composition-filters object model.

Filters are controlled by *conditions*[6]. Filter names, method headers and condition names can be made visible to the *clients* of the object, however, their implementations are defined in the implementation part and invisible. In Figure 1, a possible effect of the input filters is shown. If a message passes through the input filters it can be further delegated to internal objects, methods or external objects. In addition, Figure 1 depicts the effect of output filters on the outgoing messages. All the messages that originate from method executions within the object and are sent to objects that are outside the boundaries of the current object pass through the output filters. Without filters, our model is very similar to the conventional object model.

The implementation part contains method definitions, instance variable declarations, definitions of conditions and an optional initialization operation. The implementation part is fully encapsulated within the object.

The Interface Part

As an example of a simple class consider the interface part of class *Point*. We present our examples following the Sina language notation.

---

[6] In [Aksit et al. 92] conditions were called *states*.

```
class Point interface
    comment This class implements a graphical point;
    conditions
        Initialized;        // this condition is only valid after the object has been initialized
    methods
        moveTo(Integer, Integer) returns Nil;
                            // changes the coordinates of the point
        getX returns Integer;
                            // reads the current x location of the point
        getY returns Integer;
                            // reads the current y location of the point
    inputfilters
        disp : Dispatch = { True=>inner.moveTo, Initialized => inner.* };
end;
```

Figure 2. Definition of the interface part of class *Point*.

The methods that are to be visible at the interface of the object are declared in the interface part by *method headers* following the keyword methods. Class *Point*, for instance, declares the methods *moveTo*, *getX* and *getY* for changing and reading the coordinates of the point respectively. The actual implementations of these methods are encapsulated within the implementation part. An appropriate message must be sent to an instance of class *Point* to invoke one of these methods.

An input filter specifies conditions for message acceptance or rejection and determines the appropriate subsequent action. The output filters handle outgoing messages and are studied in section 4. After the keyword inputfilters, class *Point* defines a single input filter called *disp* of class *Dispatch*[7] using the expression

```
disp: Dispatch = { .... };
```

An input filter of class *Dispatch* is used to initiate execution of a method when the corresponding message passes successfully. The filtering condition, between the brackets "{" and "}", is specified as

```
{ True=>inner.moveTo, Initialized => inner.* }
```

On the left hand side of the characters "=>", a necessary condition is specified, denoted by the condition identifiers, *True* and *Initialized* in this case.

---

7   The current version of the Sina language provides a number of primitive filters such as *Dispatch*, *Meta*, *Error*, *Wait* and *RealTime*. The *Dispatch* filter is explained in this section. The *Meta* filter will be studied in section 4. The *Error* filter is similar to the *Dispatch* filter but it does not provide a method dispatch; it raises an error condition if a message does not pass through the filter [Aksit et al. 92]. The *Wait* filter is used for synchronization [Bergmans et al. 92]. The *RealTime* filter is used for realtime computations [Aksit&Bosch 92]. These filters can be used as both input and/or output filters. An input filter composes the signature of its object whereas an output filter specifies how its object sends messages to other objects. An important feature of all these filters is that they are orthogonal to each other and, therefore, they can be combined freely.

Conditions are similar to logical propositions. The names of the conditions are declared in the interface part following the keyword conditions and their definition is provided in the implementation part. Conditions may reflect the values of instance variables, but may reflect external variables as well. In this example, the condition *Initialized* is set to *true* if the instance variables of class *Point* have been initialized.

The received message is matched with the method names specified on the right hand side of the characters "=>". The character "*" indicates a wild-card or don't care condition; if the message matches with any of the method names provided by class *Point* it will be accepted for execution. An alternative could be to list all the method names explicitly. The pseudo-variable *inner* denotes the methods defined by *Point*.

An optional *internal* clause may be used to declare encapsulated objects whose behavior can be made (partially) visible on the interface of the encapsulating object by filter specifications. Internal objects differ from instance variables, because internals are used to compose the behavior of the object, whereas instance variables represent the local data of the object. An *external* clause may be used similarly to declare exterior objects that are to be accessible to this object. The use of internals and externals will be explained when inheritance mechanisms are introduced.

The Implementation Part

The components of the implementation part are exemplified by class *Point* as shown in Figure 3.

Instance variables are declared in the instvars clause. Instance variables are fully encapsulated and can be objects of arbitrary complexity. Class *Point* declares 3 instance variables named *x, y* and *initializeDone*. Only the methods defined within the object's class may access the instance variables directly, external clients of an object or even its subclasses cannot do this.

The implementations of the conditions are defined by message expressions. The structure of a condition implementation is similar to the structure of a method. However, a condition implementation always results in a *Boolean* value and is free of *side effects*.

The initialization method of an object is defined in the initial clause. This method is executed immediately after object creation.

The last component of the implementation part is the definition of the methods. A method consists of a series of message expressions. The control flow may be controlled by a set of standard *control statements*.

```
class Point implementation
    comment This class implements a graphical point;
    instvars
        x, y: Integer
        initializeDone: Boolean;
    conditions
        // the conditions that were declared in the interface part are implemented here
        Initialized:
            begin return initializeDone end;
    initial
        begin initalizeDone:= false;  end;
        // here the initial method is defined, which is executed immediately after object creation.
    methods
        moveTo(x, y: Integer) begin ....; initializeDone:=true end;
        getX  begin .... end;
        getY  begin .... end;
end;
```

Figure 3. The implementation part of class *Point*.

Message Evaluation by Filters

A filter is a *first-class* object that determines whether a particular message is either *accepted* or *rejected* and what action is to be performed in either case. Each filter is declared as an instance of a filter class. A programmer may define an arbitrary number of filters for an object. Each filter can be an instance of an arbitrary filter class. The complete set of input filters of an object determines the conditions for message acceptance and determines which method will be executed upon acceptance. Figure 4 illustrates how a message is evaluated by a set of filters.

This example consists of three filters *A*, *B* and *C*. A received message *m* has to pass through all the filters to result in a successful dispatch. Every filter consists of a number of filter elements (two or three in this example). When a message is to be evaluated by a filter it will be checked against the elements of the filter in left-to-right order. A filter element consists of three parts:

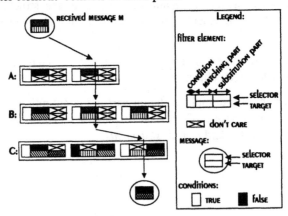

Figure 4. Message acceptance by filters.

- A *condition*, which specifies a necessary condition to be fulfilled in order to continue evaluating a filter element;

- A *matching part*, in which the evaluated message is matched against a defined pattern;

- A *substituting part*, where (parts of) the message can be replaced.

In filter *A*, the selector of the received message is matched against the selector of the matching part of each filter element; when the filter element does not match the subsequent filter element is tried. In filter *A*, although both of the conditions are *true*, only the second element matches the message since the selector of the first filter element does not match. The message is accepted by filter *A* and can then proceed to the next filter.

In filter *B*, matching is not restricted to the selector of the message, but involves the target of the message as well. The first element of B does not match but the second and third elements do. Due to the left-to-right ordering, the message matches on the second filter element and proceeds to the next filter.

Filter *C* demonstrates the full expressiveness of filter evaluation. It introduces substitution of selectors and targets. In the filter, the first filter element does not match and the second filter element has a condition that is *false*. The message is accepted at the third element and new values for the target and selector are substituted.

Since there is no subsequent filter, the type of the filter determines what will happen with the message. Commonly the last filter is of class *Dispatch*, which results in delegation of the request message to its target object.

The conditions, the matching and the substitution as provided by filters, provide a generic mechanism for selecting messages based either on their properties (selector or target), or on some condition specified by the receiving object. They also support the renaming of message selectors and redirection of messages (by substituting new targets). Based on the acceptance or rejection of a message, the filter can perform appropriate actions such as bouncing or blocking a rejected message or delegating an accepted message.

Inheritance and Delegation Through Input Filters

This section demonstrates how input filters can be applied to realize basic object-oriented data modeling techniques, such as inheritance and delegation. In section 4 we will explain how filters can be used to define ACTs.

In the composition-filters model, inheritance is not directly expressed by a language construct but is simulated by input filters. In order to inherit from a class an *internal object* must be declared as an instance of that class. Inheritance is simulated by delegating messages to the methods provided by this instance object. This is exemplified by class *ReferencePoint*, shown in Figure 5.

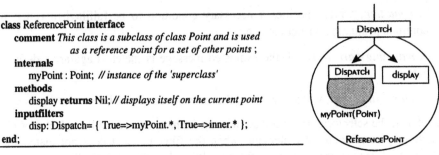

```
class ReferencePoint interface
    comment This class is a subclass of class Point and is used
                as a reference point for a set of other points ;
    internals
        myPoint : Point; // instance of the 'superclass'
    methods
        display returns Nil; // displays itself on the current point
    inputfilters
        disp: Dispatch= { True=>myPoint.*, True=>inner.* };
end;
```

Figure 5. The interface part of class *ReferencePoint*.

Class *ReferencePoint* declares an internal object *myPoint* of class *Point* and introduces one method *display*. The method *display* makes the graphical object visible at the current location.

The filter *disp* of class *Dispatch* contains two filter elements. The condition *True* preceding each filter element means that the target-selector pair(s) on the right-hand side will always be checked. These two filter elements have the following meaning:

First filter element:

The first element of the filter, *myPoint.** specifies that all the incoming messages are delegated to the internal object *myPoint,* provided that these messages are supported by class *Point.* Since the methods of *Point* are now available to *ReferencePoint* through an instance of *Point,* class *ReferencePoint* inherits the operations of class *Point.* This technique for simulating inheritance is also referred to as *delegation-based inheritance.*

When an instance of class *ReferencePoint* is created, its internal object *myPoint* is also created. An important feature here is that instance variables of the *superclass* are only accessible through operations provided by the superclass.

The second filter element:

If the first filter element does not match with the message, the second filter element is evaluated. Instead of delegating to an internal object such as *myPoint,* this filter element delegates the message to the pseudo-variable *inner*[8]. By

---

8 Apart from the pseudo-variable *inner,* two other pseudo-variables, *self* and *server,* are also available as a means of self-reference. The variable *inner* allows direct internal access on the objects' own methods. *self* refers to the instance of the class which defines the method. If, for example, *myPoint* refers to *self,* it will refer to *myPoint* but not *aReferencePoint.* We introduced *inner* to avoid infinitely nested compositions. Such nested compositions can be created if only *self* is used. In order to refer to the object that originally received the message, *server* is used as a target. For example, if *myPoint* refers to *server,* it will refer to *aReferencePoint.* Note that *server* is dynamically bound and is equivalent to Smalltalk *self.*

declaring *inner* as a target object, class *ReferencePoint* makes the methods defined and implemented by itself available to its clients.

Note that since the filter elements are evaluated from left to right, the first element prevails over the second one. The order of the filter elements can be manipulated to bind messages to the desired targets[9].

Instead of using an internal object as a target, the programmer may also delegate the incoming messages to an *external object* by declaring the target name in the *externals* clause. Because external objects are not encapsulated within the object, they can be shared by other objects. In addition, contrary to the *internals* clause, an external declaration does not result in automatic object creation.

4. Abstract Communication Types

4.1. Requirements for Abstract Communication Types

We have identified the following requirements for defining effective communication abstractions:

1. *First-class property*[10]: If the communications among objects show a well-defined, meaningful, complex and/or reusable behavior, then they must be explicitly represented by one or more ACTs. The rationale for this requirement is that if communications among objects are well-defined and meaningful, they are likely to be problem domain entities; if they are complex, then they can be managed by the object-oriented techniques such as encapsulation and inheritance; if they are reusable, they must be defined as classes (objects) since classes (objects) are the unit of reuse.

    An ACT class must be able to reuse other classes in the system so that ACT frameworks may be constructed.

2. *Large scale synchronization*: ACTs must be able to express various concurrency and synchronization schemes. We believe that distributed applications can be conveniently constructed using ACTs. Therefore, ACTs must have rich semantics to express various concurrency and synchronization mechanisms, such as asynchronous communications, broadcasts, coordinated terminations, distributed concurrency control algorithms, etc.

3. *Reflection upon messages*: An ACT must be capable of reflecting upon messages, such as for monitoring, logging, affecting synchronization semantics and message contents, or redirecting messages.

---

9 This is especially useful for solving name conflicts that are due to multiple inheritance.

10 First-class property means an ACT object is treated as an ordinary language object.

4. *Uniform integration of communication semantics*: Considering ACTs as objects only is not sufficient. Communication mechanisms defined by an ACT must be uniformly integrated with the operations implemented by the participating objects. An ACT must be considered as the *extended identity* of the participating objects[11].

4.2. Basic Concepts

An ACT class is an ordinary Sina class with the same syntax and semantics. What makes a class an ACT class is the way its behavior is composed with its participating objects. An ACT class operates on first-class representations of messages. For converting a message into its first-class representation, we introduce a new filter class called *Meta* filter. An instance of *Meta* filter has a structure similar to the *Dispatch* filter. The difference here is that if the received message is accepted by a *Meta* filter it is first converted to an instance of class *Message* and then passed as an argument of a new message to the ACT object. The conversion operation is also known as *reification*. The ACT object can retrieve the necessary information from the message argument. An ACT can also modify the contents of the message by invoking the operations of class *Message*. Finally, an ACT can convert an instance of *Message* back to a message execution. The detailed explanations of class *Meta* filter and *Message* are presented in sections 4.3 and 4.4, respectively.

ACTs can be further classified as *abstract sender types* (ASTs) and *abstract receiver types* (ARTs)[12]. ASTs and ARTs are responsible for abstracting one-way communication among objects. Various ways of composing ACTs are illustrated in Figure 6.

In Figure 6(a), each object has an output *Meta* filter which intercepts and delegates the outgoing messages to the internal AST object. The internal ASTs that are encapsulated by different objects may all belong to the same class to enforce common protocols among objects. The AST object is responsible for abstracting the communication that originates from the sender object. The sender object inherits the behavior of the AST object in object communication. This mechanism uniformly integrates the communication semantics of the AST object with the sender object. Typical applications of this architecture are asynchronous communications, encoding messages etc.

---

11 The semantics of an ACT object can not be integrated uniformly with the behavior of interacting objects just by executing message calls. After each message call, the context of the original call (such as the pseudo-variable *self*) is changed. As a consequence, this may result in a less reusable coordinated behavior since the ACT object can not polymorphically refer to the participating objects. This is equivalent to the *self-problem* as defined in [Lieberman 86].

12 This is an intuitive classification. We found out that in practice designers of ACTs tend to talk about ACTs that send or receive messages.

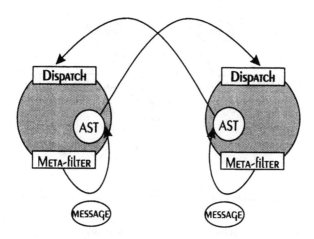

Figure 6(a). Outgoing messages are delegated to an internal AST object.

The architecture in Figure 6(b) is similar to 6(a), except that a shared external AST object is used instead of an internal one. This allows communicating objects to share the behavior with a common state. For example, this AST object can store the names of the receiver objects in a multicast implementation.

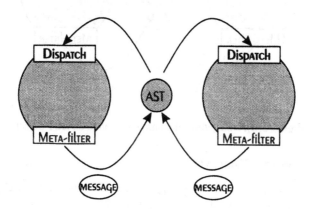

Figure 6(b). Outgoing messages are delegated to an external shared AST object.

In Figure 6(c), each object has an input *Meta* filter which intercepts and delegates the received messages to the external ART object.

The ART object is responsible for handling incoming messages. Examples are one-way constraint solvers, security protocols, data handlers in atomic transactions, decoding messages, etc.

Figure 6(d) combines the functionalities of AST and ART types into a single external ACT object. This object handles both incoming and outgoing messages. Typical examples are *coordinated behavior, multi-way constraint solvers, distributed algorithms* etc.

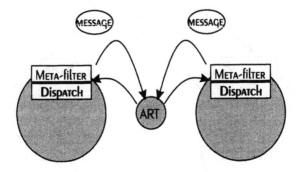

Figure 6(c). Composition of an external ART object with the participating objects.

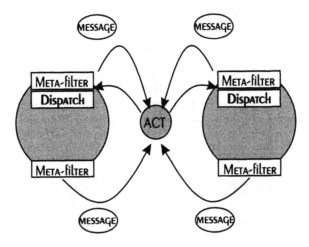

Figure 6(d). Delegating all communication to an ACT object.

4.3. Modeling Software Using ACTs.

In our analysis and design method, we apply the ACT concept as an object-oriented modeling technique. As illustrated by Figure 7(a), during the class (object) identification phase we explicitly search for classes that represent interactions among objects. Typically, these classes manifest themselves as action abstractions, distributed algorithms, coordinated behavior, inter-object constraints, etc. ACT classes are not procedural abstractions but they are problem domain entities and have a well-defined behavior.

In some cases, the analyst may fail in identifying ACT classes. After the identification of inheritance and part-of relations among classes, we specify object interaction patterns. If there is a well-defined pattern among objects and if this pattern is meaningful in the problem domain, then we represent them as ACT objects. As shown in Figure 7(b), in such a case we move the object-interaction behavior (code) to an ACT object.

Many object-oriented methods define *associations* [Rumbaugh 91] between objects. Most associations represent message exchange between these objects and can be conveniently represented by ACTs.

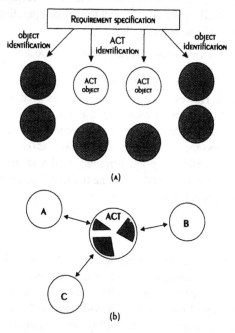

Figure 7. Identifying ACTs using (a) requirement specification and (b) object interaction patterns.

We have applied the object-oriented analysis and design techniques to a large number of applications [Aksit&Bergmans 92]. In various applications we could benefit from mechanisms that could abstract object interactions. One example was the administration system for social security services [Greef 91]. In this system, different objects were coordinating together to calculate payments. These calculations were the implementations of laws and could be abstracted by ACTs. Another example was the chemical process control system for a distillation process which was developed at the department of Chemical Engineering, University of Twente [Jonge 92]. In this system various optimization algorithms were distributed to different components. The algorithms were solving some well-defined differential equations and could be modeled by ACTs that implemented these algorithms. Distributed system design clearly demonstrated the need of abstracting interaction patterns [Aksit 89b, Bempt 91, Bergmans 90, Dolfing 90, Zondag 90]. In the distributed system design we could benefit from ACTs, for example, in building *layered architectures*, dedicated distributed *concurrency control* mechanisms and implementing *security protocols*.

4.4. Class Meta-Filter

Instances of class *Meta*-filter are used to reify messages that pass through them. The reified message is passed as an argument of the new message to an ACT object. Reification is needed to allow the ACT object to invoke operations on the instance of *Message*. Consider the following example:

aMetaFilter : Meta = { aCondition => [self.aMethod] anACT.aMethodOfAnACT };

There is no difference between a *Meta* filter and other filters in the manner a filter expression is evaluated. However, when the message is accepted by a filter element, which means both aCondition is *true* and the message is *self.aMethod*, a new message is created and the original message becomes the argument of the new message. The new message is composed of *anACT.aMethodOfAnACT(aMessage)*, where aMessage is the reified original message. If the received message does not match with a *Meta* filter it is passed to the next filter. The semantics of class *Meta* filter are presented in Appendix B.

4.5. Class Message

A message in the system becomes accessible when it is reified by a *Meta* filter and passed to an ACT as an argument of class *Message*. Class *Message* defines a number of methods for accessing and changing the *receiver, sender, server, selector* and *arguments* of the message. In addition, it provides methods for copying, reactivating and replying to the message. The accessing and changing operations are self explanatory. We will now describe the other methods.

The method *copy* returns a copy of the message. The *sender* of the copied message is undefined unless it is explicitly initialized. The reactivating method *fire* causes the message to continue with its execution. The method *reply* accepts an argument and sends this argument as a reply message to the sender, stored internally in the message. The interface methods of class *Message* are described in Appendix A.

4.6. Implementation Issues

Currently, we are carrying out a research activity for the efficient implementation of composition-filters. We are experimenting with a Sina compiler that generates C++ and Smalltalk code. In most cases, ACTs do not impose significant execution overhead, since the code that is executed by an ACT can be *inlined* into the object that owns the meta filter. This is because the name of the ACT object is explicitly named in the filter initialization part.

5. Examples of Abstract Communication Types

5.1. Example for an Inter-Object Invariant Behavior: One-Way Constraints

An instance of class *ReferencePoint* is supposed to store the reference coordinates of a figure. When the coordinates of the reference point are changed, then all the dependant graphical objects must be updated accordingly. Thus a figure can be considered as a constraint among the graphical elements that form the figure. We consider such a constrained behavior as a typical example of an ACT.

To compose this constraint behavior with *ReferencePoint*, Figure 8 extends the interface part by declaring object *figure* of class *OneWayConstraint* in the externals clause and by adding a new input filter called *constraint* of class *Meta*.

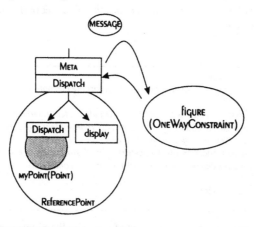

```
class ReferencePoint interface
    comment this class is a subclass of class Point and is used as a reference point for a set of other
            points ;
    externals
        figure : OneWayConstraint; // instance of the 'ART class'
    internals
        myPoint : Point; // instance of the 'superclass'
    methods
        display returns Nil; // display itself on the current point
    inputfilters
        {
            constraint : Meta= { True => [*.moveTo]figure.applyConstraint };
            disp: Dispatch= { True=>myPoint.*, True=>inner.* };
        }
end;
```

Figure 8. Redefinition of the interface part of class *ReferencePoint* .

Class *ReferencePoint* now has two filters enclosed by the characters "{" and "}". The filter *constraint* of class *Meta* contains a single filter element. The condition *True* preceding the filter element means that the target-selector pair(s) on the right-hand side will always be checked. The filter element consists of matching and substitution parts:

Matching part:

The matching part of the filter "*[*.moveTo]*" means that all the incoming messages with the selector *moveTo* will match. The received message will be converted to an instance of class *Message* if there is a match. If the received message does not match with the *Meta* filter it is passed to the next filter.

The substitution part:

After the message conversion the message is sent as an argument of the message "*figure.applyConstraint(aMessage)*". Object *figure* is declared in the externals clause and is responsible for enforcing the constrained behavior among the elements of *figure*. After updating the dependant graphical elements, *figure* converts the message back to the execution form which then passes though the second filter called *disp* of class *Dispatch*. The second filter dispatches the message to its target.

```
class OneWayConstraint interface
    comment this class implements a one way constraint enforcing mechanism ;
    methods
        applyConstraint( Message ) returns Nil; // this is the independent reference message
        putDependants( OrderedCollection(Any) ) returns Nil; // dependant objects are supplied
        size returns Integer; // number of dependant objects
        putConstraints( OrderedCollection(Block) ) returns Nil; // store constraints for dependants
        getConstraints returns OrderedCollection(Block); // retrieve constraints
    inputfilters
        disp : Dispatch = { true => inner.* };
end;
```

Figure 9. The interface part of class *OneWayConstraint*.

Class *OneWayConstraint* is an ART and is a general one-way constraint solver which provides the consistency of the dependant variables when the independent variable changes. In the following example variables y and z are dependants of x:

$$y = f1(x) \qquad\qquad z = f2(x)$$

OneWayConstraint introduces five methods. The method *applyConstraint* accepts a single argument of class *Message*. This argument is used as the independent value for the one-way constraint solver. The method *putDependants* accepts an ordered collection of objects of any type and stores them internally as dependant objects. The method *size* returns the number of dependant objects. The method *putConstraints* accepts an ordered collection of instances of class *Block* as an argument. Class *Block* represents a Sina method implementation. Each block is a constraint expression to be solved and corresponds to the object that is stored at the same index location of the ordered collection of dependants. For example, constraints on figure elements can be expressed as

[moveTo(message.argument(1) + ΔX , message.argument(2) + ΔY)]

Where *message* is the argument provided to the method *applyConstraint*. The method *argument(i)* returns the i_{th} argument of this message. ΔX and ΔY are the coordinates relative to the reference point.

The method *getConstraints* retrieves the ordered collection of *Blocks*.

Note that class *OneWayConstraint* is a generic class and can be reused in other applications.

In the following example class *BoundedFigure* inherits from class *OneWayConstraint* and restricts the coordinates of the figure within a certain frame. *BoundedFigure* introduces two new methods called *putFrame* and *getFrame* and overrides the method *applyConstraint*. The method *putFrame* accepts an argument of class *Rectangle* and stores it as the boundary of the figure. The method *getFrame* returns the current frame of the figure. The method *applyConstraint* of *OneWayConstraint* is now overridden because the allowed coordinates of the figure are restricted.

```
class BoundedFigure interface
    comment This class inherits from OneWayConstraint and extend it further by putting a frame;
    internals
        figure : OneWayConstraint;
    methods
        putFrame( Rectangle ) returns Nil;
        getFrame returns Rectangle;
        applyConstraint( Message ) returns Nil;
    inputfilters
        disp : Dispatch = { true => { inner.*, figure.* } };
end;
```

Figure 10. The interface part of class *BoundedFigure*.

5.2. Example for Inter-Object Synchronization: Asynchronous Message Send

The update messages sent by the constraint solver can be executed asynchronously. In Figure 11, class *OneWayConstraint* is extended by defining a new output filter called *send* of class *Meta*. This filter converts the outgoing messages to an instance of *Message* and passes it to the internal object *messageSender* of class *Asynchronous*. Class *Asynchronous* provides asynchronous message passing and its definition is given in Figure 12.

Class *Asynchronous* is an AST and defines a single method called *messageInput*. This method accepts an instance of class *Message* as an argument and replies to this message immediately by returning the object *nil* to the sender. It then activates the message by invoking the method *fire* on this message. Note that the matching part in the dispatch filter "*[self.*]*" will match with any message that is sent to an instance of class *Asynchronous*.

In Sina, unless mutual exclusion is provided by a filter [Bergmans et al. 92], methods may be executed concurrently. This class therefore may execute concurrent *messageInput* invocations.

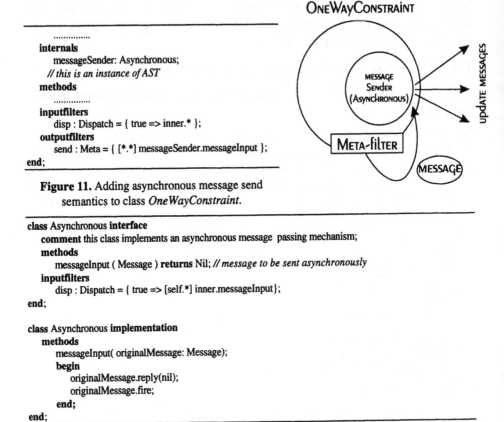

```
              ..............
              internals
                  messageSender: Asynchronous;
                  // this is an instance of AST
              methods
              ..............
              inputfilters
                  disp : Dispatch = { true => inner.* };
              outputfilters
                  send : Meta = { [*.*] messageSender.messageInput };
          end;
```

Figure 11. Adding asynchronous message send
semantics to class *OneWayConstraint.*

```
class Asynchronous interface
    comment this class implements an asynchronous message passing mechanism;
    methods
        messageInput ( Message ) returns Nil; // message to be sent asynchronously
    inputfilters
        disp : Dispatch = { true => [self.*] inner.messageInput};
end;

class Asynchronous implementation
    methods
        messageInput( originalMessage: Message);
        begin
            originalMessage.reply(nil);
            originalMessage.fire;
        end;
end;
```

Figure 12. The interface and implementation parts of class *Asynchronous.*

5.3. Example for Coordinated behavior: Atomic Transactions

For computer-aided engineering applications figures can be processed to calculate
certain features such as volume, weight, etc. In the one-way constraint
implementation of Figure 11, dependant objects are updated by sending them a
number of asynchronous messages. During the update operation the figure is
inconsistent and, if there are other processes accessing this figure, the results of their
computation may be inconsistent as well.

Atomic transactions have proven to be a useful mechanism to preserve consistency
[Haerder&Reuter 83]. *Serializability* and *indivisibility* are the two important
properties of atomic actions. Serializability means that if several actions are executed
concurrently, they manipulate the affected data as if they were executed serially in
some order. Indivisibility means that either all or none of the atomic actions are
performed.

The implementation of class *OneWayConstraint* is extended in Figure 13 by defining
a second output filter named *atomic* of class *Meta* to enforce consistent updates. This
filter converts the message that is fired by *messageSend* to an instance of *Message*
and passes it to the internal object *atomicUpdate* of class *TransactionManager.*

The interface definition of class *TransactionManager* is given in Figure 14. Class *TransactionManager* inherits from class *CommitReceive* and provides two methods called *size* and *transaction*. The method *size* accepts an integer argument and stores it internally as the size of the transaction. The method *transaction* accepts an argument of class Message and executes this message together with other messages as an atomic transaction.

In our example class *TransactionManager* has an instance variable called *commitSend* which implements a commit protocol. This protocol is explained with the help of Figure 15(a-d). In 15(a) *commitSend* receives the transaction as a message list from *TransactionManager* and *fires* them one by one.

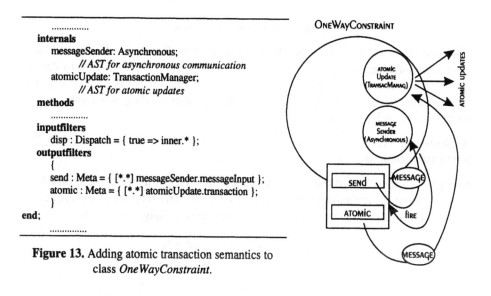

Figure 13. Adding atomic transaction semantics to
class *OneWayConstraint*.

```
class TransactionManager interface
    comment this class sends a set of messages as a transaction;
    internals
        myCommitReceive: CommitReceive; // Inherits from CommitReceive. It is used to commit or
        // abort the transaction
    methods
        size(Integer) returns Nil; // size of the transaction block
        transaction( Message ) returns Nil; // an element of a transaction block
    inputfilters
        disp : Dispatch = { true => inner.* };
end;
```

Figure 14. The interface part of class *TransactionManager*.

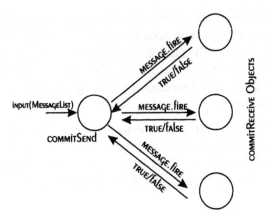

Figure 15(a). Transaction starts.

The receiver object must incorporate an ART of class *TransactionManager*. Class *TransactionManager* inherits from class *CommitReceive* which is responsible for handling *transaction commit* and *abort* messages. When a message is first received by *CommitReceive*, it goes from the *idle* to the *commit pending* state, and returns *true* as shown in Figure 15(d).

As shown by Figure 15(b), if all the responses to *commitSend* are *true*, then the transaction commits.

In Figure 15(c) is shown that when a message is returned as *false* the transaction aborts. During the *commit pending* state, if *CommitReceive* receives a new request it returns *false* and thus causes the abortion of the corresponding transaction.

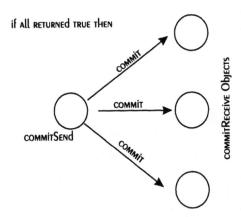

Figure 15(b). If all succeed then transaction commits.

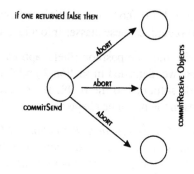

Figure 15(c). If one fails, then the transaction aborts.

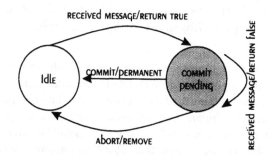

Figure 15(d). The state transition diagram of class *CommitReceive*.

Objects that require transactional behavior must incorporate an instance of class *TransactionManager* as an ART. Class *AtomicPoint*, shown in Figure 16, represents the dependant graphical points which are to be updated when their reference point is changed. This class inherits from *Point* and delegates any *moveTo* message as an instance of *Message* to its internal object *atomic* of class *TransactionManager*. The second filter dispatches to the internal objects *myPoint* and *atomic*, if the received message passes through it. Since *TransactionManager* inherits from class *CommitReceive* it responds to *commit* and *abort* messages.

```
class AtomicPoint interface
    comment This class makes point an atomic point;
    internals
        myPoint : Point;
        atomic: TransactionManager;
    inputfilters
        makeAtom: Meta = {true=> [moveTo] atomic.commitInput};
        disp : Dispatch = { true => atomic.abort, atomic.commit, myPoint.* };
end;
```

Figure 16. The Interface part of class *AtomicPoint*.

6. Evaluation and Conclusions

To illustrate the useful features of ACTs, we presented examples in 3 categories: examples of inter-object invariant behavior, inter-object synchronization, and coordinated behavior. Figure 17(a) shows the relations among the classes as defined in this paper. Figure 17(b) organizes these classes into a layered architecture.

In this section we analyze the composition-filters approach with respect to the problems and requirements we identified in section 2 and 4.1, respectively. First we discuss how ACTs provide solutions to the problems in section 2, and how this is illustrated by the examples in the previous chapter.

1. *Lack of Support for Meta-levels and Reflection:* ACTs can be used for intercepting and manipulating messages. Interception of messages is achieved by the input and output filters of an object, whereas manipulation of messages is made possible by *Meta* filters, since these transform messages into first-class objects. This will allow the software engineer to model and implement layered architectures and extend the message passing semantics of the object-oriented model if needed. Figure 17(b) shows the layered architecture as defined in this paper.

2. *Complexity and Lack of Reusability:* ACTs can make the complexity of programs manageable by moving the interaction code to separate modules. This allows for reducing the number of inter-module relations and hiding communication details. Classes *OneWayConstraint*, *Asynchronous* and *TransactionManager*, for example, represent inter-object interactions. The details of these interactions are abstracted by the methods. Note that *OneWayConstraint*, *Asynchronous* and *TransactionManager* are generic classes and may be used in various applications.

Programmers may apply object-oriented techniques, such as inheritance and delegation, to achieve a more systematic reuse of these components. Inheritance mechanisms will allow software engineers to construct *application frameworks* for different communication protocols. For example, constraint-based systems, distributed concurrency control and recovery protocols, security protocols, distributed scheduling and optimization algorithms, etc. can be expressed using ACTs. The software engineer can tailor these frameworks for his/her particular needs. Properly designed ACTs can be highly reusable.

As illustrated by *BoundedFigure*, ACTs can be extended through the use of inheritance. Another possible extension could be to subclass *TransactionManager*, for instance, to implement weak atomicity for some actions. Thus, the implementation of ACT classes can be changed without affecting the participant objects. For example the implementation of class *TransactionManager* could be changed to *two-phase commit protocol*, without affecting the instances of class *OneWayConstraint*.

3. *Enforcing invariant behavior:* It is easier to enforce the invariant behavior among objects if there is a module explicitly representing this behavior. For example, constraints among objects are enforced by a single class *OneWayconstraint*. Otherwise, all the interacting-code among display objects had to be taken into account.

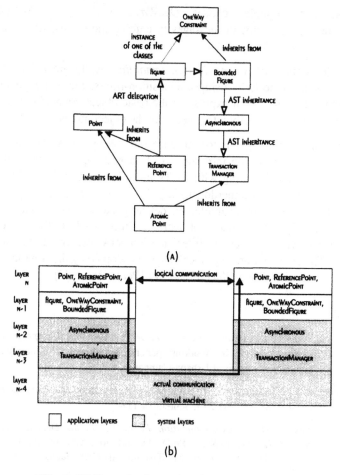

Figure 17. Example classes (a) relations among classes
(b) classified into layers of abstractions.

We will now evaluate ACTs with respect to the requirements that were stated in section 4.1:

1. *First -class property:* ACT classes are first-class modules because they are just like other Sina classes. What makes a class an ACT class is that it manipulates messages as first-class objects, and the way it is composed with other classes. Inheritance and/or delegation of behavior is provided for ACT classes through the use of composition-filters.

2. *Large scale synchronization:* ACT classes can implement large-scale synchronization among participating objects. A typical example is class *TransactionManager.* Sina provides mechanisms for concurrency and synchronization since it is a concurrent language [Bergmans et al. 92].

3. *Reflection upon messages:* Through the use of classes *Meta* and *Message,* messages can be manipulated because they are abstracted by the methods of class

Message. For example, classes *OneWayConstraint* and *BoundedFigure* manipulate the arguments of messages to enforce the consistency of dependant objects.

4. *Uniform integration of communication semantics:* ACTs are incorporated with the participating objects by using composition-filters. Since composition-filters also are the basic means for expressing the basic object-oriented data abstraction mechanisms, ACTs are fully integrated with the object model.

The contribution of this paper is to introduce the concept of ACTs. Realization of ACTs is made possible by the introduction of a new type of filter: called *Meta*. Currently, we are experimenting with ACTs in building object-oriented distributed transaction frameworks [Tekinerdogan 92]. We also investigate mechanisms to improve fault-tolerance, for example, by defining ACTs that manage replicated objects transparently. The concept of ACTS as introduced in this paper can be effectively used with the other filter mechanisms presented in our earlier publications. The composition-filter mechanism is adopted by the Sina language and an ICASE environment called *ObjectComposer* [Pool&Bosch 92].

References

[Agha et al. 92] Agha et al, *A Linguistic Framework for Dynamic Composition of Fault-Tolerance Protocols*, Working paper, Department of Computer Science, University of Illinois at Urbana-Campaign, 1992.

[Aksit&Tripathi 88] M. Aksit & A. Tripathi, *Data Abstraction Mechanisms in Sina/ST*, OOPSLA '88, pp. 265-275, September 1988.

[Aksit 89a] M. Aksit, *Abstract Communication Types*, in *On the Design of the Object-Oriented Language Sina*, Ph.D. Dissertation, Chapter 4, Department of Computer Science, University of Twente, The Netherlands, 1989.

[Aksit 89b] M. Aksit, *Atomic Delegations*, in *On the Design of the Object-Oriented Language Sina*, Ph.D. Dissertation, Chapter 5, Department of Computer Science, University of Twente, The Netherlands, 1989.

[Aksit et al. 91] M. Aksit, J.W. Dijkstra & A. Tripathi, *Atomic Delegation: Object-oriented Transactions*, IEEE Software, Vol. 8, No. 2, March 1991.

[Aksit&Bergmans 92] M. Aksit & L.M.J. Bergmans, *Obstacles in Object-Oriented Software Development*, OOPSLA '92, pp. 341-358, Vancouver, Canada.

[Aksit et al. 92] M. Aksit, L.Bergmans & S. Vural, *An Object-Oriented Language-Database Integration Model: The Composition-Filters Approach*, ECOOP '92, LNCS 615, pp 372-395, Springer-Verlag, 1992.

[Aksit&Bosch 92] M. Aksit & J. Bosch, *Issues in Real-Time Language Design*, NATO Advanced Study Institute on Real-Time Systems, Position paper to be published as LNCS, Springer-Verlag, Sint Maarten, October 1992.

[Barber 89] J. Barber, *Computational Reflection in Class-Based Object-Oriented Languages*, OOPSLA '89, pp. 317-326, October 1989.

[Bempt 91] M. v.d. Bempt, *Construction of Hierarchies in Distributed Computer Systems*, M.Sc. Thesis, Department of Computer Science, University of Twente, The Netherlands, November 1991.

[Bergmans 90] L.M.J. Bergmans, *The Sina Distribution Model*, M.Sc. Thesis, Department of Computer Science, University of Twente, The Netherlands, March 1990.

[Bergmans et al. 92] L. Bergmans, M. Aksit, K. Wakita & A. Yonezawa, *An Object-Oriented Model for Extensible Synchronization and Concurrency Control*, Memoranda Informatica 92-87, University of Twente, January 1992.

[Booch 90] G. Booch, *Object Oriented Design (with applications)*, Benjamin/Cummings Publishing Company, Inc., 1990.

[Campbell et al. 89] R. H. Campbell & et al. *Principles of Object-Oriented Operating System Design*, Report UIUCDCS-R-89-1510, University of Illinois at Urbana-Champaign, USA.

[Coad&Yourdan 91a] P. Coad & E. Yourdon, *Object-Oriented Analysis*, 2nd Edition, Yourdon Press, 1991.

[Coad&Yourdan 91b] P. Coad & E. Yourdon, *Object-Oriented Design*, Yourdon Press, 1991.

[Champeaux 91] D. de Champeaux, *Object-Oriented Analysis and Top-Down Software Development*, ECOOP '91, pp. 360-375, July 1991.

[Dolfing 90] H. Dolfing, *An Object Allocation Strategy for Sina*, M.Sc. Thesis, Department of Computer Science, University of Twente, The Netherlands, November 1990.

[Francez 86] N. Francez et al, *Script: A Communication Abstraction Mechanism and Its Verification*, Science of Computer Programming, 6, 1, pp. 35-88, 1986.

[Greef 91] N. de Greef, *Object-Oriented System Development*, M.Sc. Thesis, Department of Computer Science, University of Twente, The Netherlands, 1991.

[Haerder&Reuter 83] Haerder & A. Reuter, *Principles of Transaction-Oriented Database Recovery*, ACM Computing Surveys, Vol. 15, No. 4, pp. 287-317, December 1983.

[Helm et al. 90] R. Helm, I. Holland & D. Ganghopadhyay, *Contracts: Specifying Behavioral Compositions in Object-Oriented Systems*, OOPSLA '90, pp. 169-180, 1990.

[Holland 92] I.M. Holland, *Specifying Reusable Components Using Contracts*, ECOOP '92, LNCS 615, pp. 287-308, Utrecht, June 1992.

[Honda&Tokoro 92] Y. Honda & M. Tokoro, *Soft Real-Time Programming Through Reflection*, Int. Workshop on New Models for Software Architecture'92, Reflection and meta-Level Architecture, Yonezawa & Smith (eds), pp. 12-23, November 1992.

[Ichisugi et al. 92] Y. Ichisugi, S. Matsuoka & A. Yonezawa, *A Reflective Object-Oriented Concurrent Language Without a Run-Time Kernel*, Int. Workshop on New Models for Software Architecture'92, Reflection and meta-Level Architecture, Yonezawa & Smith (eds), pp. 24-35, November 1992.

[Jonge 92] E. Jonge, *Object-georienteerde Analyse, Ontwerp en Implementatie van een Batchdestillatiebesturing*, M.Sc. Thesis, Department of Chemical Engineering, University of Twente, The Netherlands, January 1992.

[Lamping et al. 92] J. Lamping, G. Kiczales, L. Rodriguez & E. Ruf, *An Architecture for an Open Compiler*, Int. Workshop on New Models for Software Architecture'92, Reflection and meta-Level Architecture, Yonezawa & Smith (eds), pp. 95-106, November 1992.

[Lieberherr et al. 91] K. Lieberherr *et al.*, *Graph-Based Software Engineering: Concise Specifications of Cooperative Behavior*, Northeastern University, Tech. Report: NU-CCS-91-14, September 1991.

[Lieberman 86] H. Lieberman, *Using Prototypical Objects to Implement Shared Behavior*, OOPSLA '86, pp. 214-223, 1986.

[Lieberherr&Holland 89] K. Lieberherr & I. Holland, *Assuring Good Style for Object-Oriented Programs*, IEEE Software, pp. 38-48, September 1989.

[Maes 87] P. Maes, *Concepts and Experiments in Computational Reflection*, OOPSLA '87, pp. 147-155, October 1987.

[Pool&Bosch 92] S. Pool & J. Bosch, *ObjectComposer ICASE Environment*, OOPSLA '92 conference demonstration, October 1992.

[Rumbaugh 91] J. Rumbaugh *et al.*, *Object-Oriented Modeling and Design*, Prentice-Hall, 1991.

[Smith 82] B.C. Smith, *Reflection and Semantics in a Procedural Language*, MIT-LCS-TR-272, Mass. Ins. of Tech., Cambridge, MA, January 1982.

[Tekinerdogan 93] B. Tekinerdogan, *The Design of a Framework for Object-Oriented Atomic Transactions*, Draft M.Sc. Thesis, Department of Computer Science, University of Twente, The Netherlands, 1993.

[Tripathi&Aksit 88] A. Tripathi & M. Aksit, *Communication, Scheduling and Resource Management in Sina*, JOOP, Vol. 1, No. 4, November/December 1988, pp. 24-37.

[Yokote 92] Y. Yokote. The Apertos Reflective Operating System: The concept and its Implementation, OOPSLA'92, pp. 414-434, October 1992.

[Wirfs-Brock et al. 90] R. Wirfs-Brock *et al.*, *Responsibility-Driven Design*, Prentice-Hall, 1990.

[Zondag 90] E. G. Zondag, *Hierarchical Management of Distributed Objects*, Memoranda Informatica 90-73, 1990.

Appendix A - Specification of class Message

In this appendix the relevant methods of class *Message* are described. As described, class *Message* has fields for the *receiver* object, the *sender*, the *server*, the *method selector* and the *arguments*.

- getReceiver **returns** Any;
  returns the receiver of the message object.

- putReceiver(Any) **returns** Nil;
  changes the receiver of the message object into the argument object.

- getSender **returns** Any;
  returns the object that sent the message.

- putSender(Any) **returns** Nil;
  changes the sender of the message into the argument object.

- getServer **returns** Any;
  returns the object that originally received the message, but that delegated it to the receiver object.

- putServer(Any) **returns** Nil;
  changes the server of the message into the argument object.

- getSelector **returns** Identifier;
  returns the method identifier that is stored in the message.

- putSelector(Identifier) **returns** Nil;
  changes the method identifier into the argument identifier.

- getArgument(Integer) **returns** Any;
  returns the argument refered to by the integer argument.

- putArgument(Integer, Any) **returns** Nil;
  changes the argument refered to by the integer argument into the argument object.

- copy **returns** Message;
  returns a copy of the message.

- fire **returns** Nil;
  activates the message. If the receiver object is not changed, the message is evaluated by the subsequent filter. Otherwise is the message sent to the new receiver object, where it will be evaluated as any message.

- reply(Any) **returns** Nil;
  sends the argument object as a reply message to the sender of the message.

Appendix B - The Semantics of the Message System

This appendix gives a formal description of the message system. A message is represented as

$$msg = (o_s, o_r, o_v, \sigma, [a_1, ..., a_n])$$

Where, o_s is the sender id and o_r is the receiver id, o_v is the server object id, σ is the message selector, and $[a_1,...,a_n]$ are message arguments.

The input filter set consists of filters $F_{i,1},...,F_{i,n}$ and the output filters set consists of filters $F_{o,1},...,F_{o,m}$. Each filter F_i has a message queue MQ_{F_i}. A filter of class *Error* is always added as a last filter $F_{i,n+1}$ generating an error if a message is not dispatched so far. A filter of class *Dispatch* is always added as a last filter $F_{o,m+1}$ to send a message once it passed the m output filters.

In appendix A, methods of class *Message* were introduced. Now we will describe the semantics of the methods *copy*, *fire* and *reply*. In A(1), the method *copy* results in a new message with the same structure except the *sender* object is now replaced by *nil_obj*. The method *fire* as defined in A(2), puts the message in the message queue of the next filter. This filter is determined according to the declaration order. The sender of the *fire* message receives *nil_obj* as a result of this invocation. In A(3), the method *reply* sends its argument as a reply message to the sender of the original message. Similar to the previous formula, the sender of the *reply* message receives *nil_obj* as a result of this invocation.

$$copy \rightarrow (nil\_obj, o_r, o_v, \sigma, [a_1,...,a_n])$$
$$A(1)$$

$$fire \rightarrow \begin{cases} MQ_{Q_{RF_{i+1}}} = MQ_{Q_{RF_{i+1}}} \cup \{msg\} \\ nil\_obj \end{cases}$$
$$A(2)$$

where O_R is the reifying object

and F_i is the reifying Meta filter

$$reply(rep\_obj) \rightarrow \begin{cases} rep\_obj \xrightarrow{reply} o_s \\ nil\_obj \end{cases}$$
$$A(3)$$

Each message is removed from the message queue of the current filter and evaluated according to the algorithm as described in section 4. The filter can either *accept* the message or *reject* it. In each case the filter will perform some action depending on its type. The actions performed by filters *Dispatch* and *Meta* are described in the following:

The function execute(msg) is used to start execution of the method as a result of filter evaluation. The *Dispatch* filter is defined in A(4). If the received message is accepted and if the *target* of the message is *self*, then the corresponding method is executed. If, however, the *target* object is not *self*, then the accepted message is put in the message queue of the first filter of the *target* object. If the message is not accepted, then it is put in the message queue of the next filter. The *Meta* filter is defined in *A(5)*. If the message is accepted, *msg* is converted into *msg'* and *msg'* is put in the message queue of the first filter of the specified ACT. If the message is not accepted, then it is put in the message queue of the next filter. The conversion operation creates a new message *msg'* with the current object as the *sender*, the ACT object a *receiver* and *server*, the message selector σ_{ACT} as specified in the filter expression and the original message *msg* as the argument of the message.

$$F_i(msg) : \text{Dispatch} \rightarrow \begin{cases} \text{execute}(msg) & \text{if accepted and self} = O_r \\ MQ_{O_r} = MQ_{O_r} \cup \{msg\} & \text{if accepted and self} \neq O_r \\ MQ_{F_{i+1}} = MQ_{F_{i+1}} \cup \{msg\} & \text{otherwise} \end{cases}$$

A(4)

$$\text{where } MQ_{Q_r} = MQ_{F_{i,1}} \text{ of } O_r$$

$$F_i(msg) : \text{Meta} \rightarrow \begin{cases} MQ_{ACT} = MQ_{ACT} \cup \{msg'\} & \text{if accepted} \\ MQ_{F_{i+1}} = MQ_{F_{i+1}} \cup \{msg\} & \text{otherwise} \end{cases}$$

A(5)

$$\text{where } (\text{self, ACT, ACT, } \sigma_{ACT}, [msg]) = msg'$$

$$\text{and } MQ_{ACT} = MQ_{F_{i,1}} \text{ of ACT}$$

$$\text{and ACT} = O_r$$

Object-Oriented Distributed Programming in BETA

Søren Brandt and Ole Lehrmann Madsen

Computer Science Department, Aarhus University
Ny Munkegade, DK-8000 Aarhus C, Denmark

Email: {sbrandt,olmadsen}@daimi.aau.dk

Abstract. This paper describes abstractions that have been designed
to support distributed programming in the object oriented programming
language BETA. The approach is minimalistic in the sense that a goal
is to provide the essential building blocks on top of which other distribution related abstractions may be built. This goal is made easier by
demanding for type orthogonal persistence and distribution as the full
power of the underlying language may then be used when building higher
level abstractions on top of the basic ones.

1 Introduction

This paper describes abstractions that have been designed to support distributed
programming in the object oriented programming language BETA [19]. The abstractions are relatively simple, as they are designed to cope only with distribution specifics, whereas e.g. concurrency issues are dealt with by the basic BETA
language. In general, when designing programming languages and systems, a
goal is to keep them as simple as possible, consisting of a few general orthogonal
language constructs. This was one of the main principles behind the design of
the BETA object oriented programming language, and it is one of the design
principles behind the abstractions in this paper.

In the case of distributed programs, a consequence of the orthogonality principle is that instances of any class must be remotely accessible. If this is not so,
a class designed and implemented without distribution explicitly in mind might
not be usable unless wrapped in a layer of code providing the ability to be accessed remotely. Especially in OO environments with large class libraries, the
usability of these libraries is limited if everything must be rewritten or wrapped
to be used in a distributed setting. Furthermore, if the language constructs allowed in the distributed case are limited, the expressive power of the language
is limited, leading to more clumsy classes. For example, BETA owes a lot of its
expressive power to nested virtual classes, a language construct to our knowledge found in no other programming language, and especially in no distributed
programming language.

The principle of orthogonality also applies to object persistence [5] as it
should be possible to save any object on stable storage regardless of the class to

which the object belongs. Again, a good example of this is the classes of a large library.

Another gain from the full generality of a powerful programming language is that fewer distribution specific language constructs are needed, thereby keeping the total number of language constructs at a minimum. For example, CORBA [20] includes a type system, an interface definition language and a way of handling exceptions. CORBA is referred to as "language independent". In our opinion there is no such thing as language independence. Instead CORBA defines a new language expressing a subset of a number of other languages. This is of course inevitable in an open system, but should not be confused with "language independence". As a result, a programmer using CORBA IDL to specify remote objects needs to learn and remember yet another programming language to be able to do distributed programming.

The goal thus is a general distributed implementation of BETA allowing instances of any class to be accessed remotely. Preferably, distributed BETA should, modulo network failure and server crashes, be semantically equivalent to non-distributed BETA, the only difference being that objects may be spread around on any number of network hosts and that object references may refer to objects on remote network hosts. By *object reference* we mean a unique object ID.

A number of issues more or less specific to distributed programming are not directly addressed by this work, as the primary goal is to be able to use the full power of the BETA language when doing distributed programming. Section 5 discusses some of the issues left out, and the reason why they are not regarded as mandatory.

The first applications built using distributed BETA are CSCW[1] applications. The original reason for initiating research into the area of BETA distribution, was a non-distributed hypermedia application to be enhanced to support distributed cooperative work. As the design of the hypermedia is using the full power of the BETA language, it would have required a total redesign and reimplementation of large amounts of code, if distributed access to objects was restricted. As a consequence, we decided to develop a distributed version of BETA. The demands from CSCW applications put on distributed BETA includes support for wide area and heterogeneous networks. Furthermore, it should be possible to integrate the implementation with third party libraries, such as the X window system.

We have identified the following mandatory abstractions needed to be able to describe distributed programs in BETA:

- *Ensemble*: An abstraction modeling the operating system of a physical network host.
- *Shell*: An abstraction modeling executables whose instances are large grain processes within some ensemble.
- *NameServer*: An abstraction modeling mappings from textual object names to object references.

---

[1] Computer Supported Cooperative Work

- *PersistentShell*: The primary building block for object persistence.
- *ErrorHandler*: An abstraction for handling partial failures.

Section 2 briefly describes the BETA language. Section 3 describes the abstractions introduced above in more detail. Section 4 describes our approach to object movement. In section 5 we look at some issues of distribution not directly covered by our model. Section 6 addresses related work. Having described our model for distributed programming in BETA, section 7 briefly discusses problems and implementation techniques for doing a general distributed implementation of BETA and the current state of the implementation.

2 The BETA object model

A BETA object may be either *active* or *passive*. A passive object is similar to an object in Smalltalk, Eiffel or C++. It has a number of data attributes in the form of references to other objects or part-objects. It also has a number of pattern attributes that e.g. may be used as (virtual) procedures. An object may invoke an operation in other objects. The calling object is blocked until the operation is completed.

An active object executes its own actions defined in an associated action-part. An active object thus defines an independent thread. Active objects may be executed concurrently or as coroutines. Access to shared objects may be synchronized by means of semaphores. Semaphores are, however, mainly used as a primitive for defining higher-level concurrency abstractions. The Mjølner BETA System [12] provides a library with a number of pre-defined concurrency abstractions corresponding to monitors and Ada-like tasks with rendezvous. These abstractions are all defined using BETA patterns and semaphores. If the user is not satisfied with the concurrency abstractions of the library it is easy to define new ones, see [19, 18].

A pattern is a general abstraction mechanism that unifies abstraction mechanisms such as class, generic class, procedure, function, process, coroutine, exception, etc. A pattern P is declared in the following way:

```
P: Super
    (# Decl1; Decl2; ... Decln
    enter In
    do Imp1; Imp2; ... Impm
    exit Out
    #)
```

where Super defines a possible super-pattern for P; Decl1, Decl2, ..., Decln is a list of declarations of reference attributes or patterns; In defines possible input parameters of P-objects; Imp1, Imp2, .., Impm is a sequence of imperatives (statements) associated with P-objects; and Out defines possible output parameters of P-objects.

A declaration of a reference attribute may have one of the forms:

```
R1: @ P;
R2: ^ P
```

R1 is a *static reference* denoting a *part object* which is an instance of **P**. An instance of **P** is generated as part of the generation of the object containing the declaration. **R2** is a *dynamic reference* that at different points in time may denote different objects, which may be instances of **P** or subpatterns of **P**. A static reference is similar to a data member in C++ and a dynamic reference is similar to a pointer in C++ and an instance variable in Smalltalk.

R1 and **R2** are references to passive objects. References to active objects may be declared using the | operator:

```
R3: @ | P;
R4: ^ | P
```

R3 is an *active* part object and that **R4** is a dynamic reference to an *active* object.

The enter/do/exit part of a pattern has no counterpart in e.g. C++ and Smalltalk. If a pattern **P** is used as a procedure, then the enter/exit-part describes the input/output parameters and the do-part describes the imperatives (statements) of the procedure. The enter/do/exit part also has a meaning for passive objects, but this will not be described here.

For an active object, the do-part describes the head of a new thread. This may be either in the form of a coroutine or a concurrent process. The imperative

R3

executes **R3** as a coroutine. The calling process is blocked until **R3** suspends itself or terminates. A subsequent call of **R3** will resume its execution at the point where it suspended. The imperative

R4.fork

will execute **R4** as a concurrent process. The calling process will continue its execution.

For a more detailed description of BETA, see [19]. In the next section an example of a BETA program is given.

2.1 Example

Throughout this article, most BETA code shown will be extracts from an example illustrating the development process from prototype to final application. The example consists of a *MessageDistributor*, distributing messages from and among a number of *MessageGenerators*. The BETA program constituting the logical model (see below) of this is shown in figure 1. A short description of the program is given below. Later a distributed prototype will be shown. Appendix A contains the final application.

In figure 1, the *MessageDistributor* pattern contains the two nested patterns, *registerGenerator* and *distributeMessage*. These patterns serve as the methods of

```
MessageDistributor:
  (# registerGenerator:
      (# theGenerator: ^|MessageGenerator;
      enter theGenerator[]
      do (* Add theGenerator to list of generators. *)
      #);
    distributeMessage:
      (# theMessage: @Text;
      enter theMessage
      do (for <<all generators>> repeat
              theMessage -> thisGenerator.receiveMessage;
          for);
      #);
  #);
MessageGenerator:
  (# theDistributor: ^|MessageDistributor;
    receiveMessage:
      (# theMessage: @Text;
      enter theMessage
      do (* Something useful. *)
      #);
    init:
      (#
      enter theDistributor[]
      do THIS(MessageGenerator)[]
          -> theDistributor.registerGenerator;
         THIS(MessageGenerator).fork;
      #);
  do
    cycle
    (#
    do "A nice message" -> theDistributor.distributeMessage;
    #);
  #);
(# (* Main program. Three active objects executing in parallel: *)
  theDistributor: @|MessageDistributor;
  generator1    : @|MessageGenerator;
  generator2    : @|MessageGenerator;
do
  theDistributor.fork;
  theDistributor[] -> generator1.init;
  theDistributor[] -> generator2.init;
#)
```

Fig. 1. Logical model of example application

instances of MessageDistributor. The enter parameter to the registerGenerator method is a reference to an active instance of MessageGenerator. That it is a reference parameter follows from [] in `theGenerator[]`, while the fact that it is an active object follows from | in `theGenerator: ^|MessageGenerator`. The methods of *MessageGenerator* are *receiveMessage* and *init*. receiveMessage takes a Text value as enter parameter, meaning that a copy of the actual parameter is passed to the method. The init method registers the current MessageGenerator instance by calling the registerGenerator method of the entered MessageDistributor instance and forks the MessageGenerator to make it execute in parallel with the thread calling the init method. Finally the program object contains three active part objects executing in parallel.

2.2 Logical versus physical system structure

BETA is a language for describing a system (program execution) consisting of objects and patterns, some of which represents phenomena and concepts from the application domain, and others which are for implementation purposes. The BETA objects and patterns provide the *logical structure* of a system; the BETA language provides mechanisms for describing this logical structure.

The *physical structure* of a BETA program includes its organization of the program text in terms of interface modules, implementation modules, variants, versions, etc. The basic BETA language does not include mechanisms for describing the physical structure, because the physical structure is independent of the logical structure. In [19], the mechanism for describing the physical organization of the program text is described in details.

The logical model describes the system in terms of objects and patterns, including a description of active and passive objects. Communication and synchronization of active objects are also described. I.e the logical model includes the concurrency issues.

The actual distribution of objects on processors in a distributed system is considered part of the physical structure of the system. This means that there is a sharp distinction between the logical concurrency issues and the physical distribution issues. Separation between transient and persistent objects is considered part of the physical structure.

Concurrency issues includes description of active objects and communication and synchronization between them. Distribution issues includes mapping of objects onto processors, remote communication, failure handling, fault tolerance, object movement, stable persistence, etc.

The distinction between logical and physical structure is also part of the method proposed by Booch [3].

As shown in figure 2, it is important to note that the physical structure is not just part of the implementation of a logical model. In the design phase there are issues related to *logical design* as well as issues related to *physical design*. Logical design involves identification of objects and patterns that are meaningful in the application domain. Physical design involves issues related to inherent distributed aspects of the application domain. In a banking system, it is an inherent property that the teller machines may be physically distributed at other locations than the banks. There is a similar distinction between logical implementation and physical implementation.

	logical structure	physical structure
design	logical design	physical design
implementation	logical implementation	physical implementation

Fig. 2. Logical versus physical structure

There is not always a sharp distinction between the 4 phases, since many choices may be arbitrary. We, however, think that it is useful to distinguish between the 4 phases. Design (logical and physical) relates to issues that are meaningful/inherent in the problem domain. Implementation (logical and physical) is about realizing the design on a computer system. Logical design and implementation is about objects and patterns. Physical design and implementation is about distribution aspects.

3 The abstractions

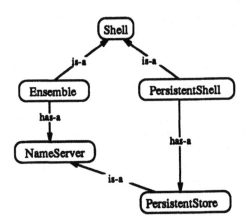

Fig. 3. Abstraction relations.

This section describes the abstractions considered mandatory for handling distribution in BETA. The abstractions so far involves no extensions to the BETA language as such, although the implicit superpattern of all patterns, *Object*, has been extended with a number of persistence and mobility attributes. Instead, the abstractions are described as library patterns for inclusion in distributed BETA programs. Relations between the abstractions described are shown in figure 3.

Figure 4 shows an example system with three ensembles. Shell objects logically "runs on" an ensemble. Other kinds of objects exist in the memory space of some shell. The arrows in figure 4 are object references.

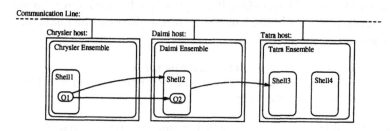

Fig. 4. Ensembles, Shells and other objects

3.1 The NameServer

All object-oriented systems with support for multiple processes need some way of handling exchange of object references. In distributed BETA, the approach to naming is the provision of an abstract superpattern, the *NameServer*. In short, the NameServer simply provides a mapping between textual names and object references. The exact semantics of this mapping depends on the actual subpattern of the abstract NameServer superpattern[2].

The NameServer *put* operation saves a (name,reference) pair given as parameters. *get* retrieves an object reference given a name and a type. Finally, *remove* deletes a (name,reference) pair.

Two subpatterns of NameServer are provided by the basic model: The *ns* part object attribute of the ensemble pattern described in section 3.3, and the *PersistentStore* attribute of *PersistentShell* described in section 3.4.

Other subpatterns of NameServer could be written on top of the basic abstractions and provided as library patterns. For example, a NameServer acting like the ANSA [1] federation based *trader*, a NFS-like distributed hierarchical name space and a replicated name server could be provided as library patterns. The point here is that programmers need not be tied to any built-in naming scheme, as is the case in e.g. Arjuna [13] and PS-Algol [5], but may define their own by implementing a special kind of NameServer. To get started, however, a system defined name server is needed, and in distributed BETA this is the NameServer part object of the ensemble described in section 3.3.

The BETA code for exporting a MessageDistributor reference to a NameServer *ns* is shown below. The object reference is named "Distributor".

```
(theDistributor[],"Distributor") -> ns.put;
```

---

[2] An abstract superpattern is a pattern supposed to be used only as a superpattern, and not directly instantiated.

The following code shows how to get a reference to a MessageDistributor from a NameServer. **MessageDistributor##** designates the *type* MessageDistributor, thereby telling the NameServer that we expect the object returned to be an instance of the *MessageDistributor* pattern: If the object in *ns* named "Distributor" is not at least a MessageDistributor, the "qualification error" exception is raised. Qualification errors are handled by further binding the quaError virtual of the NameServer get operation:

```
(MessageDistributor##, "Distributor")
-> ns.get (# quaError::< (# do <<Handle exception>> #)#)
-> theGenerator.init;
```

If a qualification error is not handled, a runtime error occurs.

3.2   The Shell·

The *Shell* pattern is the superpattern of all objects that may be instantiated directly by an ensemble, and may in most respects be thought of as modeling an executable. Instances of the Shell pattern thus correspond to large grain processes, e.g. UNIX processes, with an address space of their own.

Other kinds of objects logically exist inside Shells. As seen from other, possibly remote, objects, a Shell instance is just another kind of object with a well defined interface dependent on the actual Shell subpattern. The shell pattern is shown below:

```
shell:
  (# (* Reference to the ensemble running this shell: *)
     myEnsemble: ^|ensemble;
     (* Method for killing this shell: *)
     kill: (# ... #);
     (* The virtual global errorhandler of this shell: *)
     globalHandler:< errorHandler;
  #)
```

3.3   The Ensemble

The ensemble described in this article is based on the ensemble described in [10]. Minor changes have been made to model the reality of a distributed environment with a possibly large number of processors and network hosts. The model of persistence described in [10] has also been concretized and changed slightly.

The ensemble is a platform for executing BETA programs and should to some extend be thought of as equivalent to an operating system. However, in contrast to traditional operating systems, the ensemble provides a much tighter integration between application programs, their execution environment and other application programs. The ensemble is a program execution that can be understood entirely in terms of BETA. The program text of the ensemble constitutes an outermost block level that surrounds all application programs. Executing

```
ensemble: shell
  (# (* Application program patterns: *)
     applicationProgram1: shell(# ... #);
     applicationProgram2: shell(# ... #);
     ...
     (* Instances of application programs: *)
     app1: ^|applicationProgram1;
     app2: ^|applicationProgram2;
     ...
  do (* Instantiation and execution of application programs: *)
     &|applicationProgram1[] -> app1[]; app1.fork
     &|applicationProgram2[] -> app2[]; app2.fork;
     ...
  #)
```

Fig. 5. A tentative description of an ensemble in BETA syntax

an application program amounts to instantiating a pattern that represents the application.

The ensemble description in figure 5 is of a rather static nature with object references declared directly as part of the ensemble program text. This is of course not feasible, as the implications of adding a new appliction program would be to stop the ensemble, edit the program text, recompile, and finally restart the ensemble. Hardly something the average user would like to do in order to install a new version of his favourite word processor. The statical nature of the ensemble is removed by adding a NameServer part object to contain references to application program instances and other objects. As the Ensemble is an abstraction modeling the operating system of a network host, there is a one-to-one correspondence between Ensemble instances and network hosts[3].

In a distributed system, there may be any number of network hosts, and in addition to the mapping of textual object names to object references, the Name-Server part *ns* has the responsibility of binding the ensembles together. The way ns handles this responsibility is by having default knowledge of other ensembles in the distributed environment. This means that if the *get* operation of ns is given e.g. the internet name of a network host, a reference to the corresponding ensemble instance is returned.

In the tentative ensemble description in figure 5, the application programs (shells) are shown textually nested within an ensemble. As a consequence all instances of the application patterns have the ensemble on which they where created as static father. Logically this binds the instance to the ensemble on which it was created. In a distributed system with more than one ensemble,

---

[3] In a true distributed operating system such as Amoeba [14], the ensemble would model the operating system and therefore possibly a large number of processors/network hosts.

it should be possible to move application instances, i.e. *shell* instances, between different ensembles, and so we cannot accept that a shell is logically bound to the ensemble where it was created. Instead of textual nesting, every shell instance thus has a reference, *myEnsemble*, to the ensemble on which it is currently running.

An important operating system task is the management of processes. Therefore, an important Ensemble attribute is the ability to create new Shell instances dynamically on the operating system represented. The *createShell* attribute of an ensemble takes a pattern variable, i.e. a type, describing a subpattern of *shell* and creates an instance of this pattern on the ensemble. In non-distributed BETA, a new object is simply created using the "new" operator **&**, as in **&aPattern**. In distributed BETA, however, **&aPattern** means "create a new instance of **aPattern** in the address space of the current shell". The difference is the implicit location concept in terms of the address space of a shell. *createShell* may thus be thought of as a way to create these address spaces. Once created, a shell object may be used the same way as any other object.

```
ensemble: shell
  (# createShell:
      (# type: ##Shell; sh: ^|Shell;
      enter type##
      do ...
      exit sh[]
      #);
    ns: @NameServer(# ... #)
  #)
```

Fig. 6. Description of an ensemble in BETA syntax

The BETA code involved in dynamically obtaining a reference to the (possibly) remote ensemble named "daimi.aau.dk" followed by the creation of a shell on this ensemble is shown below.

```
(* Create an instance of the MessageDistributorShell on
 * the "daimi" ensemble *)
daimi: ^|ensemble;
...
(Ensemble##,"daimi.aau.dk") -> myEnsemble.ns.get -> daimi[];
MessageDistributorShell## -> daimi.createShell -> mds[];
```

Figure 7 shows the distributed prototype of the example application. The final application is contained in appendix A.

```
(* Distributed Prototype
 * =====================
 *
 * We are now assuming that a newly created server is registered
 * within some NameServer that in turn is  known by all relevant
 * ensembles in the distributed system. The NameServer has the name
 * "ProtoServer", and the MessageDistributor in the prototype is
 * called "Distributor".
 * MessageDistributor and MessageGenerator patterns are unchanged. *)

(* The MessageDistributor Shell: *)
Shell
(# theDistributor: @|MessageDistributor;
   ns: ^NameServer;
do
   (* Fetch the NameServer used: *)
   (NameServer##,"ProtoServer")
     -> myEnsemble.ns.get
     -> ns[];

   (* Start theDistributor. *)
   theDistributor.fork;

   (* Export theDistributor to ns. *)
   (theDistributor[],"Distributor") -> ns.put;
#)

(* The MessageGenerator Shell: *)
Shell
(# theGenerator: @|MessageGenerator;
   ns: ^NameServer;
do
   (* Fetch the NameServer used. *)
   (NameServer##,"ProtoServer")
     -> myEnsemble.ns.get
     -> ns[];

   (* Get a reference to the MessageDistributor and
    * initialize theGenerator. *)
   (MessageDistributor##, "Distributor")
     -> ns.get
     -> theGenerator.init;
#)
```

Fig. 7. Distributed prototype of example application

3.4   The PersistentShell

The building blocks for object persistence is the *PersistentShell* and the operations *checkpoint*, *revert* and *deactivate* supported by all objects. A PersistentShell contains a static part object *ps* that is an instance of *PersistentStore*. The PersistentStore in turn is a virtual subpattern of NameServer. That PersistentStore is virtual means that it may be extended in subpatterns of PersistentShell. When an ensemble running a PersistentShell crashes, the PersistentShell is automatically restarted when the ensemble comes up. When this happens, the *restart* virtual, corresponding to the *recover* operation of Argus [17] guardians, is executed.

```
PersistentShell: shell
  (# ps: @PersistentStore;
     PersistentStore:< NameServer (# ... #)
     restart:< (# ... #);
  #)
```

An object *o* is made persistent by associating it with a persistent store. A non-persistent object is called *transient*. Associating an object with a persistent store happens as a side effect of putting the object into a persistent store:

```
o: ^Object;
psh: ^|PersistentShell;
...
(o[],"aName") -> psh.ps.put;
```

It is an error to associate an object with more than one persistent store at a time as that would lead to ambiguity concerning where the object state should be fetched at activation time. If the same object is put into the same store more than once, the effect is simply to associate multiple names with the object.

A persistent object may become transient again using the PersistentStore *remove* operation. Following remove, the object may then be associated with another persistent store.

Now, the operation `(o[],"aName") -> ps.put` does nothing but associating *o* with *ps* and register the pair (o[],"aName"). The state of *o* is not saved on stable storage until the *o.checkpoint* operation supported by all objects is executed. As persistence is reachability based, *o.checkpoint* also saves the state of all objects in the transitive closure of *o* on stable storage. If an object *a* first referenced by an object *b* in a breadth first traversal of the transitive closure of *o* is not already persistent, *a* is associated with the same persistent store as *b* and the *a.checkpoint* operation performed.

The *o.revert* operation reverts the state of *o* to the state saved in the associated persistent store, and may be used as a building block for providing transactional behaviour. The *o.deactivate* operation removes the object from volatile storage. If an inactive persistent object is accessed, it is reinstantiated in the address space of the shell accessing the object unless the persistent object is a shell itself, in which case the shell is reinstantiated in its own address space. As is the case with the checkpoint operation, revert and deactivate works on the transitive closure of the object.

More on reachability In the description above, most operations involved the transitive closure of an object. The reason for this approach is that the behaviour of an object o may in principle depend on all objects reachable from o. In non-distributed applications where all objects are logically part of the same application, it is our experience that this approach works well in most cases. However, even in non-distributed programs there are situations where saving the full transitive closure of an object is not what is wanted. For example, an object representing a drawing may have a reference to the window in which it is displayed. In this case it may not make sense to save the window when saving the drawing itself. Instead of following the reference to the window, one may instead want to forget about the object referred.

In distributed applications, a reference can refer a remote server object. In this case, it may make no sense to follow the reference when saving the object containing the reference. Instead one might want to remember what object was referred, but without actually following the reference.

There are a number of possible ways to handle this problem. In the ONTOS [21] object oriented database system for C++, references to persistent objects are saved automatically, but without saving the state of the object referred. The ONTOS application programmer who needs to save the transitive closure thus has to implement the necessary book-keeping himself. As stated earlier, we believe that saving the full transitive closure is in practice the best default.

In Argus [17], persistent objects must explicitly be declared *stable*. As a consequence of the transactional semantics built into the language, the stable storage copy of any persistent object is always up-to-date. Persistence is not reachability based, and therefore it is no issue whether references should be followed or not.

The approach taken in the POET [22] object oriented database system, is to add a number of keywords to the C++ language. In POET, a reference is followed unless declared *transient*. Doing the same in BETA would mean adding keywords to distinguish between references that should be followed and references that should not. With this solution it would still be possible for all types of objects to persist. Furthermore, the POET solution would add to the expressive power of the BETA language with respect to patterns developed explicitly with persistence in mind.

In the current implementation of the BETA PersistentStore, it is possible for advanced users to taylor the graph-traversal performed when checkpointing the state of persistent objects to stable·storage. This way effects similar to the ones described for ONTOS and POET may be achieved. However, for ease of use, adding the POET solution may be considered in the future.

3.5 ErrorHandler

One of the main issues distinguishing distributed programming from "ordinary" concurrent programming is the possibility of partial failure. Partial failure is the rather probable event of a single system component failing while others in principle are able to continue doing useful work.

The ErrorHandler provides a scope in which exceptions may be caught, handled and possibly reraised in the (dynamically) enclosing errorHandler scope. Each thread has its own errorHandler chain. When a communication error occurs, the action taken is to locate the first ErrorHandler that handles the problem in the current dynamic ErrorHandler chain, and raise an exception there.

The method invocations on remote objects are thus handled as usual, with no syntactic difference at all, but in case of communication errors, these are handled by raising the exceptions provided by the ErrorHandler. A simple example of this approach is shown in figure 8. Notice that the approach very much resembles exception handling in C++ or Ada[4]. In case no exception handler has been setup by the programmer, the *globalHandler* of the current shell is invoked which in most cases will terminate the shell. The point here is that distribution related failure handling may be added to the code without changing the program logic. Only additions, as opposed to changes, are made.

Apart from the specification of exception handlers, the errorHandler scope is used to specify the amount of time to wait for an answer before raising the *timeOut* exception. This is done using the *timeOutValue* virtual.

Other physical communication aspects could be specified using this errorHandler "scoping" mechanism as well. For example "Quality of Service" and diverse communication parameters could be expressed this way, thereby gaining detailed control of different communication aspects without the need for access to the implementation of objects used.

4 Object movement

The primitives for object movement are the same as in Emerald [8]. However, instead of being expressed as language keywords as in Emerald, primitives for object movement in BETA are expressed syntactically as attributes of the objects.

For any object o, `o.location`[5] returns the shell containing o. `o2[] -> o1.move` has the effect of moving the object $o1$ to the shell where the object $o2$ resides. The convention is to recursively move an object and all its *static* part objects. `o2[] -> o1.fix` fixes $o1$ in the shell where $o2$ resides. `o1.unfix` unifixes $o1$ thereby allowing it to move again after a fix. Finally, `o2[] -> o1.refix` atomically performs *unfix, move* and *refix* operations on $o1$. The semantics of these operations are the same as in Emerald.

Moving a Shell means moving the process and address space and all contained objects. Moving a PersistentShell furthermore has the effect of moving the stable storage copy of the persistent objects to stable storage on the host represented by the target ensemble. It makes no sense to move an ensemble.

---

[4] The "exceptions" are virtual methods of the errorHandler. Handling an exception thus means further binding the corresponding virtual method by using the `::<` operator. Note that there are no special language constructs in BETA for handling exceptions. For a description of exception handling in BETA, see [19], chapter 16.

[5] Corresponding to the Emerald expression `locate o`

```
do catch: errorHandler
    (# connectionBroken::< (* Connection to 'theObj' lost. *)
        (#
        do <<Do local cleanup>>;
            (* Propagate exception to surrounding ErrorHandler: *)
            theObj[] -> prevHandler.connectionBroken;
        #);
    timeOuts: @Integer;
    (* Number of seconds to wait for an answer: *)
    timeOutValue::< (# do 5 -> value #);
    timeOut::< (* No response from 'theObj' within time limit. *)
        (#
        do timeOuts+1 -> timeOuts;
            (if timeOuts //maxTimeOuts then
                <<Do local cleanup>>;
                (* Leave current errorHandler scope: *)
                leave catch;
            else
                retry -> value;
            if);
        #);

do (* The actual method invocations: *)
    'foo' -> remoteObject.someMethod -> theResult;
    'bar' -> remoteObject.someOtherMethod;
#)
```

Fig. 8. Example usage of ErrorHandler pattern.

In addition to explicitly moving objects, Emerald allows objects to attach other objects thereby requesting attached objects to be moved together with the object itself. This way colocation of objects can be controlled explicitly by the programmer using built-in language constructs. Furthermore, to achieve efficient usage of reference parameters to remote calls, such parameters might in Emerald be declared as call-by-move or call-by-visit parameters.

In BETA, an activation record is a first-class object that is an instance of a nested pattern. The parameters to a procedure call are attributes of the nested procedure object. As will be explained in a little more detail in section 7, procedure objects are created at the caller side, parameters filled in, and then moved to the site of the enclosing object (the callee) for execution. In the case of reference parameters, only the reference itself, not the object referred, is moved along with the procedure object. This default could be changed by attaching reference attributes to the procedure object to achieve that the object referred was moved along. As a consequence the effect of call-by-move/visit may in BETA be achieved using attach-like keywords.

Emerald experience seems to show that attach and call-by-visit/move are worthwile optimizations although they add nothing to the expressive power of the language. As with the distinction between transient and persistent pointers described in section 3.4, we might therefore consider adding a couple of attach-like keywords to distributed BETA. This has, however, not been done.

5 Other issues

Assuming the abstractions introduced so far and a general implementation of distributed BETA, we now need to ask ourselves the question whether we have missed some crucial aspect of distribution.

We already have a clear model of how we would like to think about distribution with respect to BETA, as described in section 3. Furthermore, the BETA language is a concurrent language [18], and so there is no reason why we should change or add anything to the language to handle this aspect of distributed programming. Simple failure handling was covered in section 3.5. This section addresses a few of the issues that have been raised by others when discussing abstractions needed for distributed programming.

5.1 Synchronous versus asynchronous communication

The distinction between asynchronous and synchronous communication has often been addressed in the literature [7]. Proposals nearly always conform to either a single thread per process combined with asynchronous communication and futures to achieve maximum concurrency, or multiple threads combined with blocking (synchronous) communication.

BETA basicly supports the second possibility, that is multiple threads and blocking communication. It is well known that the two possibilities may easily simulate each other, but in this respect BETA goes one step further as the language is very good at building abstractions. For example, an abstraction for doing asynchronous communication in BETA may be defined and used as shown below.

```
async: (# theThread: 0|(# do this(async) #);
            forked: @Boolean;
        do (if not forked//true then
                true -> forked;
                theThread.fork;
            else
                INNER
            if)
        #);
   (* Usage: *)
   do async(# do (a,b) -> server.foo #);
```

What happens is the following: The first time the new instance of *async* is called, it forks a thread to execute it a second time. When this happens, INNER is called and the code of the specific async subpattern is executed concurrently with the rest of the caller code. Note that booleans in BETA are initially FALSE.

The async pattern may freely be combined with a *future* abstraction as described below:

```
future:
  (# sem: @semaphore;
     resultType:< Object;
     result: ^resultType;
   enter (# enter result[] do sem.V #)
   exit (# do sem.P exit result[] #)
   #);
(* Usage: *)
   tf: @future(# resultType::< text #);
   do async(# do 6 -> server.getText -> tf #);
      ... (* Do some useful work. *)
      tf -> putLine;
```

An instance of the future pattern contains a semaphore that is initially closed. When something is assigned to the future, the semaphore is opened, thereby allowing a read on the assigned value. If a read on the future is executed before a write, the reader will be blocked on the semaphore until the write happens.

Other examples of abstractions for concurrency are shown in [18]. Libraries for handling distribution should of course contain these and other relevant abstractions, but as shown they are not mandatory as basic building blocks for distributed programming.

5.2 Different interfaces to the same object

A number of object based distributed programming systems share the notion of conformity based type systems [4, 1]. Among other things this means that classes and types are distinct concepts, and that a given class may conform to different types. Alternative terms are "interface type" and "implementation type". One of the potential advantages of this approach is the possibility to hand out different interfaces to the same object, thereby restricting the methods that different users of the object may access.

In BETA, this may to some extend be achieved by handing out references to different part objects of a single aggregation object. The methods of each part object may have access to the methods and state of the autonomous object, but clients having only references to the parts are of course only able to use methods of the part. Any number of references to different part objects may be given out this way, and so it is possible to achieve different interfaces to the same BETA object. An example of this is shown in appendix A, where a reference to the MessageDistributor part of the MessageDistributorShell is exported to the NameServer.

5.3 Missing aspects

Transactions are not directly supported by the abstractions described in this paper. However, among others, the Arjuna project [13] has shown that transactions can be supported by a number of library classes. A similar approach can be taken with respect to support for transactions in BETA. Furthermore, the building blocks for persistence as described in section 3.4 combined with the general support for concurrent programming provided by the BETA language, forms a base on top of which such classes may be easily built. A distributed object oriented database for BETA objects supporting nested transactions has already been built using a prototype implementation of the abstractions described in this paper [15].

Concerning replication, Argus and Arjuna among others have shown that object replication is easily achieved on top of a transaction mechanism.

Apart from transactions, security is clearly a missing aspect needing future consideration.

6 Related work

The Arjuna [13] project focuses on the implementation of atomic actions using the inheritance mechanism provided by C++. In Arjuna, a persistent object is by definition a transactional object. While we of course agree that a transaction mechanism is often needed, we do not agree that every program using distribution and persistent objects needs transactions. Furthermore, Arjuna distribution and persistence is not type orthogonal for the following three reasons. First, only subclasses of the Arjuna *LockManager* class may persist. Secondly, although multiple inheritance could be used to mix in the ability to persist, the Arjuna programmer still needs to write methods for saving and restoring the state of the object. This may be a major effort in the case of e.g. a general graph structure. In BETA, any object may persist, and the serialization of objects is done automatically using runtime type information. Third, using an RPC mechanism for parameter passing, Arjuna has value parameter semantics. This is in our opinion a major restriction in the expressive power of any object oriented programming language. Finally, the Arjuna naming scheme, although implicitly relying on the notion of a NameServer, is hardwired into the *ArjunaName* class, thereby making it impossible for programmers to build their own naming scheme. However, Arjuna has shown that a transaction mechanism may be expressed using inheritance. This approach could also be used to build a transaction library in BETA to facilitate development of applications needing transactional behaviour.

In Argus [17], transaction mechanisms are part of the language definition. Distributed access to objects is restricted to *guardians* using an RPC mechanism for communication between guardians. Like a guardian, the *shell* described in this paper corresponds to a self contained program module, containing a number of transient or persistent objects and a number of processes (active objects). However, in Argus remote access is restricted to the guardian handlers using value parameter semantics, whereas in distributed BETA, remote access is not restricted to the methods of the shell, but is allowed also on fine grain objects inside shells to which the caller has a reference. In BETA, parameters may be passed by value or by reference, and both possibilities therefore exist in distributed BETA. The guardian *recover* method is used to restart guardians after node crashes. In distributed BETA, the ensemble only restarts instances of *PersistentShell* and its subpatterns automatically. Automatic restart of other shellTypes may be achieved by further binding the *restart* virtual attribute of PersistentShell.

Distributed BETA is in many respects very similar to the Emerald system. First, the BETA primitives for object movement are directly inspired by the Emerald primitives. Emerald has reference parameter semantics, whereas BETA has both value and reference parameter semantics. The BETA ensemble is similar to the Emerald node. However, Emerald is designed to be *the* operating system, whereas the BETA model reflects the underlying operating system. The ensemble represents the operating system itself, whereas shells represents the executable programs and shell instances the processes of the OS. The most important difference between BETA and Emerald is that Emerald is lacking support for persistent objects[6].

The proxy approach has been used in a number of implementations of distributed object systems. For example, Distributed Smalltalk [2] uses the concept of proxy objects in the implementation. In contrast to Smalltalk, BETA is a statically typed language using runtime type checks only at assignments where covariance means that type checking is not possible at compile time [11]. The pattern of a BETA object is immutable, thereby avoiding the distribution specific problems resulting from mutable Smalltalk classes.

7 The proxy approach

Until this point we have primarily been focusing on the logical model of distributed programming in BETA. This section briefly discusses a general proxy based implementation of distributed BETA.

The implementation of distributed BETA is based on the notion of proxy objects [2]. One possible alternative would be to use a single large (e.g. 64 bit) distributed shared memory [6, 9]. However, this possibility is ruled out by the CSCW applications needing support for heterogeneous wide area networks.

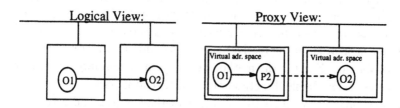

Fig. 9. The proxy view

In the proxy approach, remote references are, as illustrated in figure 9, han-

---

[6] Although an object oriented database for Emerald objects is being developed [16].

dled by actually referencing a local representative of the remote object, the proxy. It is then the job of the proxy to handle the communication with the remote object. The main advantage of this is that the compiler does not need to be aware of the difference between proxies and real objects, and so the same code may be generated to call methods in both types of objects.

As seen from the caller, a method invocation is therefore handled the same way in the remote and local cases. Calling methods in BETA is equivalent to executing instances of nested patterns, and therefore the problem to be solved is the movement of such objects into the right scope (the scope of the real object, not the proxy) before execution[7]. In the case of simple method invocations, the low level calling sequence is as described below. Figure 10 illustrates the case of a method call of the form (a,o[]) -> foo.m -> c; where "foo" is an instance of the pattern *fooPat*, a is an integer passed by value and o[] is an object passed by reference.

```
fooPat:
  (# m: (# x,z: @Integer; o: ^Object;
         enter (x,o[])
         do ...
         exit z
    #)#);
```

1. Sender side: Create an instance of the pattern corresponding to the invoked method and fill in parameters. This happens exactly the same way in ordinary local method invocations.

2. Sender side: Marshall the method object into a bytestream and send it to the Shell containing the real object. Any BETA object contains runtime type information, and therefore any object may be marshalled for transmission across a network. As the identification of the receiver is contained directly in the proxy object, and is thus visible from the method object having the proxy as static father, this does not involve any table lookups that could depend on the number of proxy objects in the actual process.

3. Receiver side: Unpack the method object. This involves a hashtable lookup to identify the object that is the static father of the method object. Furthermore, as one parameter was a reference parameter, a proxy for the referred object is created on the receiver side, if one did not already exist.

4. Receiver side: Execute the method object as in an ordinary local invocation.

5. Receiver side: Marshall method object and send it back.

6. Sender side: Unmarshall the returned method object and return exit parameters to the caller. This last step is also done exactly like in a local invocation.

---

[7] In principle one could as well move the real object to the site of the caller. This corresponds to thread migration (moving BETA method objects) versus object migration (moving the object whose method is executed).

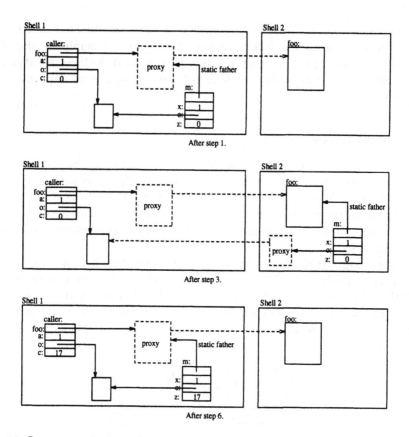

Fig. 10. Remote method execution

In most respects this very much resembles an ordinary RPC mechanism, although these usually supports only value parameters. Note, however, that because activation records in BETA are first class objects, the mechanism for object movement also takes care of remote procedure calls.

There are a number of BETA specifics that needs special consideration during this process.

First, execution of an INNER construct may mean that the scope of the executing code changes. To ensure that the executing object is still inside the scope of a real object and not a proxy, this means in some cases that the executing object may need to be moved to ensure that the static father of the object is still a real object, and not some proxy object. Even though this complicates the implementation of distributed BETA, it is no problem in the sense that if it is not used, it will not have any implications with respect to efficiency.

Second, BETA allows direct remote manipulation of non-private attributes. In non-distributed BETA, this is compiled into assembly code doing the manipulation directly on the memory of the object referred. As already described, it is the job of the runtime system to ensure that objects are always executing in the scope of real objects, and not in the scope of proxies. Therefore, the direct manipulation problem is solved by the compiler using access methods in situations where the runtime system does not ensure that the object manipulated and the (procedure) object doing the manipulation are colocated. As these situations are relatively seldom, using access methods will have no significant implications for efficiency.

7.1 Implementation status

A version of the persistent store as described in section 3.4 has been used for about two years in the EU EuroCODE and EuroCoOp projects. This version is also part of the Mjølner BETA System described in [12]. The current version of the PersistentStore supports automatic pointer swizzling using tagged pointers as well as a tailorable graph-traversal algorithm for limiting persistence as described in section 3.4.

Concerning distribution, a prototype implementation with a number of restrictions is available, and has been used to implement a general distributed OODB and hypermedia built on top of the OODB. In the hypermedia each user has a link manager on top of which a number of applications are running. This is illustrated in figure 11.

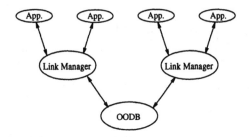

Fig. 11. The hypermedia application

Among the restrictions in our current implementation we should mention at least the following:

- Explicit object migration is not supported. Migrating passive objects poses no special problems as most of mechanisms needed are already implemented. A callable loader and linker being implemented will support movement of objects to shells not already containing the code for objects moved. Migrating active objects is still a problem, mainly due to the need to support heterogeneous networks, but also due to the fine granularity of the objects to be migrated. Most of these problems are the same as described in [8], and may be solved in a similar way.
- No distributed garbage collection. Efficient algorithms for doing distributed garbage collection are still an area open for investigation. However, there should be no special problems with doing distributed garbage collection in

BETA as compared to other distributed OO languages. The garbage collector used in non-distributed BETA is a generation scavenger based on [23], using copy-collection in the infant object area, and mark-sweep in the adult object area. The distributed garbage collector should be able to cooperate with this highly efficient local garbage collection scheme.

Some aspects of the prototype implementation are:

- The Ensemble is represented by a deamon on each UNIX host responsible for generating unique object ID's and saving (object name, object reference) pairs. When an object reference crosses a Shell boundary, the object referred is given a globally unique ID.
- Each Shell instance is a UNIX process.
- Runs on heterogenerous network of workstations. (SPARC, HP-PA RISC, Sun and HP MC680x0 based UNIX workstations using TCP communication.)

We are currently working towards a more general implementation of distributed BETA as described in this article.

8 Conclusion

A major goal in the design of distributed BETA has been to separate issues related to the logical model and the physical model. The logical model describes a given application domain in terms of active and passive objects and patterns representing phenomena and concepts from the application domain. The physical model describes the mapping of the logical model onto a given computer system. The physical model defines the distribution of objects on different host machines and it also defines which objects are to be transient, persistent and shared. The separation of issues between logical and physical modeling has several advantages:

1. Issues related to concurrency, communication and synchronization are part of the logical language model. In distributed systems based on C or C++ these issues are defined implicitly by (ad hoc) mechanism introduced to handle e.g. remote procedure calls.
2. The actual distribution of objects on different host machines is independent of the logical model. The same logical model may be realized on a single processor, a multi-processor or as a loosely coupled distributed system.
3. Better support for the application development process based on evolving prototypes. This is achieved by providing type orthogonal persistence and object distribution. This article includes a simple example evolving from a logical BETA prototype into a distributed BETA program.

We have described the building blocks believed to be basic in the sense that most other abstractions, possibly excluding security, may be built on top using pure BETA. That is, further low-level runtime support should not be necessary.

9 Acknowledgements

This work has been carried out within the DeVise project at the Computer Science Department, Aarhus University. It is supported by the Danish Research Programme for Informatics, grant no. 5.26.18.19 and by the Esprit projects EuroCoOp (5303) and EuroCODE (6155). Furthermore we would like to thank Jørgen Lindskov Knudsen, specifically for supplying the *future* abstraction discussed in section 5.1, and for numerous discussions in general. Thanks also to Jens Arnold Hem and Lennert Sloth for providing valuable input to the prototype implementation and to Timothy Budd and Anders Kristensen for proof reading. Finally, we would like to thank the people at Mjølner Informatics for low-level help during prototype implementation.

References

1. Architechture Projects Management Ltd., Poseidon Hous, Castle Park, Cambridge, UK. *The ANSA Reference Manual, version 01.00*, 1989.
2. J.K. Bennett. The design and implementation of distributed smalltalk. In *OOPSLA PROCEEDINGS*, 1987.
3. Grady Booch. *Object-Oriented Design with Applications*. New York NY: Benjamin/Cummings, 1991.
4. A. Black et al. Distribution and abstract types in emerald. *IEEE Transactions on Software Engineering*, 13(1), Jan 1987.
5. Atkinson et al. An approach to persistent programming. *Computer Journal*, 26(4), Nov 1983.
6. B. Koch et al. Cache coherency and storage management in a persistent object system. In S.Zdonik A.Dearle, G.Shaw, editor, *The Fourth International Workshop on Persistent Object Systems*, 1990.
7. E. Bal et al. Programming Languages for Distributed Computing Systems. *ACM Computing Surveys*, 21(3), Sep 1989.
8. E. Jul et al. Fine-Grained Mobility in the Emerald System. *ACM Transactions on Computer Systems*, 6(1):109–133, Feb 1988.
9. J.S. Chase et al. Lightweight shared objects in a 64-bit operating system. In *OOPSLA PROCEEDINGS*, pages 397–413, 1992.
10. O. Agesen et al. Language Level Support for Persistence in BETA. In J.L. Knudsen, O.L. Madsen, and B. Magnusson ands M. Löfgren, editors, *Object-Oriented Environments*. Prentice Hall, Sep 1993.
11. O.L. Madsen et al. Strong typing of object-oriented languages revisited. In *OOPSLA Proceedings*, 1990.
12. P. Andersen et al. The Mjølner BETA system. In J.L. Knudsen, O.L. Madsen, B. Magnusson, and M. Löfgren, editors, *Object-Oriented Environments*. Prentice Hall, Sep 1993.
13. S.Shrivastava et al. An Overview of the Arjuna Distributed Programming System. *IEEE Softwaare*, pages 66–73, Jan 1991.
14. Tanenbaum et. al. Experiences with the amoeba distributed operating system. *Communications of the ACM*, 33:46–63, Dec 1990.

15. J. Hem L. Sloth. Object oriented model for the distributed object oriented database. Technical report, EuroCODE, Workpackage WP2 - Deliverable D2.2, 1993.

16. N. E. Larsen. An object-oriented database in emerald. Master's thesis, DIKU, Department of Computer Science, University of Copenhagen, 1992.

17. B. Liskov. Distributed Programming in Argus. *Communications of the ACM*, 31(3):300–312, Mar 1988.

18. O.L. Madsen. Building abstractions for concurrent object-oriented programming (draft). Computer Science Department, Aarhus, Feb 1993.

19. B. Møller-Pedersen O.L. Madsen and K. Nygaard. *Object-Oriented Programming in the BETA Programming Language*. Addison Wesley, June 1993.

20. OMG. *The Common Object Request Broker Architechture and Specification*, Dec 1991. Document number 91.12.1, Revision 1.1.

21. Ontos, Inc. Three Burlington Woods Burlington. *ONTOS Reference Manual*, June 1991. MA 01803.

22. J. Robie and B. Witte. *The POET handbook*. Berlin, Germany, 1991.

23. D. Ungar. Generation scavenging: A non-disruptive high performance storage reclamation algorithm. In *First Symposium of Practical Software Development Environments*, pages 157–167, Apr 1984. ACM Software Engineering.

A Final version of example application

This section includes the last version of the example application used in this article.

```
(* Final application
 * ==================
 *
 * In this version we add fault tolerance to the program. For the
 * sake of simplicity we assume that the "ProtoServer" object is
 * started by the system administrator. On the other hand, clients
 * unable to connect to a MessageDistributor may  create their own.
 *)


MessageDistributor:
   (# (* registerGenerator is still unchanged. It is called
       * remotely, but is only doing local computations. *)
      distributeMessage:
        (# theMessage: @Text;
         enter theMessage
         do
             (for <<all generators>> repeat
                 callGenerator: ErrorHandler
                 (# connectionBroken::<
                       (* thisGenerator failed. For simplicity we
                        * choose to forget thisGenerator. *)
                       (#
                       do thisGenerator[] -> forgetGenerator;
                          leave callGenerator;
```

```
                              #)
                    do theMessage -> thisGenerator.receiveMessage;
                    #)
              for);
         #);
  #);
MessageGenerator:
  (# theDistributor: ^|MessageDistributor;
     (* receiveMessage is unchanged *)
     init:
        (#
        enter theDistributor[]
        do (* registerGenerator is a remote communication.
            * Errors will be handled defaultHandler of the
            * GeneratorShell. *)
           THIS(MessageGenerator)[]
             -> theDistributor.registerGenerator;
           THIS(MessageGenerator).fork;
        #);
  do
     cycle
     (#
     do
        callDistributor: ErrorHandler
          (# connectionBroken::<
                (* Distributor failed. Try again later. *)
                (# do leave callDistributor #)
             do "A nice message"
                -> theDistributor.distributeMessage;
          #);
     #)
  #);
(* The Distributor Shell: *)
MessageDistributorShell: Shell
(# theDistributor: @|MessageDistributor;
   ns: ^NameServer;
   defaultHandler::<
     (# (* This is the default ErrorHandler. Errors caught
         * here are considered fatal errors so we just shut
         * down this Shell. *)
        connectionBroken::<
          (* What to do on a broken connection. *)
          (# do (* Close down in a nice way. *); kill #)
        (* Other exceptions. *)
     #);
do
     (* Fetch the NameServer used. *)
     (NameServer##,"ProtoServer") -> myEnsemble.ns.get
     (# notFound::<
          (# (* No NameServer named "ProtoServer" found. *)
```

```
        do (failure,'"ProtoServer" not found') -> stop;
   #)#) -> ns[];
   (* Start the server. *)
   theDistributor.fork;
   (* Register the server. *)
   (theServer[],"Distributor") -> ns.put
   (# alreadyThere::<
        (# (* An instance of the name "Distributor" has already
           * been registered. The example assumes that only one
           * server is  needed, so we just give up. *)
        do (failure,'A server is already running') -> stop;
   #)#);
#)
(* The MessageGenerator Shell: *)
Shell
(# theGenerator: @|MessageGenerator;
   ns: ^NameServer;
   defaultHandler::<
     (# connectionBroken::<
          (# do (* Close down in a nice way. *) #)
     #);
do
   (* Fetch the NameServer used. *)
   (NameServer##,"ProtoServer")  -> myEnsemble.ns.get
   (# notFound::<
        (#
        do (failure,'"ProtoServer" not found') -> stop;
   #)#) -> ns[];
   (* Get a reference to the GenericServer and use it to
    * initialize the client. *)
   getDistributor: (MessageDistributor##, "Distributor") -> ns.get
   (# notFound::<
        (# (* No MessageDistributor named "Distributor" found.
           * Start a new MessageDistributorShell on myEnsemble.*)
           mds: ^|MessageDistributorShell;
        do MessageDistributorShell## -> myEnsemble.createShell
           -> mds[];
           mds.fork;
           (* To avoid race conditions we cannot use mds.theServer
            * directly as some other generator simultaneously might
            * try to start another. The result of createShell is
            * simply shown here to demonstrate that the reference
            * returned might be used in other situations. Instead
            * we retry the get operation. *)
           restart getDistributor
   #)#) -> theGenerator.init;
#)
```

A Flexible System Design to Support Object-Groups and Object-Oriented Distributed Programming*

Silvano Maffeis

Department of Computer Science
University of Zurich, Switzerland
maffeis@ifi.unizh.ch

Abstract. Under many circumstances, the development of distributed applications greatly benefits from mechanisms like process groups, reliable ordered multicast, and message passing. However, toolkits offering these capabilities are often low-level and therefore difficult to program. To ease the development of distributed applications, in this paper we propose to hide these low-level functions behind object-oriented abstractions such as *object-groups*, *Remote Method Calling*, and *Smart Proxies*. Furthermore, we describe how the ELECTRA toolkit provides such object-oriented abstractions in a portable and highly machine-independent way.

1 Introduction

Distributed systems like failure tolerant client-server applications, distributed filesystems, nameservers, groupware systems, and distributed scientific computations usually require a fine degree of synchronization between distributed, concurrent activities. These applications often benefit from the presence of process-groups [4] as a structuring mechanism, and of reliable, ordered multicast [11] to perform one-to-many communication. We shall use the term *directly distributed system* [6] to denote these sorts of applications. More specific, in directly distributed systems, distributed threads of execution interact *directly* with one another while continuously respecting constraints on their joint behavior. On the other side, in data-oriented systems like distributed data management applications, distributed threads of execution typically interact *indirectly* with one another by issuing operations on logically shared data objects. Our work primarily aims at supporting directly distributed systems, though tools for supporting purely data-oriented applications, for instance transactions and atomic objects [22, 9], could be realized on the abstractions we treat in this paper.

An intent of this paper is to propose *object-groups*, *Remote Method Calling*, and *Smart Proxies* as a widely usable and powerful abstraction mechanism for building directly distributed systems. We exemplify how these abstractions are being realized in an object-oriented toolkit, called ELECTRA [16], which is currently being developed at the University of Zurich.

This paper goes beyond previous work on object-oriented, distributed programming, for example [2, 17, 22, 9], in that it proposes a system design to support object-groups in a highly portable fashion. We have been influenced by the work carried out in the HORUS [25], ISIS [4, 5], and in the PANDA project [3], and by ideas described in [12].

The rest of the paper is structured as follows. In the next section we will give a short introduction to the ELECTRA toolkit. Throughout the paper, the toolkit serves to exemplify abstractions and mechanisms we propose. Section 3 introduces Smart Proxies and

---

* This work is supported by *Siemens AG ZFE*, Germany, and by the *Eidgenössisches Volkswirtschaftsdepartement, Kommission zur Förderung der wissenschaftlichen Forschung (KWF)*, Switzerland, Grants No. 2255.1 and 2554.1

object-groups. It also addresses problems inherent to object-group communication. The way ELECTRA supports object-groups and object-oriented, distributed programming independently from the underlying communication platform is described in Sect. 4. Finally, Sect. 5 summarizes and concludes the paper.

2 Overview of the ELECTRA Toolkit

Currently, several distributed control technologies (DCT) exist, mostly in the form of C programming libraries, which aid programmers in building reliable, directly distributed systems. Examples are AMOEBA [23], DELTA-4 [26], HORUS [25], ISIS [4], PSYNC [18], and TRANSIS [1].

However, the methods and tools offered by such DCT are often difficult to use by people lacking many years of experience in building distributed systems, since the provided functions are mostly low-level and not expressive enough for modelling real world problems. In addition, it normally takes a great effort to port applications written for a specific DCT to another one, since each DCT goes its own ways and provides its own programming paradigms and interfaces.

ELECTRA is a toolkit for object-oriented, distributed programming in C++. It consists of a run-time environment which allows to create, find, and access objects in a computer network, of a CORBA-IDL [8] stub generator, of class libraries, and of simple programming tools to monitor and control distributed applications. For a more detailed description refer to [16].

ELECTRA objects may have an *active* or a *passive* role. Applications can issue operations on remote, active objects. The invocation of an operation on a remote object is carried out using a syntax very similar to conventional C++ method invocations. We use the term *Remote Method Calling (RMC)* to designate this communication paradigm. RMCs are issued by invoking the methods of a local stub-object, a so-called *proxy* [21]. The proxy object exports a logically centralized and logically local service, even when the accessed object is remote and replicated. Although ELECTRA is implemented in C++ and although C++ is the only language ELECTRA provides a binding for at the moment, the proposed abstractions can be realized in other languages as well.

ELECTRA is conceived to run on top of different state-of-the-art DCTs such as the ones mentioned at the beginning of this section. The mechanisms we adopt therefore will be described later in Sect. 4.

2.1 Remote Method Calling

As was stated above, RMC means that the methods of a remote object or object-group can be invoked through a local proxy object. The proxy provides the same interface as the remote object it represents. Parameters of remote method invocations may include the standard C++ base types and C++ objects, and typechecking of the RMC parameters is performed at compile-time.

Human-readable names of the form <Domain>:<Path> are used to identify ELECTRA objects. The name "ifi.unizh.ch:/nameserver", for example, refers to the object "/nameserver" running within the domain "ifi.unizh.ch". An identification name can refer to a single object or to an object-group.

A special ELECTRA object known as the *master-trader* [16] manages the identification names for a domain. In our model such domain normally comprises one LAN.

ELECTRA supports three kinds of RMC: asynchronous mode, synchronous mode, and *promises* [15]. In asynchronous mode, a thread issuing an RMC proceeds without awaiting the reply to the remote operation. In this case an upcall method can be specified, which will be invoked by the sender's run-time system as soon as the reply (containing the RMC's return values) arrives. The upcall obtains an own thread of execution. In synchronous mode, the sender is blocked until the reply has arrived. Promises allow for an intermediate form of synchronization: the RMC is issued asynchronously, but invoking the method Promise::wait() blocks the sender until the reply has arrived. The following example demonstrates how an object providing a domain name service can be accessed by different kinds of RMCs:

```
DomainNameServer dns;                           // Create a proxy.
dns.bind( "ifi.unizh.ch:/nameserver" );         // Bind to the remote object.

Promise promise;
Name name; Address address;
...
dns.install( name, address, SYNC );             // Synchronous RMC.
dns.install( name, address, ASYNC );            // Asynchronous RMC.
dns.install( name, address, ASYNC, method );    // With upcall method.
dns.lookup( name, address, promise );           // With promise object.
...
promise.wait();                                 // Explicit synchronization.
                                                // Return value is
                                                // available afterwards.
```

3 Object-Groups

To achieve high availability despite host and network failures, an active ELECTRA object can be replicated over several hosts. Each replica may fail independently. The replicas belong to the same *object-group*, an object-group being a non-empty collection of object instances which cooperate to achieve some common purpose. Internally, communication with an object-group is by means of reliable multicast.

A *homogeneous* object-group consists of objects which all perform the same task, whereas the members of a *heterogeneous* object-group perform different tasks.

If a proxy object is bound to an object-group, the method calls issued on the proxy are transparently multicasted to all of the objects in the group. As depicted in Fig. 1, the programmer always deals with one proxy, which may represent a single object or an object-group.

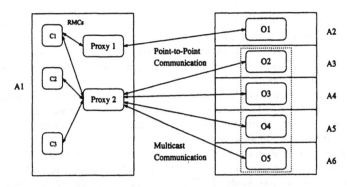

Fig. 1. Proxy 1 interfaces to a single object whereas Proxy 2 interfaces to an object-group. C*n* denotes a client object, O*n* a remote server object, A*n* an address space.

3.1 Smart Proxies

We propose the term *Smart Proxy* to denote a proxy object which provides more than just a local access point to a remote object. In addition, a Smart Proxy accomplishes at least one of the following tasks:

- *Replication transparency.* A logically non-replicated interface is provided for accessing an object-group. This ensures that single objects can be replaced by object-groups without having to modify the client applications.
- *Replication control.* The degree of replication an object-group provides can dynamically be controlled through the proxy. The proxy provides run-time replication control by closely cooperating with the group management service (see Sect. 3.4) and the naming service.
- *Caching.* To increase the performance of an application, caching can be performed within Smart Proxies. For example, a Smart Proxy interfacing to a nameserver can maintain a local list holding the most frequently accessed nameserver entries.
- *Migration transparency.* A Smart Proxy can be informed by the migration service when the object associated with the proxy was migrated. Thus, object-migration can be hidden from client applications.
- *Concurrency control.* Above tasks are normally performed by a Smart Proxy at the client site. At the server site, a Smart Proxy may allow to specify *encapsulator* objects to define concurrency control schemes [10], message filters, etc. on a per-object basis.

3.2 Benefits of Object-Groups

ELECTRA proxies provide for replication transparency, meaning that client applications need not know whether they communicate with a single object or with an object-group. Providing an object-group abstraction is interesting for the following reasons [13]:

- *Load sharing.* A non-replicated object can be replaced by an object-group whenever the object becomes overloaded, and without having to modify applications which use the object. Parallelism and load sharing can thus be increased step by step, provided that the toolkit offers abstraction mechanisms like Remote Method Calling and Smart Proxies, which allow communication with an object-group as if it was a non-replicated object.
- *Fault tolerance.* Availability and fault tolerance are increased by using a homogeneous object-group to implement a service. Each object can fail independently from the other objects in the group. The service then remains operational as long as at least one of the group members is operational.
- *Addressing construct.* Object-groups can be used for addressing a set of objects which share some common characteristics. For example, some objects might want to be informed whenever a certain event occurs. A heterogeneous object-group holding these objects can be created and a multicast be sent to the group whenever the event occurs.
- *Data publication.* Many applications, for example in the financial or flight reservation domain, need a mechanism for transmitting the same information to several recipients. This can be done efficiently by means of object-group multicast.
- *Distributed monitoring and management.* Object-groups provide a convenient way to distribute and gather monitoring and management information in distributed applications.
- *Encapsulation.* Object-groups encapsulate an internal, possibly replicated state and make it accessible through a set of well-defined methods.

– *Reusable components.* We see object-groups as reusable components for complex, failure-resilient distributed systems. New object-groups can be realized based on existing object-groups by means of inheritance.

Object-groups do present problems as well. The issues we consider next are the ordering of events within an object-group, group membership management, and the implementation of object-groups.

3.3 Ordering of Events

Within a homogeneous group, consistency of the replicated state can be guaranteed by forcing operations to occur in the same order at all the replicas, which is known as *atomically (or totally) ordered multicast* [11]. However, some applications can preserve consistency with a weaker, less expensive *causal ordering* using *causal multicast* [14, 24]. An advantage of causal multicast compared to more restrictive protocols, is that the protocol works without the introduction of extra messages.

3.3.1 Causal Multicast. Causal communication uses the *happened before* relationship described in the classic paper of Leslie Lamport [14] to order messages in a distributed system. Causal communication is a fundamental concept of asynchronous distributed systems and can be applied to settings where senders communicate with several receivers and where messages are delivered indirectly through intermediary processes.

Informally, causal communication generalizes the notion of a message depending on another one, and ensures that a message is artificially delayed by the receiver's run-time system if the message depends on one which the receiver has not seen yet.

Formally, causal dependency is defined as follows [14]:

1. If a and b are events in the *same* process, and a happened before b, then b causally depends on a.
2. If a is the sending of a message by one process and b is the receipt of this message by another process, then b causally depends on a.
3. If b causally depends on a, and c causally depends on b, then c also causally depends on a.

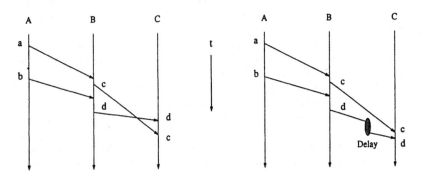

Fig. 2. Non-causal and causal communication. A, B and C are processes in a distributed system. An arrow denotes a message passed from one process to another.

Thus, a message depends on another one if there exists a *data flow* between the two messages. In Fig. 2, message c depends on message a and message d depends on message b. In the left scenario, message d surpasses message c, and d is thus delivered before c. In this situation, causality is violated. The right scenario demonstrates the case where a causal communication protocol is implemented in the distributed system. Now, the run-time system of process C artificially delays message d until c arrives, thus ensuring causality.

3.4 Group Membership Management

The problem of group membership management consists in maintaining consistent views on group membership among the objects in an object-group. At all times, an object-group member has a certain idea of which other objects belong to its group. This is called a *view*. Since objects may join or leave (terminate or fail) a group, a view is subject to *view-changes*, and these changes must be propagated to all of the group members. Therefore, a system-wide service providing consistent information on group membership must be realized. To guarantee consistency, the service delivers view changes to all of the members in the same order. Without such a service, object-group based applications may behave incorrectly and in unexpected ways.

Basically, a view change protocol consists of two phases. In the first phase, the group membership service ensures that every member which is still alive receives every message that was sent in the current view (*flush* phase). In the second phase, the view is updated and transmitted to the members (*view update* phase). Similar group membership protocols are implemented in ISIS and HORUS. The group management problem in asynchronous, distributed systems is treated in [19, 20].

3.5 Implementing Object-Groups

In this section we address the problem of implementing object-groups on distributed control technologies (DCT) such as ISIS and HORUS. We chose these two systems since they are available today and provide important mechanisms like causal communication, process groups, and reliable multicast in an efficient and stable fashion.

In the current version of ISIS, the unit of distribution is a process. On the other hand, the object-group model is of finer granularity. A process can instantiate many objects, and situations can thus arise in which a process tries to become member of a group several times. Since in ISIS the same process cannot be member of a group multiple times, one must implement a multiplexing mechanism, such that a process containing several objects forwards incoming messages to the appropriate one. This is achieved by providing an ISIS multicast-message with addressing information on the destination objects, *e.g.*, with *object-identifiers*. Multiplexing code within each receiver-process forwards the incoming messages to the appropriate objects in the process. No modifications to the ISIS system need to be made for implementing this mechanism. We believe that the performance penalty of this multiplexing mechanism is minor and that multiplexing can be realized in a way which is transparent to the programmer.

The HORUS toolkit provides light-weight processes (threads) as the unit of distribution. Threads can be grouped together and do communicate by point-to-point messages and reliable multicast. In HORUS it is thus possible to implement multithreaded objects, and a thread acting as communication endpoint can easily be created per object. In this situation, object-group communication can be implemented without having to provide a multiplexing layer. In the following section we describe how object-groups are implemented in ELECTRA independently from the underlying DCT.

4 The ELECTRA Architecture

An important goal of ELECTRA is to allow for object-group oriented, distributed programming on different state-of-the-art DCTs, and to ease the integration of new DCTs into ELECTRA.

Therefore, ELECTRA applications are based on a *virtual machine (VM) layer* which completely hides the implementation-dependent aspects of the underlying DCT (Fig. 3). The VM layer is implemented in the form of an abstract C++ class, which defines the low-level "instruction set" ELECTRA needs to support object-groups and the other abstractions we mentioned before. Comprised in the instruction set are primitives for handling threads, for message passing, reliable multicast, thread synchronization, and group management. Choosing an adequate instruction set is crucial: a small and simple instruction set requires that much more functionality must be implemented into ELECTRA. A large and complicated instruction set is difficult to map onto existing DCTs. In Sect. 4.1 we will therefore give a detailed overview of the instruction set we chose for the ELECTRA VM.

To have ELECTRA running on a concrete DCT, a so-called *concrete machine*, a specific *adaptor object* must be realized therefore (Fig. 3). The adaptor object's task is to map the VM's operations onto the operations provided by the concrete machine, and to cleanly encapsulate the program-code which is specific to the concrete machine.

Concrete machines which closely meet the requirements of ELECTRA are, for example, AMOEBA, DELTA-4, HORUS, ISIS, PSYNC, and TRANSIS. If required, there would be a possibility of implementing an adaptor object for having ELECTRA to run on the bare UNIX[2] IPC mechanisms, but this would mean re-implementing most of the functionality provided by already existing concrete machines. Such undertaking is beyond the scope of our work. Currently, an adaptor object is provided for the HORUS toolkit only.

ELECTRA Abstractions	: Object-Groups, RMC, Proxies, Class Libraries, etc.		
ELECTRA Services	: Name Server, Remote Instantiation, etc.		
ELECTRA Tools	: CORBA-IDL Compiler, etc.		
ELECTRA *VM Interface*	: Threads, Message Passing, Multicast, Groups, etc.		
HORUS *Adaptor Object*	ISIS *Adaptor Object*	AMOEBA *Adaptor Object*	Virtually Synchronous Execution
			Event Ordering Layer
HORUS Toolkit *Concrete Machine*	ISIS Toolkit *Concrete Machine*	AMOEBA Operating System *Concrete Machine*	Thread Group and Multicast Layer
			Threads, IPC, etc.
Bare Operating System (Unix, Mach, etc.)			Bare Point-to-Point IPC Mechanisms, e.g., UDP Sockets *Concrete Machine*

Fig. 3. Sample ELECTRA architecture supporting HORUS, ISIS, AMOEBA, and conventional point-to-point IPC mechanisms. The functionality in the shaded areas is provided by adaptor objects.

---

[2] Unix is a registered trademark of Unix Systems Laboratories, Inc.

To summarize, above system design allows to execute the same object-oriented application on top of a variety of more low-level concrete machines. This is achieved by building ELECTRA on a portable VM interface. Adaptor objects are used to map the VM's primitives onto the operations provided by the underlying, concrete machine.

4.1 Virtual Machine Interface

We now describe the important parts of the current ELECTRA VM interface. As stated above, the VM is encapsulated into an abstract C++ class. Adaptor objects are instances of subclasses of the VM. The VM provides interfaces for message passing, threads, thread synchronization, multicast, and group management. These are the low-level primitives we have found necessary for building a toolkit which supports object-groups and object-oriented, distributed programming.

The ELECTRA programmer is normally not confronted with the VM primitives we describe in the next sections. Rather, the primitives are called from the code produced by the CORBA-IDL compiler and from within the ELECTRA run-time system.

4.1.1 Message Passing. ELECTRA requires methods for a reliable, non-blocking transmission of unstructured data-blocks of arbitrary length. These primitives are called by the RMC module for the low-level delivery of RMCs. If the message passing mechanisms of the underlying concrete machine fail to meet a requirement, reliability for instance, the specific adaptor object must implement the requirement. This is transparent to the layers above the VM. Following the VM's message passing interface:

```
virtual Status msgSend(Entity destination, Message msg, Thread done);
virtual Status msgReceive(Entity listenOn, Thread receive);
```

A Status object reports about success or failure of an operation. To deliver a message to a specific destination, msgSend is invoked. The opaque object destination encapsulates the addressing information needed by the concrete machine for the delivery. When the message has been delivered, thread done is invoked. msgReceive registers a thread which is invoked whenever a message arrives for entity listenOn.

4.1.2 Threads. Our VM interface for handling threads is as follows:

```
virtual Status threadDeclare(Thread& t);
virtual Status threadCreate(Thread t, ThreadParam param);
virtual Status threadDestroy(Thread t);
```

Threads are declared to the concrete machine using threadDeclare, and are started using threadCreate. The creator of the thread can specify a parameter param which is to be passed to the thread once created. threadDestroy frees the internal resources associated with a thread.

The thread interface is held very simple to allow existing thread implementations to easily slide under this interface. ELECTRA uses the thread interface mainly for creating RMC upcall methods.

4.1.3 Thread Synchronization. ELECTRA's synchronization primitives, promises for example (see Sect. 2.1), all build on the simple semaphore operations provided by the VM:

```
virtual Status semaCreate(Sema& s, int value);
virtual Status semaDec(Sema s);
virtual Status semaInc(Sema s);
virtual Status semaDestroy(Sema s);
```

A semaphore is created and initially set to value using the semaCreate operation. semaDec decrements a semaphore, and blocks the issuing thread if the semaphore's value was zero. semaInc increments a semaphore. If the semaphore's value was zero, and some thread is blocked trying to decrement the semaphore, the thread is resumed.

4.1.4 Multicast. To realize object-group communication, ELECTRA requires operations for reliable, order preserving multicast:

```
virtual Status mcastSend(GroupEntity group, Message msg, Thread done);
virtual Status mcastReceive(Entity listenOn, Thread receive);
```

To low-level deliver an RMC to an object-group, mcastSend is used. The addresses of the receivers are encapsulated in the group object. In analogy to msgSend, the done thread is invoked when resources associated with the message can be released. mcastReceive is used by a group member to register a thread which is to be invoked when a multicast arrives for it.

4.1.5 Group Management. Concrete machines like AMOEBA, DELTA-4, HORUS, ISIS, and TRANSIS provide protocols for holding the view on group membership (see Sect. 3.4) each member of a group has at a certain time consistent. This is possible despite join and leave requests, and despite failures. Next, the low-level interface ELECTRA uses to manage object-groups is provided.

```
virtual Status groupCreate(GroupEntity& group, GroupPolicy policy);
virtual Status groupJoin(GroupEntity group, Entity e);
virtual Status groupLeave(GroupEntity group, Entity e);
virtual Status groupDestroy(GroupEntity group);
```

The method groupCreate is used to generate a group. A GroupPolicy object specifies parameters like the required ordering of the messages delivered to the members, *e.g.*, unordered, causally ordered, or totally ordered multicast.

Objects are inserted into and deleted from groups by the groupJoin and groupLeave methods. Finally, a group is removed using groupDestroy.

Declaring an Application's Requirements. Being able to run object-group based applications unmodified on a variety of communication platforms is enticing, but bears following problem: different concrete machines offer different services and features. AMOEBA for instance, supports totally ordered multicast, but does not provide for causal ordering of point-to-point messages in respect to multicasted messages. HORUS and ISIS support totally ordered and causally ordered multicast, and are able to enforce causality in a system which employs point-to-point and multicast communication. This can take place even in the presence of overlapping groups and failures. To cope with this incompatibility problem, we see several solutions:

- Finding the "least common denominator" of the concrete machines we want to support. We could say that all group-communication in ELECTRA is totally ordered, and that point-to-point communication will not be ordered in respect to group-communication. This solution leads to a simple programming model, but is restrictive in the sense that the ELECTRA programmer is prevented from adequately exploiting the underlying concrete machine. Furthermore, the programmer will be seduced to circumvent the VM abstraction and to directly issue operations on the underlying concrete machine, thereby limiting the portability of applications.

- Finding the superset of the capabilities provided by the concrete machines. We could say that the ELECTRA programmer can always select from a variety of ordering rules [11], such as unordered, FIFO, causal, atomic, and causal atomic multicast. Furthermore, the programmer can specify how point-to-point messages are to be ordered in respect to multicasted messages and in respect to other point-to-point messages. Clearly, developing an adaptor object would become difficult and tedious for concrete machines which do not provide such plenty of ordering rules.

- A clean solution would consist in realizing the ordering of events completely in an ELECTRA layer residing above the adaptor objects. The underlying concrete machine would then provide for unordered, reliable group-communication only. ELECTRA could offer different ordering rules using a flexible approach like PSYNC [18] or protocols like the ones implemented in ISIS [7]. The realization of such protocols as future work is under consideration.

- The solution we actually provide consists in having the programmer specifying the requirements her or his application embodies, for example the kind of multicast needed, and "asking" the underlying adaptor object whether it can fulfill the requirements.

  If an important application-requirement is not fulfilled, the programmer now may enhance the adaptor object to provide the functionality which is missing in the concrete machine, or configure the application to use another machine. Querying the capabilities of the underlying adaptor is achieved by filling out and passing an AppPolicy object to the adaptor.

  The next code fragment describes the part of the VM interface which realizes the policy mechanism. Method isSupported checks whether the application's requirements, specified in the policy object, are supported by the concrete machine. The method whatsSupported returns the characteristics of the concrete machine.

```
virtual Status isSupported(AppPolicy policy, boolean& supported);
virtual Status whatsSupported(AppPolicy& policy);
```

4.2 Multiple Virtual Machines

Another advantage of the proposed design is that an object-group based application can use different concrete machines simultaneously. Since the VM class uses virtual C++ methods, different concrete machines can be accessed from within the same application using the same VM interface.

For example, consider a banking application where some customer data shall be retrieved from a mainframe running an exotic operating system and be evaluated in parallel on a set of workstations. In ELECTRA, the parallel evaluation application could be run using ISIS as concrete machine. Most likely, ISIS will not run on the mainframe, but probably the data could be retrieved from the mainframe using a public data network protocol like X.25. Now, an ELECTRA adaptor object would be implemented which maps the message passing primitives (see Sect. 4.1.1) onto calls to operations of an X.25 programming library. The rest of the adaptor's methods would be left unimplemented. On the host side, a program would be realized[3] which interprets the incoming RMCs, issues queries on the customer database, and returns the requested data. Now, a well structured, object-oriented ELECTRA application can be realized which uses RMCs to retrieve data from the bank's mainframe, and ISIS to perform a parallel evaluation on the workstations.

The ELECTRA programmer has the illusion of communicating with a remote object, by invoking RMCs such as getCustomerData, though an exotic mainframe resides behind this abstract interface. Similarly, adaptor objects could be implemented for interconnecting different platforms like AMOEBA, DELTA-4, HORUS, ISIS, PSYNC, and TRANSIS, and practicing object-oriented, distributed programming on the resulting, virtual platform.

5   Summary

We suggested object-groups as a general structuring mechanism for object-oriented distributed systems. With the help of object-groups, programmers are less concerned about important but low-level issues like reliable multicast, ordering of events, and replication.

The Remote Method Calling (RMC) paradigm provides expressive, object-oriented communication and allows to access both single objects and object-groups with the help of Smart Proxies. With this approach, a single system component can be replaced by an object-group without having to modify applications which use the component. Thus, fault-tolerance and load-sharing can be increased step by step and complex applications become easier to realize, to modify, and to maintain.

Problems related with object-groups are the consistent ordering of messages delivered to the group-members, group view management in confrontation of joining, exiting and failing objects, and the implementation of object-groups on today's state-of-the-art platforms. Advantages of object-groups are that they allow for load sharing, fault tolerance, group addressing, data publication, distributed management, encapsulation, and reuse.

We further presented a flexible system design which we consider suited to support object-groups and object-oriented, distributed programming on various state-of-the-art platforms. This flexibility is achieved by ELECTRA's *virtual machine* abstraction. The virtual machine defines a small set of simple methods, mainly for handling threads, for message passing, multicast, thread synchronization, and group management. *Adaptor objects* are used to map the virtual machine's primitives onto the operations provided by the underlying, *concrete machine*, thus cleanly encapsulating the program-code which is specific to the concrete machine.

Acknowledgements

Henri Bal, Martin Bichsel, Ken Birman, Richard Golding, Andrew Hutchison, Robbert van Renesse, and the anonymous reviewers provided useful suggestions and comments on this work.

References

1. AMIR, Y., DOLEV, D., KRAMER, S., AND MALKI, D. Transis: A Communication Sub-System for High Availability. In *22nd International Symposium on Fault-Tolerant Computing* (July 1992), IEEE.
2. ARCHITECTURE PROJECTS MANAGEMENT LTD. *ANSAware Version 4.1 Manual Set.* Castle Park, Cambridge UK, Mar. 1993.

---

[3] Though the VM and the ELECTRA layers on top of it could be compiled and installed even on a mainframe, if it provides a C++ compiler. These modules are written in an operating system independent way.

3. BHOEDJANG, R., RUHL, T., HOFMAN, R., LANGENDOEN, K., BAL, H., AND KAASHOEK, F. Panda: A Portable Platform to Support Parallel Programming Languages. In *Symposium on Experiences with Distributed and Multiprocessor Systems IV* (San Diego, CA, Sept. 1993), USENIX.

4. BIRMAN, K. P. The Process Group Approach to Reliable Distributed Computing. Tech. Rep. 91-1216, Cornell University, Dept. of Computer Science, July 1991. To appear in Communications of the ACM, Dec. 1993.

5. BIRMAN, K. P. Integrating Runtime Consistency Models for Distributed Computing. Tech. Rep. 91-1240, Cornell University, Dept. of Computer Science, July 1993. To appear in Journal of Parallel and Distributed Computing.

6. BIRMAN, K. P., AND JOSEPH, T. A. Exploiting Replication in Distributed Systems. In *Distributed Systems*, S. Mullender, Ed. ACM Press, 1989.

7. BIRMAN, K. P., SCHIPER, A., AND STEPHENSON, P. Lightweight Causal and Atomic Group Multicast. *ACM Transactions on Computer Systems 9*, 3 (Aug. 1991).

8. DIGITAL EQUIPMENT CORP., HEWLETT-PACKARD CO., HYPERDESK CORP., NCR CORP., OBJECT DESIGN INC., SUNSOFT INC. *The Common Object Request Broker: Architecture and Specification*, Dec. 1991. Revision 1.1, OMG Document Number 91.12.1.

9. EPPINGER, J. L., MUMMERT, L. B., AND SPECTOR, A. Z. *Camelot and Avalon*. Morgan Kaufmann Publishers, Inc., 1991.

10. GUERRAOUI, R. Towards Modular Concurrency Control for Distributed Object Oriented Systems. In *IEEE Proceedings of the International Workshop on Future Trends in Distributed Computing Systems* (Sept. 1993).

11. HADZILACOS, V., AND TOUEG, S. Fault-Tolerant Broadcasts and Related Problems. In *Distributed Systems*, S. Mullender, Ed., second ed. Addison Wesley, 1993, ch. 5.

12. HAGSAND, O., HERZOG, H., BIRMAN, K., AND COOPER, R. Object-Oriented Reliable Distributed Programming. *IEEE Workshop on Object-Orientation in Operating Systems* (Sept. 1992).

13. ISIS DISTRIBUTED SYSTEMS INC., ITHACA, NY. A Response to the ORB 2.0 RFI, Apr. 93.

14. LAMPORT, L. Time, Clocks and the Ordering of Events in a Distributed System. *Communications of the ACM 21*, 7 (July 1978).

15. LISKOV, B., AND SHRIRA, L. Promises: Linguistic Support for Efficient Asynchronous Procedure Calls in Distributed Systems. *ACM SIGPLAN Notices 23*, 7 (July 1988).

16. MAFFEIS, S. Electra – Making Distributed Programs Object-Oriented. In *Proceedings of the Symposium on Experiences with Distributed and Multiprocessor Systems IV* (San Diego, CA, 1993), USENIX.

17. MARQUES, J. A., AND GUEDES, P. Extending the Operating System to Support an Object-Oriented Environment. In *OOPSLA Conference Proceedings* (Oct. 1989).

18. PETERSON, L., BUCHHOLZ, N., AND SCHLICHTING, R. Preserving and Using Context Information in Interprocess Communication. *ACM Transactions on Computer Systems 7*, 3 (Aug. 1989).

19. RICCIARDI, A. M. *The Group Membership Problem in Asynchronous Systems*. PhD thesis, Cornell University, Dept. of Computer Science, Ithaca, New York, Nov. 1992. No. 92-1313.

20. SCHIPER, A., AND RICCIARDI, A. M. Virtually-Synchronous Communication Based on a Weak Failure Suspector. Tech. Rep. 93-1339, Cornell University, Dept. of Computer Science, Apr. 1993.

21. SHAPIRO, M., ET AL. SOS: An Object-oriented Operating System – Assessment and Perspectives. *Computing Systems 2*, 4 (Dec. 1989).

22. SHRIVASTAVA, S. K., DIXON, G. N., AND PARRINGTON, G. D. An Overview of the Arjuna Distributed Programming System. Computing Laboratory, University of Newcastle upon Tyne, Newcastle upon Tyne, NE1 7RU, UK.

23. TANENBAUM, A. S. *Modern Operating Systems*. Prentice-Hall, 1992.

24. VAN RENESSE, R. Causal Controversy at Le Mont St.-Michel. *ACM Operating Systems Review 27*, 2 (Apr. 1993).

25. VAN RENESSE, R., BIRMAN, K. P., COOPER, R., GLADE, B., AND STEPHENSON, P. Reliable Multicast between Microkernels. In *Proceedings of the USENIX Workshop of Micro-Kernels and Other Kernel Architectures* (Seattle, Washington, Apr. 1992).

26. VERÍSSIMO, P., AND MARQUES, J. A. Reliable Broadcast for Fault-Tolerance on Local Computer Networks. In *9th Symposium on Reliable Distributed Systems* (1990), IEEE.

Distributed Programming in GARF *

Benoît Garbinato, Rachid Guerraoui, Karim R. Mazouni

Département d'Informatique
Ecole Polytechnique Fédérale de Lausanne
CH-1015 Lausanne, Suisse

Abstract. GARF is an object-oriented programming environment aimed to support the design of reliable distributed applications. Its computational model is based on two programming levels: the *functional* level and the *behavioral* level. At the *functional* level, software functionalities are described using passive objects, named *data objects*, in a centralized, volatile, and failure free environment. At the *behavioral* level, data objects are dynamically bound to *encapsulators* and *mailers* which support distribution, concurrency, persistence and fault tolerance. Encapsulators wrap data objects by controlling how the latter send and receive messages, while mailers perform communications between encapsulators. This paper describes how the GARF computational model enables to build flexible and highly modular abstractions for the design of reliable distributed applications.

1 Introduction

Transparency has been recognized to be a worthwhile goal in the design of distributed systems. A user of a transparently distributed system could make no distinction between local resource accesses and remote ones. From the point of view of a distributed application designer, we believe that transparency has to be provided "à la carte". That is, a distributed programming environment must provide programmers with a set of *behavioral* abstractions that hides low level features related to concurrency, persistence, distribution and fault-tolerance. Nevertheless, programmers must be able to refine such abstractions in order to obtain the desired efficiency. For example, the underlying system may decide to locate, by default, the application's components on different nodes, according to a particular load balancing policy. However, the actual distribution of the program is sometimes likely to be closely associated with the semantics of the program. Therefore, programmers must be able to explicitly locate components. There are many other examples related to concurrency and replication control where default behaviors are too restrictive and where it is often desirable to use application's semantics to refine these behaviors.

In this paper, we describe the computational model of GARF: an object-oriented distributed system that supports transparency "à la carte". GARF provides built-in *behavioral* abstractions (i.e., abstractions that deal with concurrency, persistence, distribution, and fault-tolerance), which can be used as such, or refined at programmers' convenience.

GARF promotes software modularity by separating the *functional* aspects of applications, from their *behavioral* features. The former are designed within *data objects*, similar to objects

* Research supported by the Swiss FNS as part of the project Mesures Spéciales under contract number 5003-034344.

in classical centralized languages, whereas the latter are confined within particular objects named *encapsulators* and *mailers*. *Encapsulators* are used to control how data objects send and receive messages, whereas *mailers* are used to perform communications between encapsulators. GARF provides a built-in extensible library of encapsulator and mailer classes that implement very flexible behavioral features such as client/server asynchrony, active/passive replication, semantic-based concurrency control, etc. These classes can be used as such, or refined according to application's semantics.

The remainder of this paper is organized as follows. Section 2 describes the GARF computational model. Section 3 shows its flexibility and modularity through some distribution related examples. Section 4 presents a simple distributed and fault-tolerant application implemented in GARF. Section 5 contrasts GARF with related work and section 6 concludes with some general remarks.

2   The GARF computational model

2.1   Two programming levels

The GARF computational model is based on two programming levels. A *high* level, called *functional level*, in which the programmer describes aspects of the application that could be expressed in a centralized, volatile, and sequential object-oriented system; and a *low* level, called *behavioral level*, in which programmer describes behavioral features related to concurrency, persistence, distribution, and fault-tolerance.

The functional level: at this level, the programmer focuses on all sequential aspects of the application, assuming a volatile, centralized, and failure-free environment. Such (functional) aspects are described through classes, called *data classes*, of which instances are called *data objects*. The programmer can here reuse classes designed within a classical object-oriented language (Smalltalk in our current prototype).

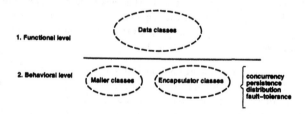

Fig. 1. Two programming levels

The behavioral level: at this level, programmer deals with features related to concurrency, persistence, distribution, and fault-tolerance. Such (behavioral) features are implemented within classes, called *behavioral classes*, of which instances are called *behavioral objects*. GARF provides two kinds of behavioral classes: *encapsulator classes* of which instances are used to wrap data objects by controlling the way they send and receive messages, and *mailer classes* of which instances are in charge of performing encapsulator's communications. GARF offers an extensible library of built-in behavioral classes that support remote communication, asynchronous invocation, concurrency control, persistence, active replication and passive replication (see section 3 below).

2.2 GARF objects

Data objects: these are passive entities that communicate in a *point to point, synchronous* request/reply manner. A request represents an operation invocation involving two objects: a client which invokes the operation and a server on which the operation is invoked. The reply (returned to the client) represents the result computed by the server when executing the invoked operation. A request or a reply communication is named *message sending* as in most object-oriented languages.

Encapsulators: these objects are used to wrap data objects by controlling how the latter send and receive messages. Each data object can be bound to an encapsulator. The encapsulator intercepts each request/reply communication (message), sent or received by its associated data object, in a transparent way[2]. So, every message sent *to* the data object by another data object passes through its encapsulator, as well as every message sent *by* the object. A data object and its encapsulator are always located on the same node. Hence, when an encapsulator is placed on a node, its associated data object is also placed on that node. According to its semantics, the encapsulator performs pre and post-actions which handle *asynchrony, concurrency control, persistence, replication,..*(section 3).

Mailers: these objects are used to perform (remote) communications between encapsulators. Each data object bound to an encapsulator, is also bound to a mailer class. A mailer of this class is created for each request sent to the encapsulator[3]. The mailer is created on the client node and is used to transmit the request to the encapsulator and to get back the reply. According to their semantics, mailers perform appropriate communications, e.g. *one to one, multicast, atomic multicast,..*(section 3).

Figure 2 depicts our basic communication model. It shows a (request/reply) communication between a client data object C, bound to an encapsulator $E(C)$, and a server data object S, bound to an encapsulator $E(S)$ and to a mailer class $M(S)$. The request sent by C is first intercepted by the encapsulator $E(C)$. The latter forwards the request to $E(S)$, through a mailer $Mi(S)$ (of class $M(S)$). The request arrives then at S which executes the required operation. The reply follows the reverse path, i.e., S, $E(S)$, $Mi(S)$, $E(C)$, and C. As we will see in the next section, the paths followed by request/reply communications provide data objects with various behavioral features, depending of the encapsulators and mailers that are involved.

---

[2] Data objects are not aware of encapsulators.

[3] There is a *one to one* correspondence between mailers and requests sent to the encapsulator.

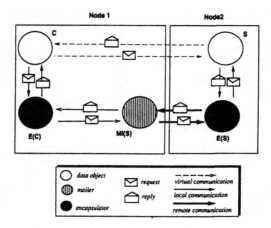

Fig. 2. The communication model

3 · Distributed programming in GARF

Distributed programming in GARF consists in:

1. designing (or reusing) data classes,
2. binding data objects, either to existing encapsulator classes and mailer classes, or to newly designed ones;
3. placing encapsulators, and the data objects bound to them, on network nodes.

Every data class is derived from the built-in class *DataObject*. The class *Encapsulator* (resp. *Mailer*) is the root of the encapsulator (resp. mailer) class hierarchy. The class *Encapsulator* defines the basic operations inRequest() and outRequest(). The operation inRequest() is invoked before each invocation of a data object bound to an encapsulator, while the operation outRequest() is invoked after each invocation of the data object. The class *Mailer* defines the operation sendRequest() which is invoked by the client encapsulator's outRequest(). All these operations take as argument the invocation itself which is considered at this point as a first class object. The class *DataObject* defines the operation garfNew() which is performed at each data object creation. This operation can be refined in subclasses to bind a data object to an encapsulator and to a mailer class.

The classes *Mailer* and *Encapsulator* do not provide any specific behavioral features except remote communications support. In other words, data objects bound to basic encapsulators (class *Encapsulator*), and to the basic *Mailer* class communicate using a RPC scheme without any concurrency, persistence or fault-tolerance characteristic. By refining inRequest() and outRequest() in *Encapsulator* subclasses, and/or by refining sendRequest() in *Mailer* subclasses, one can implement various behaviors. GARF offers a built-in library compound of a hierarchy of encapsulator classes and a hierarchy of mailer classes (fig 3) that provide support for asynchrony, intra-object concurrency control, persistence and replication. In the following, we describe this support.

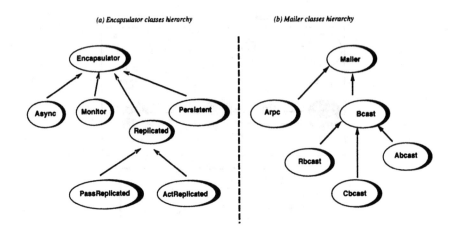

Fig. 3. Behavioral classes hierarchies

3.1 Asynchronous invocation

The synchronous request/reply communication (RPC) is based on a well understood abstraction (the procedure call). It is now a widely used communication facility in distributed systems [6,21]. Nevertheless, the client of such an invocation is always blocked during the execution of the remote operation. In many cases, it is preferable that the client turns its attention to another job in order to take advantage of the potential parallelism.

As in [23], we overcome this RPC limitation by introducing a *future* mechanism which implements the asynchronous invocation abstraction. The client of an asynchronous invocation receives immediately a future[4] without waiting for the actual result of the invoked operation. The client does not have to wait until it tries to read the value of the future: that is, until it until it invokes an operation on the future which value has not yet arrived. In this case, the client is blocked until the value (reply) arrives. Such a communication is particularly useful when the client and the server are located on different nodes since the communication delay is not negligible.

We enable two asynchronous behaviors:

Client asynchrony: asynchrony is introduced by the client's encapsulator. More precisely, when the client data object invokes an operation, its encapsulator creates a *thread* and returns a future (fig. 4). The thread is in charge of transmitting the invocation to the server's mailer, waiting for the reply and passing it to the future.

Server asynchrony: asynchrony is introduced by the server's mailers. When a mailer receives an invocation to forward, it creates a *thread* and returns a future (fig. 5). The thread is in charge of transmitting the invocation to the (remote) encapsulator, waiting for the reply and passing it to the future.

---

[4] A future is the container of the invocation result which may be not yet available.

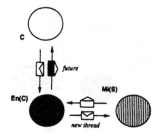

Fig. 4. Client asynchrony

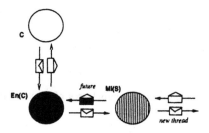

Fig. 5. Server asynchrony

We have designed an encapsulator class named *Async* which implements the client asynchrony and a mailer class named *Arpc* which implements the server asynchrony. One can provide a data object with either the first behavior by binding it to an encapsulator from the class *Async*, or the second behavior by binding it to the mailer class *Arpc*, or even both behaviors by binding it to an encapsulator from the class *Async* and to the mailer class *Arpc*.

3.2 Synchronization

Since data objects can be invoked concurrently, it is necessary to provide them with appropriate concurrency control that schedule incoming invocations. The simplest concurrency control[5] is the *monitor* like control. Such control ensures that only one invocation is treated at a time, i.e., it guarantees mutual exclusion of operation executions. While an operation is executing on the object, other invocations wishing to be treated must wait on an entry queue. When an operation terminates, the invocation at the top of the entry queue, if any, is treated, i.e., the corresponding operation is executed. As in [19], we introduce such behavior through encapsulators. More precisely, we provide an encapsulator class *Monitor*, which offers the mutual exclusion capability. An encapsulator from this class maintains an *invocation queue* in which it stores the invocations until their turn arrives.

A data object bound to an encapsulator from the class *Monitor* executes one operation at a time (fig. 6). It is obvious that such behavior might be too restrictive in many situations. One

---

[5] We are concerned here with intra-object concurrency control vs. inter-object concurrency control [12].

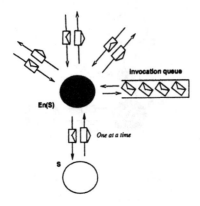

Fig. 6. Monitor like behavior

can refine the mutual exclusion policy in subclasses of *Monitor* and introduce intra-object concurrency (e.g. *readers/writer*).

3.3 Persistence

An object is persistent if it "dies at the right time" [16]. Generally, an object is said to be persistent if it does not disappear unless the programmer or user demands it explicitly. As a consequence, a persistent object can survive to the session that created it [2].

Supporting persistent objects requires global persistent names and stable storage. Persistent names are required to reference the object at any time and stable storage is required to preserve the object state between sessions. As for client asynchrony and synchronization, we provide persistence capabilities through encapsulators. We introduce a subclass of *Encapsulator* named *Persistent*. A data object bound to an encapsulator from this class is automatically made persistent. Such an encapsulator has a global persistent name, and a stable storage allocated to it. The encapsulator and its associated data objects are not deleted unless the programmer demands it explicitly by invoking the operation die() on the encapsulator.

An encapsulator from the class *Persistent* provides two operations store() and retrieve() which respectively store and retrieve the data objects' state to and from the stable storage (fig. 7). Hence, when a data object is created and bound to an encapsulator from the class *Persistent*, the encapsulator checks whether the data object has already been created within a previous session[6]; in this case it retrieves the data objects' state from the stable storage. After each operation execution, the encapsulator stores the objects' state into stable storage. This behavior can be refined in subclasses of *Persistent*, in order to be used within a transaction-based mechanism for example [11].

---

[6] The encapsulator uses its global persistent name for this purpose

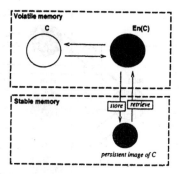

Fig. 7. To and from stable storage

3.4 Replication

Replication has been proven to be a powerful means to mask failures and increase availability [7]. Assuming *reliable communication channels* and *fail-silent nodes*, an object is reachable as long as it has a replica running on a non-faulty node.

Replication facilities in GARF are provided for data objects bound to encapsulators from subclasses of the class *Replicated*. Encapsulators from these classes can be gathered inside groups of which global names are maintained by *group managers*. A *group manager* is a particular GARF object used to store the member list of a group of encapsulators. When an encapsulator leaves the group, i.e., its node fails, the group manager removes its name from the list of members.

To replicate data objects of a class D, one must refine the operation `garfNew()` within the class D to create k copies of that object and bind them to k encapsulators of *Replicated* subclasses. The encapsulators (and thus their associated data objects) can then be located on failure independent nodes. To preserve the consistency of data object replicas, encapsulators must follow some agreements on how to forward invocations to their data objects. We have considered two kinds of agreements:

Active replication: every replica encapsulator receives the invocation and forwards it to its data object which treats it and returns a reply (fig. 8). There is no need here of inter-replicas coordination. That replication scheme is provided by the encapsulator class *ActReplica* and the mailer class *Abcast*. Mailers from the class *Abcast* transform an invocation into a reliable totally ordered multicast to the encapsulator replicas and waits for the first reply. Such a multicast guarantees that every replica treats an invocation or none, and that invocations are treated in the same order by all the replicas [5].

Passive replication: a single encapsulator called the *primary* replica receives the invocation, forwards it to its data object which treats it and returns the reply. At regular intervals, the primary replica sends checkpoints to other replicas which act as backups. If the primary replica fails, the backups elect a new primary. The class *PassReplica* implements encapsulators that behave that way. The mailer used at the client side can be simply created from

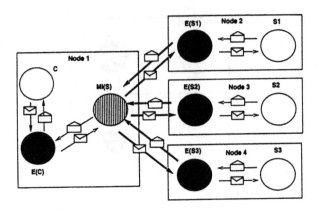

Fig. 8. Active replication

the basic class *Mailer*, since there is only a need for point to point communication between the client encapsulator and the primary encapsulator replica.

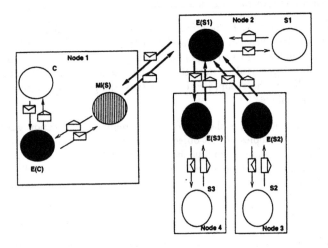

Fig. 9. Passive replication

4 Example: The Distributed Diary Manager

In this section, we illustrate our approach by describing the design of a fault tolerant distributed application built with the GARF system. The application is a distributed diary manager called the DDM. At the functional level, the application is designed in terms of data classes, assuming a volatile, centralized, and failure free environment. At the behavioral level, the programmer deals with features related to concurrency, persistence, distribution, and fault-tolerance, by using built-in encapsulator and mailer classes, or designing new ones.

4.1 Designing the DDM at the functional level

The DDM application is aimed to manage a diary for each user. A diary is associated to its owner through a diary index which manages a list of (user name, diary) pairs. A diary stores the list of meetings to which its owner participates. Each meeting is composed of a period and a list of participants. A diary service is the user-interface of DDM and enables to list all diary owners, to create or delete a diary, to plan or cancel a meeting with other owners and to list all the meetings a user is expected to attend.

At the functional level of the DDM, we designed mainly four data classes, derived from the basic abstract class *DataObject*: *DiaryIndex*, *Diary*, *Meeting*, and *DiaryService*. Class *DiaryIndex* implements operations returning a diary given a user name, listing the names of all diary owners and adding or removing a user. This class has a single instance that we will refer to as *the diary index*. Class *Diary* implements operations that allow to list all the meetings contained in a diary and to update the latter. This class has one instance per user. Class *Meeting* implements operations allowing to list its participants, to give the meeting period and to remove a user from the participant list. Each time a user plans a meeting, a new instance is created. Finally, class *DiaryService* describes the user-interface of DDM. An instance of this class is created each time a user starts to work with the application.

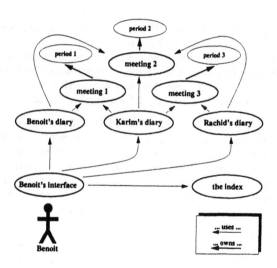

Fig. 10. Data objects of a DDM execution

Figure 10 shows data objects involved in a DDM execution. The figure points out the dependencies between instances of DDM classes. The *uses* relation expresses the client-server model in which a client object needs a server object to accomplish some services. The *owns* relation expresses a particular case of the *uses* relation, where the client is the unique user of the server object. Such relations allow to identify globally shared objects of the application. These objects are *diary services*, *index*, *diaries* and *meetings*; all other objects involved in DDM are local, e.g., *periods* and *owner names*.

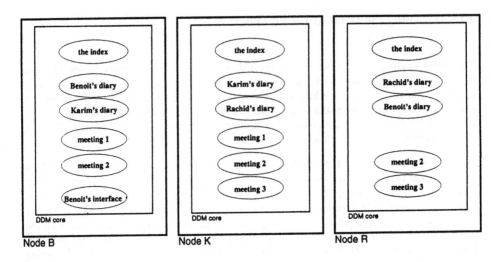

Fig. 11. Replication of DDM objects

4.2 Designing the DDM at the behavioral level

At the behavioral level, the design of DDM is extended with behavioral features, using encapsulator and mailer classes. Since DDM is intended to support several users at the same time, the diary index, diaries and meetings may be accessed concurrently. In addition, DDM is aimed to manage long-lived information, i.e., when a user terminates a session with the DDM, he expects to be able to reuse his diary in a further session. Finally, we require DDM to continue its execution despite a predefined number of node failures.

In our example, there are three potential users of DDM: Benoît, Karim and Rachid, each have a dedicated node, i.e., a workstation. Those nodes are named respectively B, K and R. A DDM core program is running on each of these three nodes, allowing to create DDM objects and to communicate with them at any time. When a user starts to work with DDM, a user-interface object (a diary service) is simply created on that node. When the user quits DDM, his diary service is deleted, while all the other objects that were created during his work, on any of the three nodes, keep on existing for later use.[7]

Fault-tolerance is achieved by replicating critical objects. An owned object can be seen as being a part of its owner (figure 10). With this in mind, we can now focus only on the replication of what we called the globally shared objects, i.e., the index, diaries, meetings, diary services. The diary index is a critical component. We want it to be replicated on each node where DDM is running. Furthermore it exists even though no user is registered. In our case, it means that a replica of the diary index is present on each of the three nodes, hence it can tolerate the failures of two nodes. A diary is always present on the node of its user, plus on one other node where DDM is running. The choice of that second node is made according to some policy of load balancing of objects. A diary can thus tolerate the failure of a single node. A Meeting's replication rate depends on the number of the meeting participants. Indeed each participant has a replica of all its meetings on his node. This way, even though all other nodes have failed, Benoît for example could still consult his list of

---

[7] The DDM core program can be seen as some kind of Unix daemon.

meetings. As said before, a diary service is the user-interface of DDM. It disappears when its user decides to stop working with DDM. Therefore it is not replicated at all and is always on the node of his user.

The difference of replication policies leads to several qualities of service depending on the operation the user wants to perform. For example listing owners and meetings is always still possible after two failures, while planning a meeting might not. It means that Karim could get the information that Rachid is registered, but could not be able to plan a meeting with him. To recover from failures, we consider persistence capabilities. Otherwise, if two nodes fail, Rachid for instance could well have irreversibly lost his diary. Furthermore, if all three nodes fail at the same time, DDM will be completely reinitialized and all information lost. In order to avoid loss of objects' states after failures, we make the diary index and all diaries and meetings persistent.

We now list the encapsulator and mailer classes used to achieve the various objects' behaviors specified above. The diary index, the diaries and meetings are shared and persistent objects. Their operations are performed in a *readers/writer* way, and their intermediate states are stored on stable memory. To support these features we designed an encapsulator class named *DDMEncapsulator*, which inherits its operations from classes *Monitor*, *Persistent*, and *Replicated*. Therefore, the diary index and each diary and meeting are bound to an encapsulator of class *DDMEncapsulator*. When a *DDMEncapsulator* instance is created, we specify both its replication rate and the locations of its replicas. We consider that strong consistency must always be insured for replicated objects, so we use a mailer class that provides totally ordered causal multicast: the *Abcast* mailer class.

5 Related work

5.1 Single level languages

Most of object-based systems designed for distributed applications provide a single programming level: both functional and behavioral features are described at the same level. This approach leads to a tradeoff between flexibility and modularity. Either behavioral features are defined in an uniform manner (reducing flexibility), or they can be modified but affecting functional aspects (reducing modularity).

Argus [15], Guide [14] and Arjuna [20] are well known examples of single level programming distributed systems. In all of these systems, objects communicate through Remote Procedure Call (RPC). As we have discussed in section 3, this is not always the desired behavior, and in many cases one might prefer an asynchronous style of communication. In addition, these systems provide transactions to maintain object consistency. In Arjuna and Guide, one has to write specific primitives that express transaction boundaries within object operations. This complicates the readability of operations and decreases modularity. Indeed, one cannot add transaction semantics to an operation without accessing it. By encapsulating all *Guardians* (large grain objects) invocations within transactions, the Argus system avoids this problem. However, as we pointed it out in [11,13], the systematic approach of nesting transactions does not always provide the best choice. In fact, there are many cases in which the requested operation does not need to lie within the client transaction boundary. A request involving a benevolent side effect, such as garbage collection, does not need to be designed as a subtransaction but as an independent top-level transaction.

5.2 Reflective systems

Apertos [22], and ABCL/R2 [18] are significative examples of object-based systems which provide powerful flexibility capabilities. These systems are said to be *reflective*. Broadly speaking, *reflection* is the process of reasoning about and acting upon the system itself [17]. In both Apertos and ABCL/R, each object is bound to a group of *meta-objects* describing the object behavior. For example, an object may be bound to a meta-object describing how the object communicates with other objects, a meta-object describing how to handle a faulty operation, and a meta-object describing how the virtual memory supporting the object is managed. Each meta-object is also bound to a group of meta-objects, and so on. This leads to a meta-tower for each object.

Although flexible, such systems have complicated semantics and may bring unnecessary additional complexity. We believe that since the only way to access to an object is to invoke one of its operations, it suffices to control the invocation process in order to express various behaviors. Hence, our encapsulator and mailer model may be viewed as a simpler reflective approach.

5.3 First class interactions

The most similar approaches to ours are those providing first class interaction supports. These are systems like SOS [8], XENOOPS [3] and Sina [1]. According to these approaches, object interactions are seen as first class citizens, i.e., at the same level as other objects.

Both XENOOPS and SOS offer some kind of flexible proxies that allow generic mechanisms for identification, location, storage, replication and concurrency control. In XENOOPS, each object is invoked through a *reference*, which is a particular object that determines the required action to be performed before the actual invocation. Nevertheless, since programmers have only control on what happens before an invocation, and never after, it is not possible to program post-actions following an operation execution, nor to control what happens on the client side when it invokes an operation. For example, it is not clear how one may compute selective *synchronous/asynchronous* invocations without accessing the client operation's code.

In SOS, distributed applications are made of *fragmented* objects. A fragmented object is a group of elementary objects which can be located at several address spaces. From its client point of view, a fragmented object appears as a single local object accessible through its exported interface. From its designer point of view, a fragmented object is seen as a collection of elementary object located at a different address spaces. Nevertheless, the proposed approach does not allow a modular distinction between functional and behavioral aspects, which are both mixed inside fragmented objects' implementations.

The model proposed in the SINA system is called the *composition-filter model*. Each object is associated to a set of *incoming filters* and *outcoming filters*. An incoming filter is performed when an object receives a request and an outcoming filter is performed when an object sends out a request. Filters may delay a message, redirect it of change the message. Since filters are locally associated to objects, programmers may only act on what happen when the message arrives at the object side. Hence it is impossible to compute a replicated object, in a transparent way from clients. More precisely, there is no way to multicast an invocation to an object, in a transparent way to its client.

6 Concluding remarks

This paper describes the computational model of GARF: an object-oriented distributed system aimed to enhance modularity and flexibility of applications. The GARF model is based on two programming levels: a functional level and a behavioral level. At the functional level, programmers focus on software functionalities, and at the behavioral level, they address concurrency, persistence, distribution and fault tolerance features. Such features are programmed within specific classes of which instances are encapsulators and mailers. These classes implements appropriate behavioral abstractions. In the paper we described some of the built-in classes provided by the GARF system which support client asynchrony, server asynchrony, monitor like concurrency control, persistence, active replication, and passive replication.

The incremental way of programming promoted by the GARF approach enhances both modularity and flexibility. Modularity is enhanced since different aspects of a same application are implemented inside independent classes. Data classes that implement functional aspects and encapsulator and mailer classes which implement behavioral features. One can modify the implementation of a behavioral class, e.g. a multicast class, without affecting the rest of the application. Flexibility is enhanced since the built-in behavioral abstractions can be refined to achieve the desirable efficiency according to application's semantics.

A GARF prototype has been implemented on top of Smalltalk [10] and the ISIS [4] toolkit for fault tolerant distributed programming. The GARF approach has been applied to a simple fault-tolerant application (see [9]), and is now applied to the design of more complex application in order to refine the model and to extend the mailer and encapsulator hierarchies.

References

1. M. Aksit, K. Wakita, J. Bosh, L. Bergmans and A.Yonezawa. Abstracting Inter-Object Communications Using Composition Filters. *Internal Report 0924-3755, Univ. of Twente.* 1987.
2. M.P. Atkinson, P. Bailey, W. Cockshott, K. Chisholm and P. Morrison. Procedures as Persistent Data Objects. In *ACM Transactions on Programming Languages and Systems.* 1985.
3. S. Bijnens, W. Joosen and P. Verbaeten. A Reflective Invocation Scheme to Realise Advanced Object Management. In R. Guerraoui, O. Nierstrasz and M. Riveill editors, *Object Based Distributed Programming*, Springer Verlag publisher. 1994.
4. K. Birman, T.A. Joseph and F. Schmuck - ISIS: A Distributed Programming Environnment, User's Guide and Reference Manual. *Internal Report, Dept of Computer Science, Cornell Univ.* 1991.
5. K. Birman, A.Schiper and P.Stephenson. Lightweight causal and atomic group multicast. In *ACM Transactions on Computer Systems.* August 1991.
6. D. Cherriton. The V Distributed System. In *Communications of the ACM.* March 1988.

7. F. Cristian. Understanding Fault-Tolerant Distributed Systems. In *Communications of the ACM*. February 1991.

8. P. Dickman and M. Makpangou. A Refinement of the Fragmented Object Model. In *IEEE Proceedings of IWOOS'92: the International Workshop on Object Orientation in Operating Systems*. 1992.

9. B. Garbinato, R. Guerraoui and K. Mazouni. Programming Fault-Tolerant Applications Using Two Orthogonal Object Levels. In *Proceedings of ISCIS'93: the International Symposium on Computer and Information Science*. 1993.

10. A.J Goldberg and A.D Robson. SMALLTALK-80: The Language and its Implementation. Addison Wesley publisher. 1983.

11. R. Guerraoui, R. Capobianchi, A. Lanusse and P. Roux. Nesting Actions through Asynchronous Message Passing: the ACS protocol - In *Proceedings of ECOOP'92: the European Conference on Object Oriented Programming*, Springer Verlag publisher. 1992.

12. R. Guerraoui. Towards Modular Concurrency Control for Distributed Object Oriented Systems. In *IEEE Proceedings of FTDCS'93: the International Workshop on Future Trends in Distributed Computing Systems*. 1993.

13. R. Guerraoui. Nested Transactions: Reviewing the Coherency Contract. In *Proceedings of ISCIS'93: the International Symposium on Computer and Information Science*. 1993.

14. S. Krakowiak, M. Meysembourg, V.H Nguyen, M. Riveill and C. Roisin. Design and Implementation of an Object-Oriented, Strongly Typed Language for Distributed Applications. In *Journal of Object-Oriented Programming*. September/October 1990.

15. B. Liskov and R. Sheifler. Guardians and Actions: Linguistic Support for Robust, Distributed Programs. In *ACM Proceedings of SOPL'82: the Symposium on Principles of Programming Languages*. 1982.

16. C. Low. A Shared Persistent Object Store. In *Proceedings of ECOOP'88: the European Conference on Object Oriented Programming*, Springer Verlag publisher. 1988.

17. P.Maes. Issues in Computational Reflection. In P. Maes and D. Nardi editors, *Meta-Level Architectures and Reflection*, North Holland publisher. 1988.

18. S. Matsuoka, T. Watanabe and A. Yonezawa. Hybrid Group Reflective Architectures for Object-Oriented Concurrent Reflective Programming. In *Proceedings of ECOOP'91: the European Conference on Object Oriented Programming*, Springer Verlag publisher. 1991.

19. G.A Pascoe. Encapsulators: A New Software Paradigm in Smalltalk-80. In *ACM Proceedings of OOPSLA'86: the Conference on Object-Oriented Programming Systems, Languages and Applications*. 1986.

20. G.D Parington and S. Shrivastava. Implementing Concurrency Control in Reliable Distributed Object-Oriented Systems - In *Proceedings of ECOOP'88: the European Conference on Object Oriented Programming*, Springer Verlag publisher. 1988.

21. R. Schantz, R. Thomas and G. Bono. The architecture of the Cronus Distributed Operating System - In *IEEE Proceedings of ICDCS'86: the International Conference on Distributed Computing Systems*. 1986.

22. Y. Yokote. The Apertos Reflective Operating System: The Concept and Its Implementation. In *ACM Proceedings of OOPSLA'92: the Conference on Object-Oriented Programming Systems, Languages and Applications*. 1992.

23. E. Walker, R. Floyd and P. Neves. Asynchronous Remote Operation Execution in Distributed Systems. In *IEEE Proceedings of ICDCS'90: the International Conference on Distributed Computing Systems*. 1990.

Object-Oriented Extendibility in Hermes/ST, a Transactional Distributed Programming Environment *

Michael Fazzolare, Bernhard G. Humm and R. David Ranson

Telecommunications Software Research Centre (TSRC)
The University of Wollongong, Department of Computer Science
P.O. Box 1144 (Northfields Avenue), Wollongong NSW 2522, Australia
Tel: (+61 42) 26 8832, Fax: (+61 42) 27 3277
Email: {faz, humm, dranson}@cs.uow.edu.au

Abstract. A major aim of transactional distributed programming environments is to facilitate the development of reliable distributed applications by shielding the developer from concerns such as failures. This paper describes the linguistic features of the Hermes/ST object-oriented distributed programming environment that further ease the development of such applications by enhancing the flexibility and extendibility of their implementations. This is achieved through the parameterisation of properties such as permanence, concurrency, transactional semantics and distribution. Parameterisation supports reuse, and enables the notion of incremental development, whereby a simple centralized sequential prototype of the application can be easily validated before being gradually extended to the final efficient reliable distributed application. An example application is included to demonstrate this approach.

1 Introduction

Concurrent and distributed applications are inherently more complex than their centralized, sequential counterparts. This added complexity manifests itself particularly in the programming and debugging of such applications. A major aim of distributed programming environments is to reduce the difficulty of programming such applications by providing constructs that shield the programmer from concerns such as fault-tolerance and concurrency control. Transactions [GR93], for example, are a common construct that distributed programming environments provide to maintain the consistency of distributed data in the presence of concurrency and partial failure.

Hermes/ST is a distributed programming environment that supports an *incremental development* strategy as a means to ease the prototyping and implementation of distributed applications. The incremental development of a distributed application involves starting with a distributed design of the application,

---

* This research was funded by Telecom Australia under Contract No. 7260.

implementing a centralized sequential prototype of that design, and then gradually extending this prototype to the final distributed, concurrent fault-tolerant application. The functional correctness of the design and initial implementation can be determined far more easily in a non-concurrent, centralized environment. Once these have been validated, Hermes/ST supports the incremental addition of features such as permanence, concurrency, transactional semantics and distribution.

Hermes/ST's incremental development strategy is flexible. The movement from one development stage to the next does not involve structural changes to code. Rather, through parameterization, Hermes/ST allows the addition of extra features simply by changing parameters. Hermes/ST provides convenient general strategies, such as implicit locking, which satisfy a large class of required behaviours. It also complements these strategies with facilities for their easy extension. Thus, for example, implicit concurrency control can be extended by the addition of explicit concurrency control. At each stage in the development process, versions of the system can be debugged and validated, and if necessary optimized. Optimization can be achieved, for example, by the fine-tuning of subtransactional checkpointing, explicit concurrency control, transactional retries and timeouts.

Hermes/ST also enhances the *reusability* of classes in different contexts. An example of reuse in Hermes/ST is the ability of Hermes/ST classes to be instantiated as both persistent and volatile objects. A further example of reuse is the ability of Hermes/ST methods to be invoked both transactionally and non-transactionally. This is achieved through parameterization.

The next section describes an example distributed banking application that illustrates and clarifies many aspects of Hermes/ST outlined in this paper. The following sections describe the linguistic mechanisms and features of Hermes/ST that support these notions of incremental development and reusability. The Hermes/ST object model (Section 3), generalized invocation scheme (Section 4) and concurrency control specification (Section 5) are described. Significant code from our distributed banking example is included in the appendix. The features are compared to other distributed transactional systems, in particular to the Argus [Lis88], Avalon/C++ [EME91], and Arjuna [Shr92] distributed programming environments.

2   A Banking Example

In order to clarify various issues throughout the paper, an example application, an international bank, is regularly referred to. This application is often used as a test application for distributed programming environments [Lis88, EME91, Hew91]. The banking example described in this paper is derived from the banking system in [Lis88].

An electronic bank is composed of branches and teller machines, which are geographically distributed. Each branch and teller can communicate with any other. Each branch stores a collection of accounts. Accounts are identified by their branch code and account name, and are either cheque or interest bearing savings accounts. Teller machines are used to open and close accounts, deposit, withdraw and (internationally) transfer money. A special teller, the main office, has knowledge about all branches in the bank, and provides special managerial functions such as conducting audits.

3 The Hermes/ST Object Model

The Hermes/ST object model has been inspired by the object model of Smalltalk-80 [GR89]. Indeed, Hermes/ST has been implemented as a set of Smalltalk classes that operate in the Smalltalk environment. However, the linguistic features of Hermes/ST described in this paper are independent of Smalltalk's features.

Hermes/ST objects contain methods, and encapsulate instance variables. Objects can have two kinds of instance variables: *named* variables and *indexed* variables, e.g., for array construction. Variables must be accessed through read and write access methods, e.g., **self accountName** (read access) and **self account-Name:newValue** (write access) for named variables[2], and **at:** and **at:put:** for indexed variables. Variables can only *refer* to other objects. This property has been called *uniform reference semantics* [Mey88].

Hermes/ST objects communicate via message passing, employing a standard or extended Smalltalk syntax. Hermes/ST's objects, variables and methods are defined in Hermes/ST classes. These classes are arranged in a single-inheritance hierarchy, and are descended from the Hermes/ST class **HermesObject**. Instance creation is achieved by calling a class method, which returns a reference to the newly created instance of that class. By using an instance creation parameter, Hermes/ST classes can be instantiated to return a reference to either a volatile or persistent instance. For example, the Hermes/ST statement **BinTree instantiate:#volatile** creates a volatile **BinTree** object and returns a reference to it whereas **BinTree instantiate:#persistent** creates a persistent **BinTree** object and returns a reference to it. Persistence or volatility of a Hermes/ST object is henceforth referred to as its *kind*.

Hermes/ST persistent objects have a back-up version on disk that closely follows their in-memory representation. This allows them to be longer-lived than their creating processes. They have state restoration handlers, which allow them to survive node or transaction failures. Because of their permanence, they must be deleted explicitly, rather than garbage collected as is the case for volatile objects. They exhibit *location transparency* [CC91], being accessible remotely, and are also remotely instantiable. Each persistent object possesses a network-wide unique persistent object reference. This reference has a symbolic representation.

---

[2] Smalltalk programmers may wish to note that specific access methods are provided for all Hermes/ST classes via a set-up routine. Redefining the semantics of the assignment and instance variable read access would have provided cleaner syntax. However, this would have required modifying the Smalltalk compiler which is beyond the scope of this work.

Clients on remote nodes can access an object provided they know its symbolic reference and its public interface. Hermes/ST persistent objects are concurrency controlled, and support transactions.

Transactions provide serializability, atomicity and permanence properties. Serializability ensures that concurrent transactions appear to have run in some serial order. Atomicity ensures that either all or none of a transaction's actions are performed. Permanence ensures that once a transaction has completed, none of its effects will be lost due to non-catastrophic failure. Together, these properties allow a system to move from one *consistent state* [Mos85] to another. Transactions are specified as parameters to Hermes/ST method invocations (see Section 4). In addition to single level transactions, Hermes/ST persistent objects support *nested transactions* [Ree78, Mos85].

Hermes/ST volatile objects are similar to traditional Smalltalk objects. They are only accessible locally, are not concurrency controlled, have no state restoration, and do not support transactions. They are not saved on disk and are automatically garbage collected by the system.

3.1 Support for Incremental Development

The Hermes/ST object model makes the system particularly well suited to incremental development. This approach was used successfully in the implementation of the distributed bank described in this paper, and is being employed in several other ongoing experiments. After completing the design of the distributed application, a single-machine sequential prototype of the application is first implemented using volatile objects. This is debugged, and the design is at least partially validated. Detection and removal of design and implementation errors, many of which are not directly related to the distributed, concurrent or fault-tolerant nature of the application, is performed. The debugging/design validation process at this stage is greatly eased because it is performed on a single machine without concurrency, distribution and fault tolerance.

This validated prototype may then be extended. Implicit concurrency control and permanence are added by changing instantiation parameters from `#volatile` to `#persistent`. Structural changes to the code, and the bugs that these tend to introduce, are avoided through Hermes/ST's parameterised instantiation approach. After testing of this new prototype, distribution can be added likewise, or explicit concurrency and fault tolerance properties can be added to the application (see Sections 4 and 5).

3.2 Reuse Advantages

Some classes, such as collections, are suitable for use as both persistent and volatile objects. Hermes/ST's parameterised instantiation allows the specification of such classes. The `BinTree` and `BinTreeNode` classes used in our bank application demonstrate this support for reuse. See Appendix A.1 for the definition of some instance methods for `BinTree`.

The classes **BinTree** and **BinTreeNode** together define a persistent or volatile sorted binary tree. A **BinTree** instance contains the root of the tree. **BinTree-Node** instances form the nodes of the tree, which contain the elements of the collection, as well as references to left and right subtrees (**BinTreeNodes**).

The instance creation **BinTree** class method, **instantiate:withContents:** creates a new binary tree instance of kind **kind** (either **#persistent** or **#volatile**) to contain **anObject**. It assigns a reference to a new binary tree node instance of the same kind to its variable **root**. The **add:ifExisting:** instance method similarly checks its own kind before creating a new node of the same kind. The **remove:ifAbsent:** instance method contains explicit invocations of method **delete**. **delete** does nothing in the case of a volatile object (which will be automatically garbage collected by the system), or removes the version of the object on disk in case of a persistent object[3].

Reusability is achieved through the parameterization of instance creation methods, and through the use of explicit deletion messages. Thus, a volatile binary tree is returned if **#volatile** is passed to **BinTree**'s instance creation method. Alternatively, passing **#persistent** to this method returns a permanent concurrency-controlled binary tree that manages highly concurrent transactional accesses. Furthermore, traditional object-oriented support for reuse through inheritance is not compromised (e.g. subclasses of **BinTree** can be instantiated as persistent or volatile by inheriting instance creation methods).

3.3 Comparison to Other Approaches

Argus, Avalon/C++ and Arjuna do not support class or type specifications that are reusable for various "kinds" of objects. Argus is object-based, and thus does not support inheritance. Argus has object-based *guardians*, and data types within these guardians. It possesses *atomic* and *volatile* data types, but "kind" is a type property. Avalon/C++ is similar to Argus, with servers comparable to Argus' guardians. "Kind" in Avalon/C++ is a static class property, with persistence properties defined through inheritance from *recoverable*, *atomic* or *subatomic* base classes. Arjuna is based on C++, and currently supports single inheritance. The "kind" of a class is also defined through its inheritance hierarchy. Arjuna supports volatile C++ classes, as well as persistent classes descended from *LockManager*.

The introduction of multiple inheritance could conceivably allow Avalon/C++ and Arjuna to reuse a class with varying "kinds" of instances. For example, a class **VolBinTree** could inherit from both classes **BinTree** and **Volatile-Object**, while a class **PersistentBinTree** could inherit from classes **BinTree** and **PersistentObject**. However, when the object model is extended to include a large number of "kinds"[4], this approach would become cumbersome. It would require a large number of new subclasses — one for every "kind".

---

[3] If the deletion of a persistent object is requested during a transaction, it is delayed until the top-level transaction commits.

[4] An extension of the Hermes/ST object model, currently being developed, extends the range of object kinds from the current extremes of "light-weight" volatile objects and "heavy-weight" persistent objects to a larger number of kinds.

4 A Generalized Method Invocation Scheme

The binary tree example of Section 3 employs only a simple form of method invocation, viz synchronous, non-transactional invocation. Hermes/ST provides a generalized method invocation scheme in which a method invocation is the central unit for thread creation, transaction creation and explicit concurrency control specification.

Three types of method invocations are distinguished: *synchronous, asynchronous* and *wait-by-necessity* invocations. In a synchronous method invocation, the invoking method is suspended until the invoked method returns a value. In an asynchronous invocation, the invoked method executes independently of the invoking method, within a new thread of control. The invoking method does not wait for a result. In a wait-by-necessity invocation [Car90], the invoked method is executed in a new thread of control and a *voucher* object is returned to the invoking method, which is not suspended. Sending the message *redeem* to the voucher object returns the result of the invoked method. This may cause the invoking method to be suspended until the invoked method completes.

Every method invocation, regardless of its type, can create a new transaction. This allows six combinations of method invocations: synchronous invocations that do or do not create a transaction, asynchronous invocations that do or do not create a transaction and wait-by-necessity invocations that do or do not create a transaction. Nested transactions result if a method within a transaction invokes another transaction creating method. For example, a transaction creating synchronous invocation may asynchronously invoke a method that does not create a transaction which in turn could invoke a method using wait-by-necessity that creates a nested transaction.

The Hermes/ST generalized method invocation scheme allows concurrency within transactions without subtransactional overheads. This can be achieved by using non-transaction creating asynchronous or wait-by-necessity invocations within a transaction. Furthermore, ancestor transactions are not suspended while asynchronous descendent transactions execute. This makes transaction creating, wait-by-necessity invocations within transactions possible. The extended invocation scheme is implemented through a novel transaction scheduling mechanism described in [Hum93].

A Hermes/ST method invocation in the generalized scheme is specified by the receiver, the message, its arguments, and optional *invocation parameters*. If no invocation parameters are specified, defaults are assumed. For example, in the invocation `branch deposit:amount to:accountName`, the message `deposit:to:` is sent to the receiver `branch` with arguments `amount` and `accountName`. The invocation is synchronous and does not create a transaction (default) since no explicit invocation parameters are specified. In the invocation `branch asynchronously; transactionCreating; deposit:amount to:accountName`[5], the mes-

---

[5] Smalltalk programmers may wish to note that we utilize the cascading construct (";") for the specification of invocation parameters in an unusual way. This is to provide a concise way of specifying such parameters without having to introduce new syntactic constructs.

sage `deposit:to:` is also sent to the receiver `branch` with arguments `amount` and `accountName`. This time, however, two invocation parameters are specified: `asynchronously` and `transactionCreating`. They specify that the invocation is asynchronous and creates a new transaction.

Method invocations that create a transaction can specify a range of additional parameters. They include `mode:`, `retries:` and `timeout:`.

- Two main transaction *modes* are distinguished: `#abortIfFail` (default) and `#performIfFail`. `#abortIfFail` specifies that an aborting subtransaction causes its parent transaction to abort. `#performIfFail` specifies that an aborting transaction does not cause its parent transaction to abort – instead, a specified exception is executed.
- `retries` allows the specification of how many times to retry a failed transactional method invocation before it is aborted.
- In Hermes/ST, network, node and software failures are not distinguished. Furthermore, Hermes/ST does not prevent or detect deadlocks. Therefore, a *timeout* mechanism has been chosen to trigger transaction aborts. The specification of timeout values can be critical for the overall performance of a system. Because of the dynamic nature of transaction nesting, it can be hard for a programmer to statically specify a timeout value for a method invocation that creates a transaction. Therefore, Hermes/ST provides *accumulative timeouts*. Every transaction is assigned a timeout value, either explicitly via the invocation parameter `timeout` or implicitly via a default value. Whenever a subtransaction starts, the parent transaction's timeout value is increased by the child's timeout value. Thus, timeouts accumulate over nested transactions. When a transaction's timeout value is exceeded, it fails, which may lead to a transaction abort, depending on the specified `mode` and `retries` parameters.

Another important Hermes/ST invocation parameter is the `lock` parameter. `lock` allows methods to be invoked using type-specific, user-defined concurrency control. Section 5.2 gives a description of such concurrency control specifications.

4.1 Specifying Invocation Parameters in Method Interfaces

Often, particular methods are always invoked with the same invocation parameters. For example, a distributed bank transfer is always invoked transactionally. Hermes/ST allows invocation parameters to be specified as part of the external method interface in the declaration of a method[6]. The syntax is as follows[7].

---

[6] Note that a client object invoking a method on a server object is expected to know the method's external interface.

[7] Smalltalk programmers may wish to note that we have implemented a special invocation parameter compiler that runs over method comments. This way of specifying invocation parameters does not require us to change the Smalltalk method declaration syntax and therefore to modify the Smalltalk compiler.

transfer: amount from: branch1 name: account1 to: branch2 name: account2

    "

    InvocationScheme
        transactionCreating: true

    "

Hermes/ST classes are defined in an inheritance hierarchy. Invocation parameters can be specified for all methods of Hermes/ST classes. When methods are overridden in subclasses, all invocation parameters specified by ancestor classes are *inherited individually* and can be *overridden individually*. Invocation parameters for a particular method that are not explicitly specified in the method definition and are not explicitly specified in the definition of the method in any ancestor class are determined by a default value. The external interface of Hermes/ST methods conceptually includes the values for all invocation parameters, determined either by explicit specification, inheritance or default values. Clients that invoke a Hermes/ST method may override invocation parameters specified in its interface.

See the example of a transfer method and auxiliary withdraw and deposit methods in Appendix A.2. The methods `deposit:to:` and `withdraw:from:` of class `Branch` are specified to create a new transaction when invoked. By default, invocations of `deposit:to:` and `withdraw:from:` are synchronous. The method `transfer:from:name:to:name:` is specified to create a new transaction when invoked. It invokes `deposit:to:` and `withdraw:from:`, overriding the interface definition from synchronous to asynchronous. When `transfer:from:name:to:name:` is invoked, a top-level transaction with two asynchronous subtransactions is created.

4.2 Support for Incremental Development

The Hermes/ST generalized method invocation mechanism supports an incremental development scheme for reliable distributed systems particularly well. A system developer can design methods with transactions in mind but implement them non-transactionally first. These non-transactional methods are easier to debug since no underlying transactional system masks software failures. After functional validation of these non-transactional methods, transactions can arbitrarily be put in place to maintain data integrity. This process only requires changing invocation parameters — no structural changes need to be made. The now transactional system can be tested, its performance can be monitored and bottlenecks can be detected. Since transactions are expensive, fine tuning may need to be performed to resolve bottlenecks.

One way of decreasing transactional expense is to cut down transactional nesting depth where possible. Consider the transfer example above. Note that `transfer:from:name:to:name:` is always invoked transactionally and the whole transaction should abort if either the withdraw or deposit operation fails. Further note that the transfer transaction is relatively short so that the checkpointing introduced by nested transactions is not necessary. Therefore, for performance reasons, the withdraw and deposit operations should not be performed as subtransactions. An alternative implementation of the transfer method is described in Appendix A.3.

Note that the more efficient implementation of the transfer method is possible because Hermes/ST allows concurrent threads within transactions without using subtransactions. Further note how the method invocation parameters specified in the declarations of `withdraw:from:` and `deposit:to:` are overridden by their invocations.

For longer, nested transactions, the probability of success can be increased by using nested transactions. `retries:` and `#performIfFail` allow parent transactions to continue when subtransactions fail. Transient failures and deadlocks[8] can be managed through retries. Longer failures can be managed by specifying appropriate compensating actions using `#performIfFail`.

4.3 Reuse Advantages

By separating method invocation parameters from method declarations, the Hermes/ST generalized invocation scheme supports convenient reuse of methods in various contexts. Examples are the withdraw and deposit methods, which create a transaction when invoked directly from a teller machine, and do not create a transaction when invoked from within a transfer.

4.4 Comparison to Other Approaches

Argus, Avalon/C++ and Arjuna all use similar syntactic constructs to declare transactions. They provide specific "begin" and "end transaction" commands[9] that are specified in the method code. All three systems allow concurrency within transactions *only* by generating subtransactions from within some sort of concurrent loop construct[10].

Neither of the three systems provides the level of flexibility and extendibility that Hermes/ST does, with respect to method invocation and transaction semantics. In all three systems, changing a non-transactional method into a transactional one entails changing the method code. A given method cannot conveniently be used both transactionally and non-transactionally.

Coupling thread creation with subtransaction creation has several drawbacks. Firstly, the overheads of subtransactions are considerable, requiring accesses to secondary storage. Secondly, adding transactional semantics to an existing

---

[8] A more effective way of combatting deadlocks is described in Section 5.2.

[9] `enter action...end` in Argus, `start transaction{...}` in Avalon/C++ and `AtomicAction A; A.Begin();...A.End()` in Arjuna.

[10] `coenter...end` in Argus, `costart{...}` in Avalon/C++.

multi-threaded application cannot be done in an incremental fashion. Structural changes are necessary where threads are created. This also means that multi-threaded applications cannot be used transactionally and non-transactionally at the same time. In Argus, Avalon/C++ and Arjuna, parent transactions are always suspended while child transactions execute. This not only restricts concurrency but also prevents subtransactional asynchronous and wait-by-necessity like constructs.

The Hermes/ST generalized method invocation scheme provides a higher level of flexibility and extendibility than other transactional distributed programming environments. It is implemented through an advanced synchronization mechanism that includes separate threads and transactions. The mechanism is described in [Hum93].

5 Concurrency Control

5.1 Implicit Concurrency Control

The easiest way for an application developer to prescribe concurrency control in a Hermes/ST application is to use system-defined *implicit locking*. Hermes/ST methods do not have to be specified as "readers" or "writers". Furthermore there is no need for dedicated lock acquisition code to be included in the specification of a method[11].

Implicit locking is currently implemented in Hermes/ST via a mechanism referred to as *minimal locking* [FHR93b]. Minimal locking achieves high concurrency due to a combination of Hermes/ST's fine-grained object model and read/write locking of individual persistent object instance variables[12].

The code for the binary search tree, introduced in Section 3, demonstrates implicit locking. See Appendix A.1. When the class `BinTree` is instantiated as a persistent object, then all instances of `BinTree` and `BinTreeNode` are persistent and concurrency controlled. Implicit locking allows concurrent add "add" and "remove" operations to different parts of the tree. Consider the example tree in Figure 1 containing values 4, 6 and 8. Insertions of the values 2 and 5 as part of different transactions can be performed concurrently since they affect different parts of the tree. The same is true for a concurrent removal of the value 4 and an insertion of the value 7. However, the removal of the value 4 and the insertion of the value 1 cannot be performed concurrently since both operations modify the same part of the tree. Implicit locking delays one of the requested operations until after the other operation's transaction has terminated.

---

[11] When and if such code is needed, it can, however, be specified. See Section 5.2.

[12] Providing such a high concurrency can be expensive. Therefore, minimal locking is currently being refined to a variable locking mechanism that can perform implicit concurrency control on a coarser grain. This coarser-grain locking decreases concurrency but it also decreases scheduling expense and the probability of deadlocks.

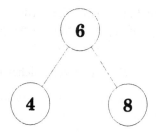

Fig. 1. An example sorted binary tree.

Support for Incremental Development. Hermes/ST implicit locking allows the transition from (non-concurrent) volatile objects to fully concurrency controlled persistent objects without changing method definitions or adding concurrency control specifications. However, when explicit concurrency control is desired, e.g. for deadlock avoidance, it can be specified as described in Section 5.2.

Reuse Advantages. The fact that concurrency control is not specified within method declarations allows methods to be conveniently used in a non-concurrent and concurrent context. Again, the binary tree implementation of Section 3 serves as an example.

Comparison to Other Approaches. Argus, Avalon/C++ and Arjuna do not provide implicit locking. In all of these systems, the acquisition of a lock is an explicit part of the operation definition. In Argus an *atomic type* is accessed via an explicit call to `read_lock(atomic_object)` or `write_lock(atomic_object)` [Lis88]. In the Avalon/C++ system, operations that are subclassed from the `atomic` class acquire read or write locks for the operation through `read_lock()` and `write_lock()` methods of the atomic class [DHW88]. Locks so acquired are easily thought of as pertaining to the method. Thus a read only method should acquire a `read_lock()`, and a method that changes object state should acquire a `write_lock()`. In Arjuna, classes derived from `LockCC`[13] acquire locks through calls to its `setlock()` method. Thus `setlock(new Lock(READ))` acquires a read lock for an operation while `setlock(new Lock(WRITE))` acquires a write lock [PS88].

Implicit locking is attractive for the following reasons:

- The first and most obvious is that implicit locking relieves the programmer of the burden of specifying concurrency control. For many data types, implicit locking provides adequate concurrency control for "free".
- Implicitly locked data types are always correctly concurrency controlled. The possibility of concurrency control specification errors is eliminated. Such errors can be hard to identify. Some examples include: declaring an operation

---

[13] `LockCC` is renamed `LockManager` in [Shr92].

to be a reader instead of a writer; forgetting to declare a method as a reader or a writer; over-specifying a method because the lock granularity is inappropriate.

Implicit locking, although attractive, is deficient in the following ways.

- Some abstract data types have synchronization constraints that are not expressed by implicit locking. For example, a "get" operation on a bounded buffer[14] has to be delayed until after a "put" operation has been performed. Such behaviour is not expressed by implicit locking.
- Implicit locking may introduce deadlock and starvation problems.

These problems are addressed by Hermes/ST explicit locking as described in the following section.

5.2 Explicit Concurrency Control

Hermes/ST explicit concurrency control is achieved through the *programmable lock approach* [FHR93b]. In the Hermes/ST programmable lock approach, type-specific concurrency control is defined in the class specifications of *programmable locks*. Programmable locks form a hierarchy with the abstract class **ProgrammableLock** as the root. Hermes/ST provides a set of system-defined programmable lock classes. They include classes for mutual exclusion, traditional read/write locking, fair read/write locking and bounded buffer synchronization [FHR93c]. The class **ProgrammableLock** defines two methods, **isSchedulable:** and **isCompatibleWith:**, which return boolean values, in this case **true**. These methods can be overridden by subclasses. The method **isSchedulable:** allows a programmable lock to make scheduling decisions on the basis of persistent object state. The method **isCompatibleWith:** defines a programmable lock's "compatibility" with other programmable locks.

Programmable locks are associated with Hermes/ST methods via the **lock:** invocation parameter (see Section 4) and instantiated when such a method is invoked. This association allows the specification of *parameters* that will be passed to a programmable lock. Arbitrary objects can be passed as parameters to a programmable lock. Two types of parameters deserve a special mention. These are the arguments of a method invocation and guard methods.

Passing Arguments of a Method Invocation to a Programmable Lock. Consider the example of programmable lock class **AccountWriteLock** which is associated with method **deposit:to:** of class **Branch** (see Appendix A.4). The lock association in **deposit:to:** specifies that the argument **accountName** is passed to **AccountWriteLock**. The argument (**accountName**) is used by **AccountWriteLock**'s **isCompatibleWith:** method to test whether **otherLock** refers to the same account as the lock itself. This re-defined behaviour of **isCompabibleWith:** only allows **AccountWriteLocks** to be granted over different accounts within one branch.

---

[14] A bounded buffer is a fixed size, first-in first-out (FIFO) queue.

Passing Guard Methods to a Programmable Lock. Guard Methods [Atk91] are read-only methods that allow programmable locks to inspect object state. Consider the example of programmable lock class **SavingsAccounts-WriteLock** which is associated with method **addInterest** of class **Branch** (see Appendix A.5). **addInterest** accesses all savings accounts of a branch to add any outstanding interest. **SavingsAccountsWriteLock** conceptually locks all savings accounts of a branch in write mode to allow **addInterest** to be performed atomically. **SavingsAccountsWriteLock isCompatibleWith:** checks the type of **otherLock**'s account (**#cheque** or **#savings**) using the guard method **type-CheckMethod**. This guard method is passed as a parameter to **SavingsAccounts-WriteLock** in the **lock** invocation parameter specification of method **add-Interest**.

Using Programmable Locks for Deadlock Avoidance. Hermes/ST implicit locking may cause deadlock if, for example, a branch-internal transfer operation from one savings account to another savings account interferes with and **addInterest** invocation. Associating **addInterest** with a **SavingsAccounts-WriteLock** and associating **withdraw:from:** and **deposit:to:** (the two methods invoked in a transfer operation) with an **AccountWriteLock** avoids such a deadlock. This is because **SavingsAccountsWriteLock** conceptually locks all savings accounts of a particular branch in write mode. A **SavingsAccountsWriteLock** is incompatible with every **AccountWriteLock** that controls the access to a savings account. Thus, in case of a conflict, the execution of one of the operations (**transfer** or **addInterest**) is delayed until after the other operation's transaction has terminated (committed or aborted).

Support for Incremental Development. If it is necessary to add explicit concurrency control to an implicitly concurrency controlled Hermes/ST application, the incremental strategy still applies. First, simple system-defined programmable locks like mutual exclusion locks or read/write locks can be employed. Performance analysis of the simply concurrency controlled system may detect bottlenecks. These bottlenecks can then be alleviated by the introduction of more sophisticated application-specific programmable locks such as **Savings-AccountsWriteLock** and **AccountWriteLock**.

Reuse Advantages. The Hermes/ST explicit concurrency control mechanism does not only support the reuse of methods that are explicitly concurrency controlled. It also facilitates reuse of concurrency control specifications themselves.

- The association of programmable locks and Hermes/ST methods is separated from the method definition. This allows one to conveniently use a method in a sequential and concurrent context.
- The concurrency control specification for a Hermes/ST class is *composable*: subclasses that add and/or override methods can individually add/change programmable lock associations. Composability is achieved by a combination

of separating the programmable lock association from method definition and associating programmable locks with methods individually.

- Programmable locks are specified separately from the Hermes/ST classes in which they are applied. This allows a common concurrency control behaviour (e.g. mutual exclusion) to be applied in different classes where appropriate.
- Since programmable locks are defined in an inheritance hierarchy, concurrency control behaviour can be reused through "programming by difference". Examples are the implementations of `SavingsAccountsWriteLock` and `AccountWriteLock` which utilize the locking behaviour of their superclass `WriteLock` and weaken the compatibility predicate using a logical "or" operator.

Comparison to Other Approaches. Argus, Avalon/C++ and Arjuna all support user-defined concurrency control. Type-specific concurrency control in Argus [WL85] has a different goal to its counterpart in Hermes/ST. The goal of Argus' user-defined atomic types is to permit higher concurrency than strict two phase locking allows. One goal of Hermes/ST's user-defined programmable locking is to further *restrict* concurrency allowed by implicit locking in order to avoid problems such as deadlock and starvation. Therefore, the mechanisms are not further compared.

Similar arguments apply to Avalon/C++. However, some aspects of Avalon/-C++'s approach to user-defined locking [DHW88] do compare with the Hermes/ST approach. The idea that locks are specified via inheritance is shared. Avalon/C++ provides the *subatomic* class as a starting point for defining a user-defined hierarchy of locks. This use of inheritance is analogous with Hermes/ST programmable lock inheritance. However, since method declarations contain concurrency control information in Avalon/C++, it lacks composability and does not allow classes to be reused sequentially.

User-defined locking in Arjuna [PS88] is similar to the Hermes/ST programmable lock approach. The lock concurrency controller class `LockCC` exports operations `setlock` and `releaselock`. `releaselock` is called implicitly at transaction termination time. An application calls `setlock` which then calls `lockconflict` which in turn calls the `!=` operator. The `!=` operator is analogous to the `isCompatible:` method in the Hermes/ST programmable lock approach. It can be overridden in user-defined locks.

Arjuna, like Hermes/ST, permits object state to be passed to locks during the instance creation of a lock. However, it does not support inspection of object state through guard methods. Thus, it is not clear how an operation such as a bounded buffer "get" can be specified.

Consistent with programmable locks in Hermes/ST, locks in Arjuna are organised in an inheritance hierarchy and are specified independently of their use. Thus Arjuna's user-defined lock specifications can be re-used and can be extended via inheritance. Locks, however, are not associated with a method but are a part of the method definition. Thus, concurrency specifications are not composable. Therefore, Arjuna lacks some of the reuse advantages that Hermes/ST provides.

6   The Banking Example in Hermes/ST

This section discusses some method definitions of the main classes **Branch** (Appendix A.6) and **Teller** (Appendix A.7) as coded in the banking example, introduced in Section 2. The class definition for **Branch** specifies an instance variable **accounts** which is initialized to an empty persistent binary tree in the **Branch** instance creation method (not shown). All accounts contained in a particular branch are stored in **accounts**, ordered according to their **accountName**.

Methods like **deposit:to:** and **withdraw:from:** (not shown) use an auxiliary method **lookUp:**. **lookUp:** descends the accounts tree to return a Hermes/ST object reference to the specified account. In the case that the account cannot be found, **abortCurrentTransaction:** is invoked. In the case of a transactional invocation, this causes the current transaction to abort and the specified symbol **#noSuchAccount** to be passed to the client of the aborting transaction. In the case of a non-transactional invocation, an exception is raised. Methods **deposit:to:** and **addInterest** are explicitly concurrency controlled using programmable lock classes **AccountWriteLock** and **SavingsAccountsWriteLock**, as described in Section 5.2.

The class definition for **Teller** specifies an instance variable **interface**, which is initialized to a volatile graphical user interface whenever a teller is started up (e.g. after a node crash). This volatility is specified in an initialization method (not shown).

The method **transfer:from:name:to:name:** performs a traditional fund transfer with the optimization described in Section 4.2. The method **internationalTransferFrom:name:to:name:** implements a more complex international transfer operation that involves a currency exchange. This method is interesting since it uses all three types of method invocations, viz synchronous, asynchronous and wait-by-necessity. Assume that every branch keeps a currency table for all traded currencies which might be slightly out of date. A currency table which always keeps the exact current exchange rate can be remotely accessed at the head office. Assume that for small transfers, i.e. transfers that do not exceed a particular limit, the locally stored exchange rate can be used whereas for large transfers, the exact rate must be used. In order to optimize the performance of the transfer method, the exchange rate request to the head office is performed concurrently with the amount request to the source branch — using a wait-by-necessity and a synchronous invocation. If the amount to transfer does not exceed the limit, then the actual transfer can go ahead without waiting for the exact exchange rate to be returned. The voucher exactRate is only redeemed when necessary. The actual transfer is performed concurrently using asynchronous invocations with the optimization described in Section 4.2.

7 Conclusions

In this paper, linguistic features of the Hermes/ST distributed programming environment have been presented. It has been shown that parameterisation in Hermes/ST leads to extendibility and flexibility of reliable distributed applications. These support incremental development and reuse. This has been demonstrated throughout the paper with reference to a simple distributed application, a distributed banking system. This paper has concentrated on Hermes/ST's linguistic features rather than on their implementation details. The implementation of the mechanisms to support the Hermes/ST distributed programming model are described in [FHR93a, Hum93, FHR93c].

All of the code presented in this paper has been compiled, tested and run on a Hermes/ST installation over a cluster of work stations linked via a local area network. Furthermore the development techniques proposed were successfully utilised during the development of the banking application.

Future extensions to the Hermes/ST distributed programming model will be directed at attempting to parameterize more features of the distributed programming environment. The current implementation supports volatile objects and persistent objects only. The introduction of other kinds of objects is currently being performed. Similarly, an investigation into the usefulness of parameterizing serializability, atomicity and persistence in the process model is being undertaken. Thus the application developer will have a broader process choice than just "transactional" or "non-transactional".

References

[Atk91]   Colin Atkinson. *Object-Oriented Reuse, Concurrency and Distribution – An ADA-based approach*. ACM Press, New York, 1991.

[Car90]   Denis Caromel. Concurrency and reusability: From sequential to parallel. *Journal of Object-Oriented Programming*, pages 34–42, September/October 1990.

[CC91]   Roger C. Chin and Samuel T. Chanson. Distributed object-based programming systems. *ACM Computing Surveys*, 23(1):91–124, March 1991.

[DHW88]   D. L. Detlefs, M.P. Herlihy, and J.M. Wing. Inheritance of synchronization and recovery properties in Avalon/C++. In *Proceedings of HICSS-21*, January 1988.

[EME91]   Jeffrey L. Eppinger, Lily B. Mummert, and Alfred Z. Spector (Eds.). *Camelot and Avalon*. Morgan Kaufmann Publishers, Inc., San Mateo, CA 94403, 1991.

[FHR93a] Michael Fazzolare, Bernhard G. Humm, and R. David Ranson. Advanced transaction semantics for TINA. In *Proceedings of the Fourth Telecommunications Information Networking Architecture Workshop (TINA 93), Volume 2*, pages 47–57, L'Aquila, Italy, September 27-30 1993.

[FHR93b] Michael Fazzolare, Bernhard G. Humm, and R. David Ranson. Concurrency control for distributed nested transactions in hermes/st. In *Proceedings of the 1993 International Conference on Parallel and Distributed Systems (ICPADS'93)*, National Taiwan University, Taipei, Taiwan, Repubic of China, December 15-17 1993.

[FHR93c] Michael Fazzolare, Bernhard G. Humm, and R. David Ranson. Hermes/st user manual and technical manual. Technical Report No. 4, Telecommunications Software Research Centre, Department of Computer Science, University of Wollongong, Wollongong NSW 2500, Australia, 1993.

[GR89] Adele Goldberg and Dan Robson. *Smalltalk-80: The Language.* Addison-Wesley, 1989.

[GR93] Jim Gray and Andreas Reuter. *Transaction Processing: Concepts and Techniques.* Morgan Kaufmann, USA, 1993. ISBN 1-55860-190-2.

[Hew91] Carl Hewitt. Open information systems semantics for distributed artificial intelligence. *Artificial Intelligence*, 47:79–106, 1991.

[Hum93] Bernhard G. Humm. An extended scheduling mechanism for nested transactions. In *Proceedings of the 1993 International Workshop on Object-Orientation in Operating Systems (IWOOOS'93)*, Ashville, North Carolina, USA, December 1993.

[Lis88] Barbara Liskov. Distributed programming in Argus. *Communications of the ACM*, 31(3):300–312, March 1988.

[Mey88] Bertrand Meyer. *Object-Oriented Software Construction.* Prentice Hall, Cambridge, Great Britain, 1988.

[Mos85] J. Eliot B. Moss. *Nested Transactions – An Approach to Reliable Distributed Computing.* MIT Series in Information Systems. The MIT Press, Cambridge, Massachusetts and London, England, 1985.

[PS88] Graham D. Parrington and Santosh K. Shrivastava. Implementing concurrency control in reliable distributed object-oriented systems. In *Proceeding of the Second European Conference on Object-Oriented Programming, ECOOP'88*, Oslo Norway, August 1988. (Also in: Lecture Notes in Computer Science, Vol. 322 Springer Verlag, pp. 233-249).

[Ree78] David P. Reed. *Naming and Synchronization in a Decentralized Computer System.* PhD thesis, M.I.T. Department of Electrical Engineering and Computer Science, September 1978. Available as M.I.T. Laboratory for Computer Science Technical Report 205.

[Shr92] Santosh K. Shrivastava. The Arjuna system programmer's guide. Technical Report Public Release 1.0, Computing Laboratory, University of Newcastle upon Tyne, Newcastle upon Tyne, UK, February 1992.

[WL85] William Weihl and Barbara Liskov. Implementation of resilient, atomic data types. *ACM Transactions on Progamming Languages and Systems*, 7(2):244–269, April 1985.

A Hermes/ST Code Examples

A.1 Instance Methods for BinTree

class name   **BinTree**
superclass   **HermesCollection**
instance variable names **root**

Class methods

instantiate: kind withContents: anObject
    "*create a new binary tree instance of the specified kind,*

initializing the root node to refer to anObject"

```
| inst |
inst := super instantiate: kind.
inst root: (BinTreeNode instantiate: kind withContents: anObject).
^inst
```

Instance methods

add: anObject ifExisting: aBlock
"Add anObject to the binary tree. If the object already exists, execute aBlock instead."

```
self root isNil
    ifTrue: [self root: (BinTreeNode
                instantiate: self kind
                withContents: anObject)]
    ifFalse: [self root add: anObject ifExisting: aBlock].
^anObject
```

remove: anObject ifAbsent: aBlock
"Remove anObject from the binary tree, and execute aBlock if it didn't exist in the tree."

```
| nextNode nodeToRemove |
self root isEmpty ifFalse: [self root contents = anObject
        ifTrue: [self root right isNil
                ifTrue: [(nextNode := self root left) isNil
                        ifTrue:
                            [self delete: self root.
                            self root: nil]
                        ifFalse:
                            [nodeToRemove := self root.
                            self root: nextNode.
                            self delete: nodeToRemove]]
                ifFalse: [self root contents: self root
                                removeLeastFromRightSubtree]]
        ifFalse: [self root remove: anObject ifAbsent: aBlock]]
    ifTrue: [aBlock value]
```

A.2 Invocation Parameters for Transfer Methods

Teller instance methods for teller operations

transfer: amount from: branch1 name: account1 to: branch2 name: account2
"

```
InvocationScheme
    transactionCreating: true
"
```

branch1 asynchronously; withdraw: amount from: account1.
branch2 asynchronously; deposit: amount to: account2.
^#done

Branch instance methods for account operations

deposit: amount to: accountName
```
    "
    InvocationScheme
        lock: [AccountWriteLock account: accountName]
        transactionCreating: true
    "
```

...

withdraw: amount from: accountName
```
    "
    InvocationScheme
        lock: [AccountWriteLock account: accountName]
        transactionCreating: true
    "
```

...

A.3 A More Efficient Implementation of the Transfer Method

**transfer: amount from: branch1 name: account1
                to: branch2 name: account2**
```
    "
    InvocationScheme
        transactionCreating: true
    "
```

branch1 asynchronously; nonTransactionCreating;
                withdraw: amount from: account1.
branch2 asynchronously; nonTransactionCreating;
                deposit: amount to: account2.
^#done

A.4   Definition and Usage of `AccountWriteLock`

class name	**AccountWriteLock**
superclass	**WriteLock**
instance variable names **account**	

isCompatibleWith: otherLock
    ^(super isCompatibleWith: otherLock)
        or: [self account ~= otherLock account]

Branch Protocol for account operations

deposit: amount to: accountName
    "

    InvocationScheme
        lock: [AccountWriteLock account: accountName]
        transactionCreating: true
    "

A.5   Definition and Usage of `SavingsAccountsWriteLock`

class name	**SavingsAccountsWriteLock**
superclass	**WriteLock**
instance variable names **account typeCheckMethod**	

isCompatibleWith: otherLock
    ^(super isCompatibleWith: otherLock)
      or: [(self
               performGuard: self typeCheckMethod
               with: otherLock account)
               = #cheque]

Branch Protocol for account operations

addInterest
    "

InvocationScheme
    lock: [SavingsAccountsWriteLock
             account: #allSavingAccounts
             typeCheckMethod: #typeOf:]
    transactionCreating: true
    "

A.6   Hermes/ST Class Branch

class name   **Branch**
superclass   **Root**
instance variable names **name accounts**

Protocol for account operations

lookUp: accountName

      ˆself accounts detect: [:account | account name = accountName]
          ifNone: [self abortCurrentTransaction: #noSuchAccount]

deposit: amount to: accountName
     "

    InvocationScheme
       lock: [AccountWriteLock account: accountName]
       transactionCreating: true
  "

    | account |
    amount < 0 ifTrue: [self abortCurrentTransaction: #negativeAmount].
    account := self lookUp: accountName.
    account balance: account balance + amount.
    ˆ#done

addInterest
 "

InvocationScheme
   lock: [SavingsAccountsWriteLock
           account: #allSavingAccounts
           typeCheckMethod: #typeOf:]
   transactionCreating: true
"

    self accounts do: [:account | account type = #savings
       ifTrue: [account balance: account balance * 1.025]].
    ˆ#done

A.7   Hermes/ST Class Teller

class name   **Teller**
superclass   **Root**
instance variable names **name currencyTable interface**

Protocol for teller operations

transfer: amount from: branch1 name: account1 to: branch2 name:

account2

        "

InvocationScheme
    transactionCreating: true
        "

    branch1 asynchronously; nonTransactionCreating;
                withdraw: amount from: account1.
    branch2 asynchronously; nonTransactionCreating;
                deposit: amount to: account2.
    ˆ#done

**internationalTransferFrom: branch1 name: account1
            to: branch2 name: account2**

        "

InvocationScheme
    transactionCreating: true
        "

    | currency1 currency2 exactRate amount newAmount |
    currency1 := self currencyOf: branch1.
    currency2 := self currencyOf: branch2.
    exactRate := self headOffice waitByNec;
                exchangeRate: currency1 to: currency2.
    amount := branch1 balanceOf: account1.
    newAmount := amount * (amount > 10000
                    ifTrue: [exactRate redeem]
                    ifFalse: [self exchangeRate: currency1 to: currency2]).
    branch1 asynchronously; nonTransactionCreating;
                withdraw: amount from: account1.
    branch2 asynchronously; nonTransactionCreating;
                deposit: newAmount to: account2.
    ˆ#done

Author Index

Lecture Notes in Computer Science

For information about Vols. 1–719
please contact your bookseller or Springer-Verlag

Vol. 756: J. Pieprzyk, B. Sadeghiyan, Design of Hashing Algorithms. XV, 194 pages. 1993.

Vol. 757: U. Banerjee, D. Gelernter, A. Nicolau, D. Padua (Eds.), Languages and Compilers for Parallel Computing. Proceedings, 1992. X, 576 pages. 1993.

Vol. 758: M. Teillaud, Towards Dynamic Randomized Algorithms in Computational Geometry. IX, 157 pages. 1993.

Vol. 759: N. R. Adam, B. K. Bhargava (Eds.), Advanced Database Systems. XV, 451 pages. 1993.

Vol. 760: S. Ceri, K. Tanaka, S. Tsur (Eds.), Deductive and Object-Oriented Databases. Proceedings, 1993. XII, 488 pages. 1993.

Vol. 761: R. K. Shyamasundar (Ed.), Foundations of Software Technology and Theoretical Computer Science. Proceedings, 1993. XIV, 456 pages. 1993.

Vol. 762: K. W. Ng, P. Raghavan, N. V. Balasubramanian, F. Y. L. Chin (Eds.), Algorithms and Computation. Proceedings, 1993. XIII, 542 pages. 1993.

Vol. 763: F. Pichler, R. Moreno Díaz (Eds.), Computer Aided Systems Theory – EUROCAST '93. Proceedings, 1993. IX, 451 pages. 1994.

Vol. 764: G. Wagner, Vivid Logic. XII, 148 pages. 1994. (Subseries LNAI).

Vol. 765: T. Helleseth (Ed.), Advances in Cryptology – EUROCRYPT '93. Proceedings, 1993. X, 467 pages. 1994.

Vol. 766: P. R. Van Loocke, The Dynamics of Concepts. XI, 340 pages. 1994. (Subseries LNAI).

Vol. 767: M. Gogolla, An Extended Entity-Relationship Model. X, 136 pages. 1994.

Vol. 768: U. Banerjee, D. Gelernter, A. Nicolau, D. Padua (Eds.), Languages and Compilers for Parallel Computing. Proceedings, 1993. XI, 655 pages. 1994.

Vol. 769: J. L. Nazareth, The Newton-Cauchy Framework. XII, 101 pages. 1994.

Vol. 770: P. Haddawy (Representing Plans Under Uncertainty. X, 129 pages. 1994. (Subseries LNAI).

Vol. 771: G. Tomas, C. W. Ueberhuber, Visualization of Scientific Parallel Programs. XI, 310 pages. 1994.

Vol. 772: B. C. Warboys (Ed.),Software Process Technology. Proceedings, 1994. IX, 275 pages. 1994.

Vol. 773: D. R. Stinson (Ed.), Advances in Cryptology – CRYPTO '93. Proceedings, 1993. X, 492 pages. 1994.

Vol. 774: M. Banâtre, P. A. Lee (Eds.), Hardware and Software Architectures for Fault Tolerance. XIII, 311 pages. 1994.

Vol. 775: P. Enjalbert, E. W. Mayr, K. W. Wagner (Eds.), STACS 94. Proceedings, 1994. XIV, 782 pages. 1994.

Vol. 776: H. J. Schneider, H. Ehrig (Eds.), Graph Transformations in Computer Science. Proceedings, 1993. VIII, 395 pages. 1994.

Vol. 777: K. von Luck, H. Marburger (Eds.), Management and Processing of Complex Data Structures. Proceedings, 1994. VII, 220 pages. 1994.

Vol. 778: M. Bonuccelli, P. Crescenzi, R. Petreschi (Eds.), Algorithms and Complexity. Proceedings, 1994. VIII, 222 pages. 1994.

Vol. 779: M. Jarke, J. Bubenko, K. Jeffery (Eds.), Advances in Database Technology — EDBT '94. Proceedings, 1994. XII, 406 pages. 1994.

Vol. 780: J. J. Joyce, C.-J. H. Seger (Eds.), Higher Order Logic Theorem Proving and Its Applications. Proceedings, 1993. X, 518 pages. 1994.

Vol. 781: G. Cohen, S. Litsyn, A. Lobstein, G. Zémor (Eds.), Algebraic Coding. Proceedings, 1993. XII, 326 pages. 1994.

Vol. 782: J. Gutknecht (Ed.), Programming Languages and System Architectures. Proceedings, 1994. X, 344 pages. 1994.

Vol. 783: C. G. Günther (Ed.), Mobile Communications. Proceedings, 1994. XVI, 564 pages. 1994.

Vol. 784: F. Bergadano, L. De Raedt (Eds.), Machine Learning: ECML-94. Proceedings, 1994. XI, 439 pages. 1994. (Subseries LNAI).

Vol. 785: H. Ehrig, F. Orejas (Eds.), Recent Trends in Data Type Specification. Proceedings, 1992. VIII, 350 pages. 1994.

Vol. 786: P. A. Fritzson (Ed.), Compiler Construction. Proceedings, 1994. XI, 451 pages. 1994.

Vol. 787: S. Tison (Ed.), Trees in Algebra and Programming – CAAP '94. Proceedings, 1994. X, 351 pages. 1994.

Vol. 788: D. Sannella (Ed.), Programming Languages and Systems – ESOP '94. Proceedings, 1994. VIII, 516 pages. 1994.

Vol. 789: M. Hagiya, J. C. Mitchell (Eds.), Theoretical Aspects of Computer Software. Proceedings, 1994. XI, 887 pages. 1994.

Vol. 790: J. van Leeuwen (Ed.), Graph-Theoretic Concepts in Computer Science. Proceedings, 1993. IX, 431 pages. 1994.

Vol. 791: R. Guerraoui, O. Nierstrasz, M. Riveill (Eds.), Object-Based Distributed Programming. Proceedings, 1993. VII, 262 pages. 1994.

Vol. 792: N. D. Jones, M. Hagiya, M. Sato (Eds.), Logic, Language and Computation. XII, 269 pages. 1994.

Vol. 793: T. A. Gulliver, N. P. Secord (Eds.), Information Theory and Applications. Proceedings, 1993. XI, 394 pages. 1994.

Vol. 794: G. Haring, G. Kotsis (Eds.), Computer Performance Evaluation. Proceedings, 1994. X, 464 pages. 1994.

Vol. 796: W. Gentzsch, U. Harms (Eds.), High-Performance Computing and Networking. Proceedings, 1994, Vol. I. XXI, 453 pages. 1994.

Vol. 797: W. Gentzsch, U. Harms (Eds.), High-Performance Computing and Networking. Proceedings, 1994, Vol. II. XXII, 519 pages. 1994.

Vol. 800: J.-O. Eklundh (Ed.), Computer Vision – ECCV '94. Proceedings 1994, Vol. I. XVIII, 603 pages. 1994.

Vol. 801: J.-O. Eklundh (Ed.), Computer Vision – ECCV '94. Proceedings 1994, Vol. II. XV, 485 pages. 1994.